T0398452

# Musicians and their Audiences

How do musicians play and talk to audiences? Why do audiences listen and what happens when they talk back? How do new (and old) technologies affect this interplay? This book presents a long overdue examination of the turbulent relationship between musicians and audiences. Focusing on a range of areas as diverse as Ireland, Greece, India, Malta, the US, and China, the contributors bring musicological, sociological, psychological, and anthropological approaches to the interaction between performers, fans, and the industry that mediates them. The four parts of the book each address a different stage of the relationship between musicians and audiences, showing its processual nature: from conceptualisation to performance, and through mediation to off-stage discourses. The musician/audience conceptual division is shown, throughout the book, to be as problematic as it is persistent.

**Ioannis Tsioulakis** is a Lecturer in Anthropology at Queen's University Belfast. In the past he has lectured at University College Cork and University College Dublin on topics including ethnomusicology, popular music and politics, Mediterranean music, and ethnographic research methods. His research focuses on cosmopolitan aspirations among local music practitioners, the concept of music professionalism, and the impact of crisis on music and politics in Greece. Ioannis is currently Associate Editor of the *Irish Journal of Anthropology*. He is also a professional pianist, composer, and arranger who has performed and recorded extensively within the Greek popular music scene.

**Elina Hytönen-Ng**, a cultural researcher and an ethnomusicologist, is a university researcher at the University of Eastern Finland. She has been studying the contemporary British jazz scene and musicians' flow experiences. She received her PhD in 2010, and since then has been an academic visitor at the Faculty of Music, University of Oxford, and a visiting research fellow at King's College London.

# Musicians and their Audiences

## Performance, speech and mediation

**Edited by
Ioannis Tsioulakis and
Elina Hytönen-Ng**

Routledge
Taylor & Francis Group

LONDON AND NEW YORK

First published 2017
by Routledge
2 Park Square, Milton Park, Abingdon, Oxon OX14 4RN

and by Routledge
711 Third Avenue, New York, NY 10017

Routledge is an imprint of the Taylor & Francis Group,
an informa business

British Library Cataloguing-in-Publication Data
A catalogue record for this book is available from the British Library
Library of Congress Cataloging-in-Publication Data
Names: Tsioulakis, Ioannis, editor. | Hytönen-Ng, Elina, editor.
Title: Musicians and their audiences: performance, speech and
mediation / edited by Ioannis Tsioulakis & Elina Hytönen-Ng.
Description: Abingdon, Oxon; New York: Routledge, 2017. | Includes
bibliographical references and index.
Identifiers: LCCN 2016029088 | ISBN 9781472456939 (hardback:
alk. paper)
Subjects: LCSH: Music audiences – Psychological aspects. | Music
audiences – Social aspects. | Music – Performance – Social aspects.
Classification: LCC ML3830 .M986 2017 | DDC 780.9 – dc23
LC record available at https://lccn.loc.gov/2016029088

ISBN: 978-1-472-45693-9 (hbk)
ISBN: 978-1-315-59701-0 (ebk)

Typeset in Sabon
by Florence Production Ltd, Stoodleigh, Devon, UK

Printed and bound by CPI Group (UK) Ltd, Croydon, CR0 4YY

# Contents

# Figures

# Tables

# Contributors

**Barbara Bradby** is a retired lecturer in sociology, where a major thread of her teaching and writing sought to use popular song to understand the society that created it. In particular, her work has focused on gender as one of the most ubiquitous social differences that is reproduced and sometimes challenged in popular song. However, the meaning of popular music is voiced only by the people that hear it, and her work has tried to keep up a conversation between the 'texts' of popular song, and the audiences that make meaning out of them.

**Nancy Bruseker** is completing her PhD at the University of Liverpool, on the subject of Vesta Tilley and her audience. Swayed by the richness of the sources examined here, she has become an expert in Victorian history. However, her abiding intellectual interest is devoted to popular music audiences in any era, particularly the women who helped constitute them.

**Mark Duffett** is Reader in Media and Cultural Studies at the University of Chester. His research interest is primarily in fandom and the dynamics of popular music audiences. Mark is the author of *Understanding Fandom* (Bloomsbury, 2013). In 2012 he was keynote speaker at the MARS conference in Finland. He is currently finishing a book on Elvis Presley for Dave Laing's Equinox Press series and co-writing another with Dr Jon Hackett on music and monstrosity for Bloomsbury.

**Jonathan Henderson** has had a distinguished career touring throughout Europe and North America as a solo guitarist and in a number of ensembles. During his musical journeys he developed a deep love of Spanish guitar and added Spanish and South American music to his repertoire of Classical, Jazz and Pop. He was resident guitarist at the Café Royal's Green Room in London from 1995 to 1997 where performers included Patti Boulaye, Alan Price, George Melly, Cybil Shepherd and Rita Coolidge. He has toured with David Soul, Gwen Dickey (Rose Royce), Francisco Yglesias (Los Paraguayos), and the Spanish gypsy rumberos band, El Adivinio.

**Elina Hytönen-Ng** is a cultural researcher and an ethnomusicologist. She's been studying the contemporary British jazz scene and musicians' flow experiences. She received her PhD in 2010 and has since then been an academic visitor at the Faculty of Music, University of Oxford and a visiting research fellow at King's College London.

**Bruce Johnson**, formerly a Professor in English, is now Adjunct Professor, Communications, University of Technology Sydney; Visiting Professor, Music, University of Glasgow; Docent and Visiting Professor, Cultural History, University of Turku. His research lies in music, acoustic cultural history and the emergence of modernity. A jazz musician, broadcaster, record producer and arts policy advisor to Australian state and federal governments, he was co-founder of the International Institute for Popular Culture. His publications include *The Oxford Companion to Australian Jazz*; *Dark Side of the Tune: Music and Violence* (with Martin Cloonan) and *Earogenous Zones: Cinema, Sexuality and Music* (editor).

**Laura Leante** is a Lecturer in Ethnomusicology at Durham University (UK). Her research interests range over Indian classical and folk music, music of the South Asian diaspora, performance analysis, music and globalisation, and popular music. In 2005–2009 Laura Leante was team member working on the AHRC-funded research project 'Experience and meaning in music performance', developing her interest in processes of meaning construction in music through the analysis of performance in Hindustani classical music. In 2009–2012 she directed the AHRC-funded project 'The Reception of Performance in North Indian Classical Music'.

**Mary Louise O'Donnell** holds a doctorate from the University of Limerick and is a former Irish Research Council postgraduate scholar and postdoctoral fellow. Her first book *Ireland's Harp: The Shaping of Irish Identity c.1770 to 1880* was published by University College Dublin Press in 2014 and other research on the history and performance practice of the Irish harp has been published in *Utopian Studies*, *Éire-Ireland* and the *Journal of the Society for Musicology in Ireland*. She has also published on topics relating to Irish cultural history, semiotics and performance studies. She is an accomplished harpist and has given recitals and lectures throughout Europe and North America.

**Richard Osborne** is Senior Lecturer in Popular Music at Middlesex University. Prior to becoming a lecturer, he worked in record shops, held various posts at PRS for Music and co-managed a pub. His blog on popular music is available at: http://richardosbornevinyl.blogspot.co.uk. His book *Vinyl: A History of the Analogue Record* was published by Ashgate in 2012.

**Andrew Pace** is a PhD candidate at the University of Manchester, England, where he is completing his research into the transmission of Maltese traditional guitar music, *prejjem*, under the supervision of Dr. Caroline

Bithell. Since 2010 he has conducted fieldwork in Malta and among the Maltese diaspora in Australia. He studied for an MA in Mediterranean and Middle Eastern Music Studies at City University, London (2011).

**Hillegonda C. Rietveld** is Professor of Sonic Culture at the School of Arts and Creative Industries, London South Bank University, UK. She is also the Editor of *IASPM Journal*, the international peer-re-viewed open-access journal of IASPM (International Association for the Study of Popular Music), and a member of the international advisory board of *Dancecult: Journal of Electronic Dance Music Culture*. Involved professionally in club and DJ culture since the early 1980s, she initially released electronic production work with Quando Quango, for Manchester's Factory Records. Her publications address the development and experience of electronic dance music cultures, including the co-edited collection *DJ Culture in the Mix: Power, Technology, and Social Change in Electronic Dance Music* (Bloomsbury Academic) and the monograph *This Is Our House: House Music, Cultural Spaces and Technologies* (Ashgate).

**Jonathan P. J. Stock** is Professor of Music and Head of the School of Music and Theatre at University College Cork, having previously worked at the University of Sydney (Associate Dean for Research, Sydney Conservatorium of Music) and the University of Sheffield. An ethnomusicologist specialising in the music of East Asia, China and Taiwan, he is also interested in applied research, English folk music, music education, musical analysis, research ethics, and the global history and theory of ethnomusicology.

**Ioannis Tsioulakis** is a Lecturer in Anthropology at Queen's University Belfast. In the past he has lectured at University College Cork and University College Dublin on topics including ethnomusicology, popular music and politics, Mediterranean music, and ethnographic research methods. His research focuses on cosmopolitan aspirations among local music practitioners, the concept of music professionalism, and the impact of crisis on music and politics in Greece. Ioannis is currently Associate Editor of the *Irish Journal of Anthropology*. He is also a professional pianist, composer and arranger who has performed and recorded extensively within the Greek popular music scene.

**Walter van de Leur** is the author of the award-winning *Something to Live For: The Music of Billy Strayhorn* (Oxford University Press). He teaches at the Conservatorium van Amsterdam and is Professor of Jazz and Improvised Music at the University of Amsterdam. He is a member of the *Rhythm Changes* jazz research group. His research interests revolve around the reception of jazz, jazz and identity and jazz historiography. Two book manuscripts are in preparation: an edited volume on the reception of jazz in interbellum Europe, and a monograph on jazz and narratives of death.

# Foreword
## Audiencing

*Jonathan P. J. Stock*

Imagine you're seated among the audience at a traditional Chinese theatre a hundred years ago. An accustomed operagoer, you're necessarily intimately familiar with the divide between onstage and offstage inscribed into the very architecture of the venue itself, and with the behavioural (and financial) expectations that accompany this division. Discounting the areas where performers and audience members do not normally mix, the performance space essentially comprises a square courtyard: the raised stage occupies most of one side, with audience seating in booths on two levels on each of the other three. Some further rows of viewers, exposed to the elements, are seated directly in front of the stage itself. You can see behind the stage too, as there's only a light gauze curtain as backdrop. Habitually, you choose not to peer through the curtain, but today you do, detecting singers in scenes yet to come listening critically to the semi-improvised performance so that their own contributions fit seamlessly into the whole and beside them a senior figure whose role is to remind the performers of the action in the next scene before they go on. There's an assistant ready to help with props, although these are few in traditional opera, and two young apprentice singers looking on in the hope of capturing some content they can one day make their own. And there are the accompanying instrumentalists in full view on one edge of the stage.

Meanwhile, you're equally cognisant of divisions and distinctions within and among the audience around you, and of how those impact on who attends to whom or to what during the operatic performance. For instance, there are the connoisseurs, ostensibly there to *ting xi*, literally, to hear the drama. The phrase emphasises these enthusiasts' deep attachment to the poetics of the lyrics and the associated skills of rhyme, pace, metaphorical nuance, recitation and song. From this ear- and text-centric position, those present to enjoy the visual qualities of the drama (*kan xi*) – bright and elaborate costumes, graceful gestures and breathtaking acrobatic combat – are mere spectators, a lesser kind of audience indeed.

Notwithstanding this traditional typology of elevated listener versus vulgar onlooker, you know there are dedicated and potentially very knowledgeable viewers who appreciate the visual and sonic dimensions of operatic performance all at once, not least the groups of fans of the lead singers. Regular attendees, they can expect to be known, at least by sight, by those onstage, and probably by many offstage as well. Their actions as a group within the theatre subtly cue their claim of a special position and relationship. Meeting and exceeding these fans' expectations is both a pleasure and a continuing burden for the targeted musicians, and satisfying these fans poses an even more significant challenge for the troupe's other vocalists. A young woman holding a baby in the women's section of open seats below your vantage point wipes a tear from her eye – some theatres still segregate men and women viewers, although it's a rapidly declining custom. Dramas that portray the many obstacles to true love are all too prevalent, and experience tells you they resonate particularly strongly for women in a society built upon the custom of arranged marriages, most particularly in rural areas where the norm was for women to 'marry out', spending the rest of their lives away from their natal home and childhood friends. Opera may be full of artifice, fantastic make believe and stereotypical roles handed down by tradition, but a skilled opera actress evokes profoundly genuine personal responses in the hearts and minds of those around her.

The audience beside you, then, is hardly one unified listenership, except insofar as you've all chosen to attend this performance and gained entrance to it. Factors like personal outlook, expertise, dedication, dress and gender all play significant roles in shaping how you're listening to the opera performance and how you view the other people who surround you. You can readily imagine that there must be a correspondingly varied set of expectations among the performers, and among those others whose input further determines the framing and character of the performance event, from promoters to censors, and from directors to costume designers. Now that you think about it, there are others present too who fit neither category entirely well, musician or audience. Even in a purpose-built artistic venue like this, the close environs of the stage are sites for highly variegated work habits. In among those listening and watching the onstage performers ply their trade, the venue's waiters serve tea and set out chairs for newly arrived customers, and freelance hawkers offer sundry hand-crafted fans and miscellaneous small refreshments. They can't avoid hearing the performance, even if they're listening out for the calls of customers or co-workers: what do they make of it, hearing live music as background noise day after day?

Unable to address those questions personally, you gaze further around the theatre. You rather suspect that the heavily made-up young women in the front row of the women's section are courtesans, presumably from a nearby establishment. You understand that certain customers enjoy singing opera with some of these women, and so the women may be here to learn the latest repertory, but perhaps they're also placed on public display as an embodied advert for their other, more private services. Their visibility reminds you of others who wish to be seen even while you hear the performance – a prominent actor's patron (and lover?), students recently returned from study overseas dressed garishly in the latest Japanese or European fashions, a politician staging his own conspicuous display of cultural rootedness, a gangster and his henchmen silently marking out the space as one that falls under their protection. Or perhaps this particular Big Brother is simply an opera aficionado, and the thugs are there to ensure his personal safety, nothing more.

In tracing the relationships that arise between musicians and their audiences in a wide series of settings, this collection of essays reminds us how central the work of seeking an audience/gathering to listen is to human music making more generally. Listening to music or making music for a body of listeners involves undertaking an act richly encircled by other musical and social actions, one where deeply established taste affiliations and ethical standpoints become engaged, and disputed, by participants on each side of the equation as well as by others who may not be present at all. Incidentally, if we're accustomed to assessing musicians' special training and skills, we've typically paid less attention to the acquisition of knowledge over a lifetime by the people we may collectively refer to as audiences. This set of essays contributes to that gap by raising our consciousness as to the areas that deserve analysis in coming to better understand what audiences bring to each new listening act.

Additionally, the volume demands that we think further on just how varied the types of participation in musical listening actually are, whether worldwide or through time, and how multivalent our roles can become in such situations – that term 'audience' is probably the best collective word we have, its roots suggesting that we don't just perceive sounds but actively evaluate them, but it still feels far too limited, as if everything seen, known and imagined before, during or in response to the performance soundtrack is always less focal a part of a musical experience. As the contributors to this volume note, in some events we would describe ourselves more as participants; in others as diners, dancers, revellers, celebrants or members of a congregation; elsewhere as adjudicators, critics or examiners; and elsewhere again, we're primarily just those musicians who're temporarily not playing along. Accordingly, the writers give significant and welcome attention to moments when audience action extends well beyond listening and when the musicians do more than produce audible sound, showing how the complex relationships that take shape between those who produce or provide music and those who hear it cohere, endure and develop over time.

# Acknowledgements

Not unlike the relationship between musicians and audiences in performance, this edited volume was shaped by a synergy. The work included herein is the result of a long process of discussions and debates across disciplines, geographical regions, languages and musical genres represented by the contributing authors. We would like to thank all of the authors for their dedicated and meticulous work, as well as for their patience during the long process that led to the present volume. We are also indebted to Ashgate and Routledge, and particularly Music Editor Heidi Bishop for her enthusiasm about our project and constant support throughout the writing and editing process. All chapters in this volume have been anonymously reviewed by specialists in the fields of ethnomusicology, musicology and popular music studies; we are extremely thankful for the reviewers' time and attentive feedback.

This volume sprung out of a One-Day Workshop entitled 'Musicians and their Audiences', which was held on 1 December 2012 at King's College London. That workshop, and the present edited volume as its outcome, would not have been possible without the help and support of the Department of Music at King's College, and particularly Martin Stokes, Roger Parker and Frances Morton, to whom we are deeply grateful. Additionally, we would like to thank Laudan Nooshin, Jason Toynbee and Andrea Dankic for their participation in the workshop; their work might not be included in this book, but their contributions were instrumental in shaping this work and are echoed in the pages to follow. Finally, we owe special thanks to Jonathan Stock and Walter van de Leur for their inspiring Foreword and Afterword.

# Introduction to musicians and their audiences

*Ioannis Tsioulakis and Elina Hytönen-Ng*

More than 60 years ago, sociologist Howard Becker (1951) pointed out that jazz music was a service occupation in which musicians had to satisfy audiences' demands. Becker stated that there were two parties at work in every performance: first, the musicians 'whose full-time activity was at the heart of the occupation and whose self was in some ways deeply involved in it' and, second, the audience whose relationship with the occupation was 'much more casual' (Becker, 1951: 136). Even though much has changed in the past 60 years, the negotiation of roles and power between musicians and audiences has far from vanished. Similar types of relationships exist across genres and cultures, especially as 'presentational performance' (Turino, 2008) and the professionalization of music-making become the norm. In the meantime, new technologies and types of music have changed the ways in which these negotiations take place and become mediated.

The idea that audiences are as intrinsic to music-making as performers has achieved consensus in culturally/socially-based musicological writings. Key texts in ethnomusicology and popular music studies (Frith, 1998; Hesmondalgh and Negus, 2002; Middleton, 1990; Nettl, 2005; Turino, 2008) dedicate substantial lengths to describe musicians and audiences by focusing interchangeably on either side of this participatory schema, revealing in the process some of the key aspects of their relationships.

The central thesis of this edited volume is that the musician–audience relationship should be regarded as a continuum rather than a dichotomy. The multiplicity of modalities of engagement, discourses on roles and appropriate behaviour, and avenues through which performers and audiences find each other call for theorisations that break clear from rigid patterns and allow for descriptive flexibility. However, complementary to this view is a certainty that despite the plethora of their manifestations and conceptualisations, we are not done with distinctions between musicians and audiences. Through an emphasis on *continuum* rather than dichotomy, contributors to this volume avoid overly focusing on one or the other category, but instead attempt to see their dynamic relationship through its constant renegotiation. Extremely important in this direction is the work of Thomas Turino (2008) and Christopher Small (1998). Through his distinction between 'presentational' and 'participatory' performance, Turino (2008: 23–65) manages to break down taxonomies of genre in favour of an in-depth analysis of how performance unfolds involving participants in different roles and capacities. Small's earlier conceptualisation of 'musicking' (1998) had paved the way by showing that, even in art music performances that tend to belong in the least interactive end of performance spectrum, audiences have agency over the unfolding of the event, as well as the perception of musical stimuli.

Recent research has productively focused on the interaction between performers and audiences across genres (see for example Burland and Pitts, 2010; Pitts, 2005; Pitts et al., 2013), while some work dealing with musical audiences has sprung out of an interest in music education and the phenomenon of performance anxiety (LeBlanc et al., 1997). In recent years there has also been research emerging on venue owners and entrepreneurs. Such studies, focusing on the commercial side of music-making, have tended to concentrate on the audience's and club owners' perspectives.[1] The musicians' experiences and their interaction with the audience, however, has been scarce in these instances. Music psychologists have also looked at audiences and musicians providing useful and diverse perspectives. Some have examined musicians during performance (see, for example, Van Zijl, 2014), while John Sloboda's recent research programme has also investigated the communication between performers and audiences in a variety of expressive genres (Sloboda and Ford, 2012). The aim of that particular project was to deepen the musicians' understanding of the audiences that they encounter in their performances. The emphasis of the project, therefore, was on facilitating a better understanding of the audience's reactions and desires for performing musicians.

Another lens for the examination of the intersection between musicians and audiences has been offered by the study of music fans. Influential work has focused on Bruce Springsteen's (Cavicchi, 1998) or The Grateful Dead's (Weiner, 1999) fans and their preferences, behaviours and modalities of community-making (see also Maxwell, 2002). More recent work by Mark Duffett (2013) has also contributed to the deconstruction of the fetishism of the performer in popular music studies, and to an understanding of audiences beyond simplistic dichotomies of producer versus consumer. Research on fandom and audience ideologies and behaviours has been extended to cover other aspects of popular and high-art culture including theatre (Mackintosh, 1993; Barker, 2003), cinema and TV audiences (Gordon, 2009; Napoli, 2003; 2011), fans of actors and specific programmes such as Star Trek and Dr Who (Tulloch and Jenkins, 1995), as well as sports fans and audiences (see for example Crawford, 2005 and Quinn, 2009). The boundaries between music fans and sports fans are often flexible, providing fertile soil for interdisciplinary research projects. Kytö (2011), for example, has looked at the ways that soccer fans use music and sound as part of their activities.

Still, fairly few publications have attempted to describe the holistic process of performer–audience interaction by seeing all its elements: the performative, the rhetorical and the imagined. Musicians' expectations and experience of audience interaction can be hugely important in the subjectivity of performance. Terms such as 'supportive' and 'familiar' versus 'neutral' or even 'hostile' are often invoked with reference to the audience, and portrayed as having an adverse effect on the performance, with some performers explicitly arguing that the success of their music-making relies on a supportive audience (Butler and Baumeister, 1998: 1225). Furthermore, the behavioural codes for audiences tend to vary between genres. In a classical music concert, for example, the audience's possibilities for interaction during the performance are much more limited than in a jazz or a rock gig. In jazz or folk/ traditional music performances the audience is often allowed to negotiate with the musicians which songs will be performed, as well as offer different types of acknowledgements during the performance. As musicians often point out, a jazz performance is a joint creation, directly influenced by the attitudes of both the musicians and the audience (Hytönen-Ng, 2013: 97). On the other hand, various genres can also act as background music, while the audience's attention is focused on other types of interaction. This kind of 'ubiquitous listening' (Kassabian, 2013) is a central formative factor in the resulting music-making practice and experience. Such variations between genres demand closer study in conjunction with the types of relationships that they foster.

Our analytical tools for looking at the ways in which audiences and performers affect each other are still quite limited. This edited volume sets out to explore how the interaction between musicians and audiences constructs subjectivities, divisions, and affinities. The underlying logic of this collection of essays stems from an analytical conviction that, in order to understand what happens when people make music, we need to look at the unfolding of the whole 'communicative event' (Gourlay, 1980: 142), which does not only include the current performance but also a limitless range of parallel discourses, historical and contemporary. Through a triple spectrum of musical performance, speech and mediation, the chapters of this book examine a diverse range of current and past case studies in order to shed light on the different ways in which musicians and audiences imagine, treat, and ultimately produce each other.

Moreover, the increased de-territorialisation and re-territorialisation (Inda and Rosaldo, 2008) of cultural phenomena connected to cultural flows (Hannerz, 1996) and the 'ideoscapes' (Appadurai, 1990) characteristic of late modernity, dictate that our approach to musician/audience relationships engages with a cross-cultural array of case studies. Our intention, however, is not to reinvent arguments of cultural particularism by simply showing that different contexts produce different relationships. On the contrary, what this collection of chapters illustrates is that, very often, preoccupations regarding these relationships are strikingly similar in the way that they invoke issues of knowledge, authority and power. At the same time, discourses around these relationships are far from shared and uniform; they often reveal schisms of ideology and aesthetics that can be found even within the smallest affinity groups. For this purpose, the present volume deals with the relationship between musicians and audiences as an inter-cultural and transnational discussion. Some genres and scenes examined here remain local, while other musicians reach a variety of different audiences through the press, music industry, internet and social media. In order to capture global and local aspects of contemporary musicians' relationship with their audiences, this volume moves across localities from India to the United Kingdom and from Greece to Australia, and across genres from jazz improvisation to congregational hymnody and from folk/traditional to electronic dance music.

## Relationships in performance

The volume's emphasis is on performance as a multidimensional process of continuous feedback. This resonates with Simon Frith's (1998: 203) view that listening should also be conceptualised as 'performing', a proposition further supported by Christopher Small's idea of 'musicking' (1998) which is constructed as a wider analytical category beyond what we would traditionally think of as 'performance'. Frith further concurs that 'the term performance defines a social – or communicative – process. It requires an audience and is dependent, in this sense, on interpretation; it is about meanings' (1998: 206). In order to describe a performance as a communicative event between performers and audience, while always keeping in mind the multiple mediations between them, we need to account for the ambiguity of this communication. As Steven Feld reminds us, hearing is a social process:

> all sounds are structured, performed, and heard through organized patterns of anticipation. . . . A range of social and personal backgrounds, some shared, some complementary, of stratified knowledge and experience, and of attitudes . . . enters into the social construction of meaningful listening through interpretive moves, establishing a sense of what the sound object or event is and what one feels, grasps, or knows about it.
>
> (1994: 89)

Thus, the challenge is in finding ways to construct dynamic and flexible models of participation which take into consideration the audience. Regula Qureshi (1987) had proposed an early such model, where she tried to understand the ways in which performers' and audience's input were imperative in what she called 'operationalizing' music and context. She proposed a three-step process of examination moving from music (as structure) to context (as an assemblage of units and codes of behaviour) and then to the actual performance event which was examined through the vantage point of the performer, 'the music maker, who converts the musical structure into a process of sound performance on the basis of his apprehension of all the factors relevant to the performance context' (1987: 65).

In her examination of the British indie music scene Wendy Fonarow (2006) has proposed a different model of examining participation in performance events, this time adopting the audience's perspective and intentions. Her analysis divides the live-music venue into three zones: zone one features the members of the audience closer to the stage, zone two includes the spectators further away from the stage who are focusing on the performance, while zone three includes the disengaged participants who are closer to the bar and pay little or no attention to the music. For Fonarow, these three types of spectorial engagement each carry their respective ideological connotations, in turn making the venue space 'not neutral but socially, historically, and semiotically produced' (2006: 80). Her discussions with audience members from zones one and two point to a reproduction of the western body/mind dichotomy: zone one members claim the achievement of an altered state of consciousness through their intense bodily participation while zone two participants favour their method of music appreciation due to its intellectualised character. Zone three serves, according to Fonarow, as the social space of the professionals of the indie industry. It is within this zone that an intense power drama is carried out among established and prospective members of the scene's social hierarchy. Accordingly, Fonarow's analysis is extremely informative insofar as it sheds light not only on the experience during performance, but also some of the strategic motivations behind modes of engagement.

The effects that the audience has on the musicians' performance and specifically the achievement of peak experiences have been previously discussed by Elina Hytönen-Ng (2013). Her research shows the importance of the audience's role in the creation of a successful performance; a social practice that is not deemed enjoyable without the presence of cooperative spectators. David Pattie (2007) has further suggested that some rock musicians even consider the term 'performance' negatively. For them, the way that the word is being used seems to imply that the event is one-sided: musicians create while the audience receives. According to Pattie, the word 'experience' would better describe the communication that takes place between the performer and the audience. Pattie argued that, particularly in rock performances, musicians attempt to achieve direct communication rather than a one-way transmission towards their audiences (Pattie, 2007: 15–16, 18).

The examination of performance as a sociocultural event has contributed to a widening of the scope of performance studies, often incorporating an emphasis on theatre audiences (Turner, 1982; Schechner, 1985; Hamilton,

2000). In these efforts, anthropological conceptualisations of 'performance' have provided a multifaceted theoretical paradigm for the study of audience interaction. In his pioneering work, sociologist Erving Goffman (1959) has extended the term performance in order to analyse everyday human behaviour.[2] Drawing on Goffman's work, Richard Schechner argues that the performance in fact starts quite earlier and finishes later than the designated event might have us believe. He asks: 'How do specific audiences get to, and into, the performance space; how do they go from that space? In what ways are gathering/dispersing related to preparation/cooling off?' (1988: 189). Additionally, performance entails more than a communication between the audience and the performer. Tsioulakis (2013), for instance, has discussed how the performance occasion is shaped by a range of antagonistic players including, apart from musicians and audiences, a collective of entrepreneurs such as agents, venue owners and record producers. The variety of experiences and subjectivities that are in turn produced by these events are dependent on the power struggles that manifest themselves within those venues. Focusing on the perspective of professional instrumentalists, Tsioulakis (2013) has proposed the term 'performative mutuality' as an optimal experience of live music-making.

As the global music industry shifts back towards an economy of live rather than recorded music-making (Holt, 2010), the interaction between the audience and the performer is increasingly formulated by decisions made by event organisers. Questions such as 'what kinds of audience do we want to attract' and concerns over the marketization of an event affect the end results. This process includes not only wider strategies of promotion and industry design, but also practical decisions that shape the performance event such as the physical space, the presentational norms, and the visual and aural configurations. The shaping of the performance setting is also a contested issue among performers who have often expressed concerns that physical contact with the audience can be 'contaminating'. The jazz musicians examined by Howard Becker in the 1940s and 1950s consistently presented physical segregation as a strategy of artistic integrity and freedom (Becker, 1951). This view has evidently not vanished in the twenty-first century:

> This close proximity of audience to performer was problematic for some of the jazz musicians who felt the intimacy had the potential to breed over familiarity or intrusion. They spoke of experiences where audience members would call out music they expected to hear.
>
> (Brand et al., 2012: 643)

These utterances testify to the charged character of performance as a terrain for the negotiation of values, authenticity and ideology. This makes musicking a privileged locus for the observation of the construction of human subjectivities. Richard Middleton has elaborated on the dependence of value and pleasure on the 'operation of ideology' (1990: 247). More specifically, Middleton argues that the 'involvement of subjects in particular musical pleasures has to be constructed; indeed such construction is part and parcel of the production of subjectivity' (ibid: 249). The ways in which subjects (such as individual persons, but also notions such as 'tradition', 'knowledge' and so on) are constructed within performance interactions form a core concern of this volume.

## Relationships in speech

The relationship between performers and audiences, however, extends beyond the performance event and its dynamics. Authors in this volume are also concerned with the verbal discourses that develop between musicians and audiences, but also the ways in which speech is employed as a medium of representation between the two. Although speech and musical performance cannot be separated, an analysis of speech acts outside the performance event is necessary in order to describe how musicians and audiences construct themselves and one another.

If performance, as discussed previously, includes a multiplicity of negotiations – from message to interpretation(s) which create a variety of interpolated meanings – then speech about music and performance creates an additional meta-level. As such, speech deserves particular focus. According to Feld, 'speech about music represents an attempt to construct a metaphoric discourse to signify awareness of the more fundamental metaphoric discourse that music communicates in its own right.' (1994: 93) These 'metaphoric discourses' are not simply *about* music/musicians/audiences, they also effectively *make* music/musicians/audiences. According to the Foucauldian approach, subjects (by which here we mean both individual persons and concepts) are produced in discourse and cannot be conceived outside it (Hall, 1997: 41–51; Foucault, 1982). Tsioulakis (2011a) has illustrated how musicians' discussions within the 'safe' space of their own (homo-)sociality can often operate as a way of resistance to the outside pressure which is often portrayed as imposed by audiences and entrepreneurs. This is a discursive process that constructs both the instrumentalists' self-conception and the domains within which they operate.

By looking at speech acts as examined in discourse analysis, we can pay attention to how people 'express judgements, for instance moral judgements', and how these speech acts are 'used to perform social acts, for instance protesting' (Harré and Stearns, 1995: 2). The emphasis is 'not only the wide expressive functions of emotions but also their dependence on specific functional and cultural contexts' (ibid). This perspective can be enormously productive for the examination of the musician-audience relationship. Given the fact that the interaction between the two counterparts oscillates continuously between brief moments of 'live' co-existence and lengthy periods of preparation, anticipation and imagination, it is evident that talking about music/musicians/audiences is far more common and frequent than actual musicking.

## Mediated relationships

After conceptualising the relationship between musicians and audiences as it is produced within performance and verbal discourse, we turn to the question of mediation. Music production from live events to recordings and from music journalism to online communities requires the efforts of multitudes of people and is realised through the utilisation of diverse technologies. This relates to what Howard Becker calls 'art worlds' which always include 'patterns of collective activity' (1982: 1). Preoccupied with deconstructing the myths of the solitary genius in art, Becker's influential work has shed light on the mechanisms that are involved in the production, circulation and appreciation of cultural works. In line with that view, work in this edited volume illustrates ways in which the relationship between musicians and audiences is mediated and ultimately shaped by technologies and the social actors who operate them. Central in this examination is the thesis that mediations are neither value-free nor purely operational; on the contrary they are imbued with ideology and power, often with the explicit intention to shape and control the relationship between musicians and audiences.

In her important work, Georgina Born (2005) alerts us to three orders of musical mediation. Music, she argues, 'produces its own social relations . . . inflects existing social relations . . . bound up also in the broader institutional forces that provide the basis of its production and reproduction' (2005: 7). These three processes, namely the creation of social circumstances, the recalibration of pre-existing domains and the interaction with broader institutions, are intrinsic in the mediation of the relationship between musicians and their audiences. For example, George Lipsitz (2007) recounts the relationship between boy/girl bands and their highly gendered audiences as a tale of capitalist negotiations between artists, the industry and particular types of audiences. Thus, the scene that he describes only acquires meaning through (and because of) its mediations in both micro- and macro-scales. On the other hand, subcultures are often constructed on a negation of mediation, which can be actual or imagined but always ideological.[3] Punk and indie's technophobia could be interpreted as a type of stylistic counter-mediation (Fonarow, 2006; Shank, 1994).

What is the role of technological mediations in the production of musician/audience subjectivities? Georgina Born stresses 'the ubiquity and prominence of technological mediation in each element of contemporary musical experience – creation, performance and reception' (2005: 9). Discussing karaoke and other 'mediated-and-live' musical expressions in Japan, Keil has remarked that 'what I find striking in these instances of mediated-and-live musical performances is, first, the humanizing or, better still, the personalization of mechanical processes' (1994: 253). However, Keil's perspective is not devoid of scepticism as is illustrated in his preoccupation with what he termed 'mediated-and-mediated' (ibid: 255) music: where even the 'live' element of music-making is in essence a pretence.

The issue of 'liveness', however, is at least as much a sociocultural as a musicological debate: it is always contested on the ground in ways unveiling the omnipresent issue of authenticity. Auslander's (1999) seminal work on 'liveness' productively engages with these debates, showing that their conceptual pitfalls and paradoxes do not diminish their sociological potency to divide. Auslander suggests that 'within our mediatized culture, whatever distinction we may have supposed there to be between live and mediatized events is collapsing because live events are becoming more and more identical with mediatized ones' (1999: 32). This, Auslander argues, directly affects the experience of audiences and often impedes the emergence of community in live performances, exactly because new forms of mediatization emphasise separation between performers and audiences (ibid: 55). Martin Barker (2003), however, has criticised Auslander's reinvigoration of the authenticity debates, arguing for more attention to audiences' primary testimonies regarding participatory experiences.[4] Christopher Morris' work on spectators of the Metropolitan Opera's 'Live in HD' cinema broadcasts has suggested that the absence of physical co-existence between performers and audience does not necessarily stop an event from being 'a shared experience, a performance' (Morris, 2010: 107).

The increasing blurring between 'live' and 'recorded' music through the use of recordings in live performance and the simulation of liveness in studio production (Porcello, 2005; Meintjes, 2005; Turino, 2008: 66–91) situate issues of mediation at the core of the construction of authenticity. As Born suggests,

> the illusory organicism and simulated 'co-presence' of the resulting recordings, in which the edits are imperceptible, has made critics reach for the concept of ideology: for whatever its governing vision, this is in reality a music made of bits and pieces of players and performances, rendered as the idealized image of 'community' and technical perfection in music.
>
> (2005: 26)

These debates of authenticity are only magnified with the increased reliance of music circulation upon digital media and the domination of the visual element on music production. Simon Frith has characterised commercial music videos as performances of artists 'playing themselves' (1998: 225). In other words, the mediation of performance becomes itself a simulation, a meta-performance. This process entails multiple levels of interpretations: the musicians interpret the song while the audience is interpreting them as personas. If until the late 1990s this interpretation used to be a socially confined process (audiences watching videos in small groups and commenting on them among their peer groups) the wake of internet technology has made this process faster and magnified its impact. Thus, Baym (2012) argues that social media have created new places for the negotiation of authenticity. Artists are not seen any more as distant and fictional personas, but have the opportunity of direct communication with fans (or 'friends', 'followers' and so on). At the same time, the refusal to avail of such opportunity might create new distances and demolish relationships. In Baym's words, artists 'do not just affect audiences. Audiences affect them' (2012: 312). In close relation with the above debates, authors in this volume investigate how authenticity becomes renegotiated through mediated performances and circulation strategies, and examine how understandings of materiality and virtuality are embedded in this process.

## Organization of this volume

Chapters in this volume are divided into four sections, each focusing on a different aspect of the relationship between musicians and audiences. Rather than separating sections between genres or localities – divisions all too familiar in ethnomusicology and popular music studies – we propose that looking at the different processes involved in constructing this multifaceted continuum is a more fruitful perspective.

Contributions in Part 1 entitled 'Conceptualising the audience–performer engagement' shed light on the ways in which participants constitute and think about their divisions. In the first chapter, Bruce Johnson ponders on the ways that contexts of 'vernacular' music-making can challenge conventional participatory roles and understandings. Applying cognitive theory to observations of everyday music-making, Johnson provides ways out of some of the conceptual dichotomies that have tantalised the study of musicians and audiences, and proposes an alternative view of shared, 'coalescent creativity'. In her contribution to this volume, Laura Leante examines issues of 'knowledge' and participation in Hindustani classical music. Building upon ethnography in West Bengal and Maharashtra, Leante scrutinises the way in which audiences with different levels of musical literacy are valued by performers, thus shaping webs of authority, but also how performance interactions momentarily break down some of the strict divisions characteristic of this formalised classical tradition. Mary Louise O'Donnell and Jonathan Henderson also shed light on an under-examined issue of musical performance: the phenomenon of the 'background musician'. Their work comments on the unique set of strategies and challenges involved in playing for an audience whose primary participatory goal does not include communication with (or even acknowledgement of) the musicians.

Part 2, entitled 'Live relationships: negotiations of performance' looks more closely at the relationship as it unfolds within the live performance event. Elina Hytönen-Ng advances the examination of 'audience' and 'musician' as performative categories, by focusing on how jazz musicians in Britain articulate their views and expectations of audience members. By using Alfred Schutz's phenomenology as a theoretical tool Hytönen-Ng raises issues of intimacy and boundaries, entertainment practises and negotiations as they are evoked in the interplay between speech and practice. Based on an example of a live concert in Dublin, Barbara Bradby's chapter examines how both talk and music are used in establishing a locally situated interaction between performer and audience. Focusing on both ritualised and spontaneous modalities of behaviour, Bradby illustrates that an improvised, live conversation between the star and the audience is essential for the constitution of the popular music event. In the third chapter of this section, Andrew Pace describes the ways in which Maltese folk-fusion band Etnika invoke nostalgia as a cornerstone of their performances. Through careful utilisation of the performance space and references to a historically charged repertoire, Etnika forge new audience subjectivities through large-scale public events.

The authors of Part 3, 'Technological mediations: the virtual and the material' comment on the different ways in which technology in past and current times has shaped musician-audience relationships. Examining the implications that electronic technology has on live performativity, Hillegonda Rietveld's chapter analyses issues of 'authenticity' as they manifest themselves between DJs and audiences within electronic dance music events. With a focus on what she terms 'Digital DJ', Rietveld brings back themes of physical movement into a consideration of software-based performance and comments on the interplay between the human body and digital technology in the production of visual and sonic entertainment. Richard Osborne's chapter concerns the ways in which televised performances have shaped modalities of audience behaviour. Analysing examples from across the second half of the twentieth century, Osborne illustrates how the TV was instrumental in educating audiences on ways of participating in performances and comporting themselves in the presence of popular musicians. In the final chapter of this section, Ioannis Tsioulakis focuses on the renegotiation of musician-audience relationships through electronic media in the wake of political turmoil in recession Greece. The essay examines five case-studies of political utterances by well-established popular singers and traces the audience's virtual and physical reactions and the ways in which they shape new alliances and communicative channels.

Finally, Part 4 entitled 'Off-stage discourses and the power of fandom' looks at the construction of 'fan' and 'star' roles and the power negotiations involved in the process. Nancy Bruseker's chapter contributes to debates about the mutual construction of 'fan' and 'star' subjectivities through speech. Through a linguistic examination of audience's letters to nineteenth-century popular performer Vesta Tilley, Bruseker tells a tale of gender, class and agency, as unfolded within the until now invisible domain of private star-fan correspondence. Finally, Mark Duffett's contribution revisits *Starlust* (Vermorel and Vermorel, 2011 [1985]), a seminal historical documentation of star-fan relationships, in order to propose a Durkheimian analysis which focuses on 'effervescence' and the circulation of totemic energy between audience and performers. Deconstructing some of the literature on mass culture, Mark Duffett's chapter readdresses issues of power from the perspective of the fans' subjectivity, and illustrates how inequality can be intrinsic to the pursuit of pleasure.

A central aim in writing this edited volume is to challenge a unilateral view of the relationship between musicians and audiences, one that would maintain an easy dichotomy between active agents and passive gazers. Ultimately, this is a book about music participation; it illustrates how the established ends of the continuum musician-audience can often be challenged and even demolished, while on other occasions they become reinforced and tightly grasped by the imaginations of both collectives. Even though the contributors are driven by a common intention to interrogate the ways in which we understand musicians and audiences, their voices, writing styles, and theoretical backgrounds are not uniform. On the contrary, this work is strengthened by the complementarity between approaches that prioritise direct observation and experience, and paradigm-defining theoretical essays. Through a multiplicity of cultural localities and periods, genres and social groups, the authors of this edited volume illustrate that the division between performers and spectators is not as stable and self-explanatory as musicologists might have once thought, but the well-established ideological discourses behind it suggest that we are far from done with it.

## Notes

1   See for example Heather Maitland's website: www.heathermaitland.co.uk/category/understanding-audiences/.
2   Laura Leante and Barbara Bradby discuss Erving Goffman's work at length in their contributions to the present volume.
3   The works of Dick Hebdige (1979) and Peter Wicke (1990) offer in-depth analyses of such ideologies.
4   Auslander's theses are also challenged by Johnson, Osborne and Rietveld in this volume.

# Part 1
# Conceptualising the audience–performer engagement

# 1 In the body of the audience

*Bruce Johnson*

## Introduction

The objective of this discussion is to re-affirm the qualitative and quantitative significance of live music and its audiences, in the face of an emphasis in the scholarly literature on the mediatisation of music that sometimes even questions the existence of live performance.[1] Two recent quotations from press interviews exemplify some of the basic arguments prosecuted here. Tom Pickard, 13-year-old member of the Choir of King's College, Cambridge, described his experience, 'When we're singing, well it feels like one big mind'. The choirmaster, Stephen Cleobury amplified the point in relation to performing in the College chapel: 'One of the most astonishing buildings in the world to sing in. The music just seems to bloom inside it' (*Sydney Morning Herald*, 'Spectrum', 19–20 July 2014: 9).

My documentation of corporeal interactivity in music events foregrounds the role of audible and visible gestures in the cognitive relationship between participants, in conjunction with approaches to the analysis of social practices which draw on extended mind theory (EMT) and related models. These challenge the assumption that cognition is confined to the 'mind', arguing rather that it is to a decisive degree conducted in and through the body and its interactions with the material world. I then identify a category of musical event which illustrates the point most intensely, in which the distinction between audience and performer is entirely demolished, a category which I define here as 'vernacular'. I conclude by foreshadowing the potential explanatory power of this suite of conceptual models for our understanding of the dynamics of live music events.

## Live music performance

Discussions of music performance have become increasingly enveloped by the phenomenon of mediatisation. In a 2005 online forum of the International Advisory Editors of the journal *Popular Music* (Advisory Editors, 2005), the most frequent point of reference for popular music was music that was mass-mediated and commodified. A recent scholarly essay on popular music declared: 'Music in the twenty-first century does not exist for popular culture if it is not online nor amenable to the iPod' (Robertson, 2011: 32). The study of music audiences, already relatively neglected in music studies, is overshadowed by the media, as audiences are conceived of as accessing music by way of recordings, TV, film, video and internet files. In a recent collection of studies on audiences, apart from the first essay on ancient Greece, every contribution links the notion of audiences with modern media, ranging from print to internet (Butsch and Livingstone, 2014). It is reasonable to take as the standard in this tendency Auslander's (2008) influential study *Liveness: Performance in a mediatized culture*. Now in its second edition in English, it argues that the 'progressive diminution of previous distinctions between the live and the mediatized . . . raises for me the question of whether there really are clear-cut ontological distinctions between live forms and mediatized ones . . . ultimately I find that not to be the case' (ibid: 7).

The jump from live music as problematic to non-existent (as a phenomenon separate from mediatisation), prompts questions regarding definitions of the terms 'mediatised', 'performance' and 'live events'. Is the use of a PA a form of mediatisation? For Auslander this seems to be so 'to some degree' (ibid: 25), a nuance not evident in his declaration above. A generalisation like 'the live now derives its authority from its reference to the mediatized' (ibid: 43) simply doesn't stand up, as I document below. Of course, the interrelationship of live and mediatised performance is complex (see for example Krueger, 2005). Auslander recognises the complementarity of the live and the mediatised event, and that concerts are opportunities to promote recordings and vice versa. However, the broad picture is that since 2009 the economic value of live music in the UK appears to be increasingly in excess of recorded music (Page and Carey, 2010: 3–4). Live music remains at the very least economically significant, if not dominant. Auslander's argument rests upon an understanding of performance as something formally staged as public entertainment, as in the case of rock performance, 'which is predicated on the distinction between performers and spectators' (Auslander, 2008: 65). He argues that 'the effort to eliminate that distinction destroys the very possibility of performance' (ibid). While the broad argument that our contemporary performance cultures have been massively infiltrated by mediatisation is undeniable, it is untrue to declare that live performance 'can claim little in the way of cultural presence or power' (ibid: 46).

This conception of audiences neglects a massive amount of music performance and its audiences that occurs daily across the planet. These events, far from being marginal, are of vital importance in the global experience and function of music, in a way that cannot be said of mediatised music. As such, these events have distinctive and significant lessons about music and its social roles and thus also provide insights about individual and collective social practices to which mediatised music supplies no access. If one idea underscores the following argument it is, to appropriate the title of a recent novel by Hilary Mantel, that I am 'bringing up the bodies': musics which are made and listened to by bodies, without mediatisation. Although they all share this characteristic, their occasions and formal properties are immensely diverse. They include: domestic celebrations, chants at sports grounds and political demonstrations, locker room singing, street busking, children's playground songs, hymn-singing, live-music-serviced dances and émigré national club events, small folk and jazz pub gigs, jam sessions and rehearsals, concerts where filming and recording are forbidden, domestic music-making from group celebrations to solitary household or in-the-car singing and whistling. All these, however academically sidelined, are ubiquitous forms of live music-making that serve a significant purpose or they would not occur. I am one of many musicians I know who present such music at benefits, at rest homes and hospitals, at promotions ranging from used car yards to sports events, at regional jazz festivals. We can read more about such events in an immense body of work including by, inter alia, Ruth Finnegan (1989), Steven Feld (1988), Thomas Turino (2008), Martin Stokes (1994), Sara Cohen (1991), Michael Brown (2012) and multitudes of other ethnomusicologists and anthropologists.

Pace Auslander's dismissal of non-mediatised music experiences on economic, social, and even ontological grounds, I want to argue that they are essential forms of music making/listening in the process of individual and collective identity integration, precisely because they are non-mediatised. There is abundant literature on the psychic and somatic benefits of live, voluntary unmediatised music-making, samples of which are cited by the Australian Bureau of Statistics (ABS) with child participation figures increasing well after the advent of the mediatisation takeover as identified by Auslander.[2]

Let me briefly exemplify these live music events and their audiences. The first is so familiar and, for scholarly music discourse, unglamorous, that it has received little attention (but see for example Evans, 2006). I refer to music in churches. It is certainly the case that religious institutions and activities have to varying extents been mediatised, including through websites. In Australia, Hillsong Church is a prime example, a major mediatised international production industry, incorporating CD production, online sermons and gospel music presented in the manner of a rock/stadium concert, with giant TV screens.[3] Many other churches now include online sermon libraries.[4]

Let us sample, however, the local parish churches which cumulatively account for most of the community's weekly worship. In my own area of Leura and Katoomba in the Blue Mountains, 100 kilometres west of Sydney, there are about a dozen small churches, with regular services that may in their own right be described as performance events, and in particular they incorporate live music. At St Alban's Anglican church, Leura, during two successive services on 14 and 18 August 2013 in which I took detailed notes, there were included a total of five hymns, as well as a number of episodes of performative antiphonal dialogue (prayers, readings from *The Book of Common Prayer* and *The Bible*) which incorporated musicality, such as modifications of pitch, rhythm, volume and pace.

These were not mediatised events, with not even an active PA in use. Performances like these (for example 'Choral Evensong' on Sundays) are repeated, just in this one congregation, up to four times each week. These local churches service a local community (Katoomba and Leura) totalling about 12,400. This is neither a negligible community nor a trivial activity for its participants. A household survey conducted by the ABS during the period March to July 2006, found that '20% of adults participated in religious or spiritual groups or organisations during the 12 months prior to interview'.[5] The research organisation, National Church Life Survey (NCLS) reports that 'Around 19% of Australians are in church at least monthly'.[6] With a national population of 22.68 million in 2012, this means that every month in Australia alone (a relatively secular society in global terms[7]) at least 4.3 million people participate in that devotional live performance, including singing, every month.

If church singing is relatively neglected in popular music studies because it is so familiar, I now turn to another forum for live performance, including music, which is overlooked simply because it is not on the radar of western performance and music scholarship, yet its community benefits are sufficient to attract major government support. Participatory theatre has long been used in community development programmes in Latin America, Africa and Asia. Seeds of Life (SoL) is one such project that began in 2000, funded by the Australian and Timorese governments, and trialled among subsistence farmers in rural communities in Timor Leste in July 2013 to address food security issues. It uses staff and students from Charles Sturt University in Australia, and members of Teatru Timor Leste.[8]

Access to electronic media in the region is minimal and there is a high rate of illiteracy. The primary means of circulating information about SoL's activity is therefore word-of-mouth, and the activity itself consists of participatory theatre (PT) to provide information about ways to improve food security by using improved crop varieties. In community development in such environments, PT has long proven to be 'a dynamic and evolutionary tool for change which can facilitate dialogue and reflective participation' (McCarthy, 2004 cited McGillion, 2013).

The SoL Timor project seeks to promote awareness of higher-yielding varieties of corn and different planting techniques in farming communities south of the capital Dili. The Australian and Timorese members of the team would process into a village marketplace to attract attention and create the performance space, greeting the locals in their own language. They then presented a performance re-enacting seasonal cycles, in particular the harvest, acting out tensions between, for example, the desire to eat the corn and the need to preserve it for replanting. The triumph of the second alternative led to a celebration of prudent farming and gestures of respect to the audience-farmers. There then followed 'playback theatre', in which the audience members told their own stories about difficulties in growing their crops and the troupe would act out the stories, inviting the storytellers to comment on their accuracy and refining the performance until the storytellers were satisfied that they had been properly understood. There would then be discussion and enactment of different, preferred outcomes, based on more effective farming methods. Finally, each member of the troupe enacted a key theme presented. The performance lasted about 45 minutes.

There are several points to be made about this live theatre. It is intensely interactive and corporeal, relying on expressive action and gesture, and often physical slapstick comedy. The troupe also used dance with audience participation, and songs written by members of the troupe – in short, the theatre included musical performance. It is also entirely unmediatised, which is crucial to its success. Through word-of-mouth, over the week of presentations confined to small villages, total attendances were over 1000. Post-performance surveys conducted by the Timorese themselves indicated a very strong increase in interest in improved farming techniques, and strong approval of the manner in which the message was presented, in view of the high rate of illiteracy and poor access to any media. The local Minister for Agriculture was sufficiently impressed with the efficacy of the experiment to contract for an extension of the project into other districts.

The two cases above are unequivocal exemplifications of the robust health and importance (economic and social) of live music and its audiences, in which mediatisation plays, if any, a negligible role. It is music to which analytical models constructed on the basis of mediatisation are therefore irrelevant. These cases also provide a point of departure from which to explore two conceptual models that have rich potential for an understanding of the audience/performer dynamic.

## Thinking outside the (brain)box: theories of gesture and extended mind

My objective is to break down distinctions that misleadingly reinforce the separation between various parties to a collective activity, and in this instance specifically between audiences and performers. At the most obvious level, the simplistic conceptualisation of the musical event as constituted of performers and audiences is misleadingly schematic. It implies, among other things, that performers are not 'auditing' and that audiences are not 'performing', in ways that affect the musical and broader experiential content. Less obviously, the associated lacunae in the discourse of music and its audiences are the outcome of traditional conceptions of cognition, ultimately traceable to the mind/body binary. By reference to studies of gesture, extended mind and related concepts, I wish to challenge this model and at the very least sketch ways in which such enquiries might enlarge our understanding of the audience/performer dynamic.

A number of the terms clustering around this discussion are culturally contingent, including 'music' itself, for which some societies have no equivalent word, or for whom, unlike English, it refers only to a process rather than a commodity (Turino, 2008: 2, 24). Likewise notions of performance: the question of how to translate the word 'performativity' or 'performance' into Polish for example was debated for many years, and, as I am informed by Justyna Stasiowski (see endnote 1), the word is still used differently in Warsaw and Krakow. Furthermore, the Anglophone idea of 'audience' has no 'ready-made' equivalent in either Chinese or Arabic (Dawoud, 2014; Xu, 2014; Wu, 2014). These terms are thus cultural constructs. In English, the performer/audience binary derives primarily from the highly regimented art music concert model, in which audiences play an apparently passive role in relation to the musicians who are actively involved in performing the music, a clear distinction between producers and consumers. While the model remains robust in public and even some scholarly discourse, it has come under challenge from various quarters.

The notion of performance itself has been opened up to a broader range of social interactions (see for example Goffman, 1959; Butler, 1993; Small, 1998) and the audience/performer binary has been broken down, as for example through the coinage 'prosumer', which, however, has not been primarily applied to live performance.[9] It is in popular music studies and ethnomusicology, relating to live and particularly improvised performance situations, that the active/passive distinction is obviously so much more difficult to sustain (see for example Keil, 1987; Feld, 1988; Fonarow, 2006; Turino, 2008; in jazz: Stebbins, 1969; Berliner, 1997; Johnson, 2002; Hytönen-Ng, 2013). Consequently, it would be repetitive to argue here against that binary. Rather, I want to add to the alternative models available in a way that complements my further argument regarding the relationship between cognition and gesture, by foregrounding the importance of corporeality in the relationship between audiences and performers. This in turn needs to be framed by some more general observations regarding the relationship between corporeality and cognition, the mind/body distinction which continues tacitly to underpin theories of social practice (see further Johnson, 2013).

This is however increasingly understood to be an untenable distinction. In her study of anxieties among people whose bodies have been surgically altered, Manderson argues that these anxieties manifest

> an existential dilemma in the relationship between body and soul, corporeality, memory and emotion. . . . The notion of bodily integrity and the possibility of organic (or cellular) memory is a common concern among people who have had transplants and among their partners.
>
> (Manderson, 2011: 83; see further 231–5)

All of her case studies destabilise the simplistic distinction between the body and the 'inner' self (ibid: 183, 185, 199–200). 'The body remembers', as dramatically manifested in the phantom pain experienced by people who have lost a limb (ibid: 105). But this runs deeper than just the memory of something experienced and now lost. Goldin-Meadow recounts the case of a young woman who was born without arms, 'who should know nothing of gesturing firsthand'; nonetheless she experienced the sensation of gesturing, and even the small stumps moved as she spoke (Goldin-Meadow, 2003: 243–4). Similarly, McNeill's account of the congenitally blind, who, having never seen gesture, nonetheless gesture as they speak (McNeill, 2005: 25–6). Manderson cites the words of Fisher: 'human identity cannot be separated from its somatic headquarters in the world. How persons feel about their somatic base takes on mediating significance in most situations' (Fisher, 1990, cited in Manderson, 2011: 121).

Such data prompt the hypothesis that cognition may be usefully thought of as not confined to the 'mind' or the 'brain'. Rather than the body simply being a manifestation of cognition, in conjunction with its interactions with the material world it is an instrument of cognition. This line of enquiry destabilises a whole array of conceptual dichotomies that underpin cultural theory in its dominant forms, including 'subjective/objective', 'self/other', 'culture/nature' and of course 'mind/body'. Conventionally we think of bodily gestures as representations of thoughts that have already been generated in the mind. But we might understand social practices, including the way we respond to music, in a different way if we think in terms of extended material cognitive systems rather than bodies simply as representations of internal cognitive activity. The lines of enquiry that I want to flag converge in a number of terms including Extended Mind Theory (EMT), Distributed Cognition and Cognitive Ecology, which model human thought as 'inextricable tangles of feed-back, feed-forward, and feed-around loops, that promiscuously criss-cross the boundaries of brain, body and the world' (Clark, 2011: xxviii). That is, all three advance the proposition that cognition does not stop at the border of the individual skull.

To outline EMT most succinctly, I cite some of its theorists and, in keeping with the developmental objective of research, refer the reader to these sources, rather than waste space in extended reiteration. To further condense, I shall focus primarily on two texts by Clark (2011) and Menary (2010), both of which reprint what is regarded as the seminal text on EMT, Clark's and Chalmers' (1998) essay 'The Extended Mind'. The latter also gathers together the debates framing EMT. The definition of 'cognition' is of course often contested; even the etymology of the word itself is disputed.[10] What matters here is not a comprehensive definition of cognition, but one generally agreed constitutive aspect of it. That is, cognition is understood to occur within the skull, and does not take place outside that locus.

The traditional Cartesian model of cognition is that 'it has a natural boundary: it is contained in the brain' (see Adams, Azaiwa and Rupert, cited Menary, 2010: 229, 242–3). Menary further asserts that '[m]ost philosophers and cognitive scientists take cognition to be a clump of mental acts or processes' (Menary, 2010: 229). Cognition is thus a processing of the data from 'out there' mediated by the body's sensory mechanisms, but taking place wholly in 'the mind', which is located in the individual brain pan. This processing completed, the mind then expresses or represents the outcomes to the world 'out there' through the body (speech, gesture) and its manipulation of appropriate technologies (pen, brush, musical instrument, keyboard). This model distally underpins the audience/performer binary. That is, performers conduct acts of musical cognition – processing musical ideas – which are then expressed through various physical competencies. And there are those who audit that information, received via the body's sensory mechanisms, each cognitively evaluating it in an individual brain pan. Each 'cognitive unit', each mind, is operating separately, isolated by the body in which it is contained. As noted, the art music concert spaces and protocols appear to confirm this model. While it has certainly been recognised that in, for example, folk, pop, jazz performances, the relationship is more complex, nonetheless, studies based uncritically on the performer/audience binary implicitly subscribe to the distinction: body as 'mediator', mind as 'cogniser'.

It is a model that emphasises separation between elements of the individual, between members of a group and between the animate and inanimate world. Its ascendancy is so powerful as to have become deeply rooted in our conceptual and verbal apparatus. There have, however, always been less positivistic, more holistic and supple approaches in the understanding of the human-in-the-world from ancient times, through to the modern era in various enquiries including in the work of Bateson (1973), in field theory (Lewin, 1951), gestalt therapy (Perls, 1976), phenomenological anthropology (Jackson, 1996), vibrant matter (Bennett, 2010), forms of artistic creativity (Pressing, 1987; Johnson, 2002; Ball and Kuhlman, 2010), and in the concept of 'flow' (Hytönen-Ng, 2013). These alternative models challenge an ontology of separation, but have generally been articulated discretely and often only implicitly in a wide range of studies. While they gust over the topsoil of cultural studies, they have barely begun to aerate the impacted soil through which the roots of models such as audience/performer reach down invisibly into the paradigms like 'mind/body' and 'self/other' which nurture them.

EMT extends the challenge to the separations between mind, body and the material world, not by abolishing them, but by proposing a need to 'reconceive the mind' (Menary, 2010: 232). John Sutton cites Bruno Latour:

> in abandoning dualism our intent is not to throw everything into the same pot, to efface the distinct features of the various parts within the collective. We want analytical clarity, too, but following different lines than the one drawn for the polemical tug of war between subjects and objects.
>
> (cited in Sutton, 2010: 217, fn. 8)

This reconfiguration of our understanding of the mind asks 'where does the mind stop and the rest of the world begin?' (Menary, 2010: 1). EMT proposes a 'function-centric' rather than 'location-centric' model of cognition: 'the human organism is linked with an external entity in a two-way interaction, creating a *coupled system* that can be seen as a cognitive system in its own right' (Clark and Chalmers, 2010: 29; italics in original). This is

> not just a weak claim about the causal dependence of some cognition on external factors . . . It is a stronger claim involving the constitution of cognition, at least in part, by external factors . . . It is a thesis that takes the bodily manipulation of external vehicles as constitutive of cognitive processes.
>
> (Menary, 2010: 21)

Menary surveys a second wave in the evolution of EMT incorporating what he calls 'cognitive integration' and characterised by, inter alia, increasing interdisciplinarity including a convergence with studies of childhood development (Menary, 2010: 13, 20, see also 227–244). Sutton also foreshadows a further broadening of case studies in a third wave of development (2010: 213).

Studies of gesture reinforce such approaches. David McNeill argues that gesture is 'part of the speaker's current cognitive being, her very mental existence, at the moment it occurs' (McNeill, 2005: 92). One does not think first then find the utterance or gesture to express the point, 'rather, thinking, as the source of meaning, emerges throughout the process of utterance formation' (ibid: 125). The complicity between gesture and cognition is reinforced by the fact that the former also improves memory and learning (ibid: 128). This has been apparent in studies of childhood development, such as those of Goldin-Meadow, who argues that gestures 'would not only reflect a child's understanding, but play a role in shaping it as well. Gesture would be part of the mechanism that brings about cognitive change' (Goldin-Meadow, 2003: 116; see further Chandler, 2013). Thus one of the most effective mechanisms of assimilating information is by sharing gestures. This is part of how we learn to understand each other. As Cox argues, 'mutual imitation fosters mutual understanding. In mutual imitation we become like those we are trying to understand – we understand (in some measure) what it must be like to be them because we are being like them' (2006: 48).

Clearly these arguments have particular significance in how we understand sonic experience and cognition. It is well understood that music is potentially a powerful vehicle for individual and collective integration (see for example Hytönen-Ng, 2013: 63–76; similarly Turino, 2008: 1–2). Studies of gesture and EMT tend to confirm what everyday experience also teaches: that the power of music to integrate audiences and performers is maximised in situations of corporeal interaction.

This is one reason that group music making and dance so often form the center of rituals, ceremonies, and activities intended to strengthen and articulate social bonds – ranging from the chanting of military cadences by recruits while jogging, to singing in churches, to Shona ceremonies and Aymara festivals, to the Nazis' use of collective singing. It is *in the doing* that the feelings and direct experience of being in sync with others is most pronounced.

(Turino, 2008: 44; italics in the original. See similarly
ibid: 3, 41–2, 135–6)

Live music experience thus crucially differs from mediatised music experience (ibid: 42–3). Spontaneous and immediate interactive gesture is crucial to the social contracts created by music (see also Laura Leante's chapter in this volume).

I cite Turino not as a cognitive theorist, but as a scholar whose work as an ethnomusicologist tends to confirm the EMT model in musical terms. The recognition of the importance of corporeality in the formation of these audience/performer relationships closely parallels models of EMT, Distributed Cognition (see Spurrett and Cowley, 2010) and Cognitive Ecology (see Tribble and Keene, 2011). I want to push the idea of Turino's phrase 'in the doing' a little further, to suggest that audiences in live music events come into being in an act of collective gestural cognition. As with Turino, Arnie Cox is another scholar whose work on a parallel track gives further impetus to EMT. He draws many of these ideas together in arguing that 'our embodied experience is not only necessary for experiencing meaning that is somehow inherent in the music itself, but that meaning arises in our conceptualizations of embodied musical experience and that abstract meaning is the *product* of embodied reasoning' (Cox, 2006: 45–6; italics in the original). He recounts a concert in which a man in the audience began singing along to a performance of 'Old Man River', to the great embarrassment of his wife. That he sang along exemplifies the importance of 'imitative participation that is a regular part of musical experience *and comprehension*' (ibid: 46; my italics); that is, this is part of the process of comprehending music. That his wife was so embarrassed exemplifies the inhibitions against it and thus the radical intellectualisation or cerebration of music experience in out art music tradition. The singing of which he writes:

part of *how we understand* music involves imagining making the heard sounds for ourselves, and this imagined participation involves covertly and overtly imitating the sounds heard and imitating the physical actions that produce these sounds. Mimetic participation occurs in three forms: (1) covert and overt imitations of the actions of the performers (whether the performers are seen and heard, or heard only, or recalled); (2) covert and overt subvocal imitation of the sounds produced, whether the sounds are vocal or instrumental (likely to include an imitation of timbre as well as pitch, rhythm and dynamic level); and (3) an amodal, empathetic, visceral imitation of the exertion patterns that would likely produce such sounds.

(ibid: 46; my italics)

Cox continues: 'Mimetic participation is fundamental to human comprehension, and its role in musical experience is very much simply a special case of how the embodied mind works ... *our comprehension of the sounds* involves comprehension of the relevant motor actions' (ibid: 47–48; my italics). What is usually conceptualised as a physical response to music is thus more organically implicated in the process of coming to know it. Gesture 'seems to match best the level at which we grasp (comprehend) music most viscerally and intimately, and in this way it highlights a kind of musical knowing that is distinct from out more visual and quasi-objective conceptualizations' (ibid: 57).

The potential explanatory power of the EMT model is broad and extensive. In addition to providing new ways of understanding the 'infant–carer dyads' in childhood development (Menary, 2010: 23), more generally Clark suggests that it promises to produce 'a new kind of cognitive scientific collaboration involving neuroscience, physiology, and social, cultural, and technological studies in about equal measure' (cited in Sutton, 2010: 191). It has been deployed to productive effect in telerobotics and neuroprosthetics, and in various forms of historical studies including economics, sociology, and media theory (Sutton, 2010: 192–3). Given its fundamental premises, EMT has promise for work in any field whose underpinnings are still sustained implicitly by the mind/body binary, which covers pretty much all culture-based research. In the present instance, this includes the study of music experience and affect, as impressively demonstrated in Tribble and Keene's study of the importance of utterance and gesture in metrical psalm-singing in the formation of a community of beliefs in the English reformed church, particularly germane to this paper (Tribble and Keene, 2011: 89–106).

Congregational hymn singing was central to worship in the reformed churches. Bishop John Jewel recorded with approval that religion 'is somewhat more established now than it was', and that this was reflected in the spread of congregational hymn singing, and hearing at St Paul's Cross, 'six thousand persons, old and young, of both sexes. All singing together and praising God' (cited in Tribble and Keene, 2011: 97). These were an early form of popular music, sung in the vernacular and often derided by sophisticated commentators as childish, and probably often set to popular tunes, and referred to as Geneva jigs (ibid: 99–100). They were grassroots examples of the collapse of the distinction between producer and consumer, as may also be said of singing that accompanied 'rhythmic work including weaving, kneading' (ibid: 105). Tribble and Keene provide an elegant case study in the distinctive power of sound (as compared with vision) and in particular of embodied song in which there is the most intimate connection between singer and auditor, as a site of EMT. Referring to the totality encompassed by EMT, what they refer to as the 'cognitive ecology', Tribble and Keene demonstrate that 'close attention to the entire cognitive ecology – insides, objects, and people – allows us to fully appreciate the range of factors in play and develop a more comprehensive understanding of the forces that shaped the English Reformation for ordinary worshipers' (ibid: 106).

Notwithstanding the seeds sown by this richly instructive study, EMT has not explicitly developed a systematic relationship with music practice. Here I want to argue that these models of cognition have a particular resonance with sonic experience in general and live music in particular, as exemplified succinctly in the quotes opening this essay. Like EMT it is increasingly understood that sonic information processing and the generation of sonic affect raise fundamental questions about the validity of the mind/body binary. Music provides an excellent platform for the development and application of EMT, not only because the body and external material vehicles are central to its production (voice, fingers, instruments, setting), but also because of the distinctive character of sonic phenomenology and physiology. Again, in elaborating this I must, in the interests of space, rely on a forest of citations for fuller detail. Menary declares that '[t]he primary motivation for cognitive integration is the brute fact of our embodiment' (Menary, 2010: 228–9).

The close link asserted here between mind and body chimes suggestively with scientific studies of affect. In his influential 1980 paper 'Feeling and thinking: preferences need no inferences', R. B. Zajonc postulated that 'the very first stage of the organism's reaction to stimuli and the very first elements in retrieval are affective' (Zajonc, 2004: 254). Neuroscience tells us that this emotional reaction is physiological, generated in the amygdala when it receives the sonic signal. But the sound takes two paths to the amygdala. One is via the auditory cortex, a high level information processor that can sort through our memories to identify the precise nature of the stimulus – which band we might be listening to. But the other path is direct from the ear to the amygdala, called a quick and dirty path. Quick, because that signal arrives first. Dirty, because it has a lower level of discrimination, telling the amygdala just that this is scary, happy, safe, threatening – it is the primary response we make to an auditory stimulus. We all recognise it in sensations like goose pimples, hair prickling, and like our pets as their hackles rise, it can occur before we are even conscious of the precise cause. It is a primary pre-cultural survival mechanism, preparing us for fight-or-flight. So, there is a primary reaction to a sonic stimulus, which is physiological, involuntary, and almost irrevocable. It creates a foundation on which a secondary and cognitively mediated response draws on cultural memory to articulate the precise nature of the stimulus (see further LeDoux, 1999: 138–78).[11]

Clearly, before sound studies start addressing the effects of cultural mediations, something else transcultural (and even trans-special) has already taken place at the level of spatiality and physiology to establish an interpretive foundation on which the cultural scaffolding can be constructed. These involuntary affective interpretations that I have been describing are physiological not cognitive, according to the models we deploy. A study of sound production, transmission and reception thus discloses that, first, it is not the judiciously discriminating 'mind' that initially shapes sonic affect. It is what, in that model, we would call the body.

But this raises interestingly awkward questions. If it is the body that lays down the platform for music affect, this means that the most fundamental of the mediations is also the most fundamental interpretive mechanism. This raises in turn the radical question: in sonic experience, where do the physical mediations stop and the interpreting 'Me' begin? The body evidently cannot be usefully understood simply as a mediator. It is already an 'interpreter', functioning in ways that we habitually assign to the process of cognition. In effect, while we are operating with a mind/body paradigm, there seem to be two ways of hearing that are not only barely connected, but sometimes in tension. As has been noted in music theorisations that go back to the ancient debates as represented by Aristoxenus and Pythagoras, roughly the debate is between a sensuous, 'emotional' way of understanding the experience of music and a 'rational' one based on mathematical ratios, and as wittily implied in the apophthegm 'I'm told Wagner's music isn't as bad as it sounds'.[12] Judith Becker has written that the study of 'Music and emotion ... dissolves intractable dichotomies concerning nature versus culture, and scientific universalism versus cultural particularism' (Becker 2001:154). Sound studies destabilise a whole array of conceptual models that underpin cultural theory in its dominant forms. These models involve binaries like 'subjective/objective', 'self/other', 'culture/nature' and of course 'mind/body'. In sonic processes, where does the material become the cognitive?

These questions raised by sonic experience are precisely the questions raised by EMT, which suggest that there is a special symbiosis between the two, a potential for mutual nourishment. EMT posits a much more deeply intimate connection between subject and object, cognition and gesture, mind and body than the deep flowing current of thinking that atomises the world into discrete units. In this discussion, those units are audiences and performers, and to present my argument in its most vivid form, I want to consider musical events in which that distinction simply does not exist: audiences and performers are fully coalesced.

I suggest that some degree of that coalescence is present in all live music events in a way that is not true of mediatised music. That is, in live music events, even those in which the division between audience and performer is strategically emphasised, there is at least some degree of direct reciprocity.[13] Even symphonic concert audiences create applause that is heard, unmediated, by the performers. If we proceed along a spectrum through more intimate reciprocities – folk, jazz, pub rock, for example – ultimately we come to musical events where we can no longer make a distinction between audiences and performers, a point at which the intimate relationships posited by EMT can be most clearly heard and examined. Far from being uncommon, I argue that these constitute the most ubiquitous category of music events and, because of their corporeality, the most intense sites of individual and collective identity formation.

## Vernacular performance

The point of the foregoing has been to reinstate the idea of live music and its audiences as a quantitatively and qualitatively significant phenomenon, and as a uniquely instructive site for the understanding of music experience, where EMT and gesture come into play and yield significant insights into musical dynamics in ways that media-centric models cannot. The potential usefulness of studies of music is glimpsed in Clark's example of the connections between 'brain, body and local environment. Think of a dancer, whose bodily orientation is continuously affecting and being affected by her neural states, and whose movements are also influencing those of her partner, to whom she is continually responding' (Clark, 2011:24). As a suggestive site of EMT, the convergence of 'brain, body, local environment' and – not extrapolated explicitly by Clark – improvised musical activity, in which the 'performers' are also each other's 'audience', provides impetus to the next stage of my argument. It is suggested here that EMT is most instructively manifested in practices which involve improvised collectivity and, in particular, involve corporealised music where production and consumption are most closely entangled.

I conclude, then, with a musical model complementary to those dynamics, in the most intense, and therefore instructive, form of what Cox calls 'mimetic participation', the form in which the explanatory potential of EMT and gesture is most evident. I wish to focus on what I will be calling in a very specific sense 'vernacular performance' because it brings to bear and exemplifies so clearly all the dynamics unique to live performance. Having elaborated this model in arts policy discussions (Johnson, 1996) and more recently in conjunction with ideas set out earlier in this paper (Johnson, 2013), I don't need to do so again here, but to draw out implications for the study of audiences. The term is of course not my own (see for example Hitchcock, 1969; Illich, 1981; Pickering and Green, 1987; Bohlman, 2001). I deploy it here, however, with specific inflections which place it outside the capitalist and mediatised framework within which the 'prosumer' model is located. It is difficult to argue that, say, children involved in playground games involving nonsense sounds or old nursery rhymes is either significantly intersected by capitalism or mediatised.

As in this example, expressed in its simplest form, I define 'vernacular' here as being live music in which the categories of consumers and the producers approach complete overlap. This intimate connection invokes the origins of the term 'vernacular': 'verna', a slave born on the estate in which he or she lives and labours, emphasising the intimacy of the link between subject, agency and function. The usage of the term 'vernacular music' is already malleable enough to accommodate that linkage in this broader sense. In applying that model, we exclude none of the musics to which it is usually applied, but by transcending the constraints of genre (for example 'folk music') and framing the term through the production/consumption dynamic, it becomes a way of understanding the term more generously, and in a way that bypasses the misleading dilemmas posed by genre, in an era in which genre itself has become so permeable and evasive as a way of locating musical practices (are the Three Tenors a classical act or a popular act? What 'genre' is *Carmina Burana* when it is used to advertise coffee, to open a sports event, as a soundtrack for a film or as a military recruitment advertisement?). A non-generic approach to an understanding of vernacular music enables us to secure it more instructively in a mediatised, globalised environment.

In the most fully realised forms of vernacular music in this sense, the distinction between hearer and performer collapses. They are the same: from the person singing to themselves while doing the housework to the example of the church congregations that I discussed above, the audiences and the performers are identical. I begin with this in order to present my argument in its clearest form, but then wish to project the model into the more general situation characterised by the live presence of 'audience' and 'performer'. And the argument is that in all these cases, in all live music situations, it can be useful to think of them as extended cognitive systems, examples of EMT, in which the corporeal elements (sounding, gesturing) are not simply the representations of cognitive processes, but are themselves the cognitive processes.

The link between vernacular music as articulated here and EMT lies in the intimacy of the connection that they both postulate between thought and gesture, incorporating the material environment in and through which gesture operates. EMT proposes that gesture (and associated material objects, like a musical instrument) and thought constitute an indivisible 'coupled system' (Clark and Chalmers, 2010: 29). Put simply, the one cannot exist without the other. The musical thought requires the body/instrument in order to be realised; but likewise, the musical thought cannot come into being without the body/instrument. In a complementary dynamic, in vernacular music, the 'gesture' (the music) and the 'consumption' of the gesture are indivisible. The producer/consumer coupling is totally intimate, each wholly for and of the other.

The point here is to raise attentiveness to the role of 'gesture' in the production of the musical experience. A useful point of departure from which to develop this is what Turino calls participatory performance:

actively contributing to the sound and motion of a musical event through dancing, singing, clapping, and playing musical instruments when each of these activities is considered integral to the performance. In fully participatory occasions there are no audience-artist distinctions, only participants and potential participants. Attention is on the sonic and kinesic interaction among participants. Participatory performance is a particular field of activity in which stylized sound and motion are conceptualized most importantly as heightened social interaction.

(Turino, 2008: 28)

Turino's emphasis on the social cohesiveness that is generated by participatory performance takes us very close to the idea of performance as a manifestation of extended mind: 'Being in and out of sync with others results more in what we *feel* than in what we can verbalize about a given situation – what we *know* about it with a different part of ourselves because of the types of signs involved' (ibid: 42; italics in the original). This 'knowing with a different part of ourselves' comes within an ace of recognising the EMT and the possible link between gesture and cognition.

Turino's 'participatory performance' recognises live music as a social rather than an artistic practice. It does not however correspond with what I mean by vernacular music, but overlaps so much that some account of the differences will help to identify the distinctive qualities of the latter. If I refer back to the music events that I listed in my opening discussion, the following exemplification of the differences between, and the usefulness of both, Turino's 'participatory' and my 'vernacular' musics will be clear. For Turino, '[m]ost people go to participatory events because they want to make music and/or dance' (ibid: 29). My understanding of vernacular music differs from this; it can be the case, but more often the musical participation is not the primary objective – as in a birthday party, a church congregation, a sporting event, a political demonstration. My term thus encompasses a wider range of events. For Turino, '[t]o keep everyone engaged, participatory musical and dance roles must have an ever-expanding series of challenges, or a range of activities that can provide continuing challenges' (ibid: 31). Again, not in my model, where the music is collateral rather than central, so it is not necessary that the challenges it presents should increase. 'Participatory music' would thus not include many forms of music activity that are embraced by my 'vernacular'. Additionally, in Turino's model '[t]he music and dance of participatory performances are not scripted in advance' (ibid: 43, see also 37). This is a matter of degree, but arguably does not correspond to what happens in hymn singing, playground singing and sports stadium singing. A jazz performance is usually scripted to the extent of an agreed head and chord sequence, a congregation 'performance' is scripted more tightly, although there is a high level of what Keil (1987) calls 'participatory discrepancies'.

The relationship between repetition and improvisation is always very unclear, and even in individual jazz solos, as in speech, certain licks and phrases generally recur. But my 'vernacular' model diverges here, in that repetition or scripting can be an essential component in the socialising process of performance. In summary, while Turino's 'participatory perform-ance' is an invaluable categorisation, it does not identify the same practices as my sense of 'vernacular performance', nor does it go quite so far as to suggest that the gestures it comprises (both audible and visible) actually constitute a form of extended cognition, as opposed to the representation of cognition.

I conclude by returning to the Timorese performance as reported by McGillion (2013) above, to refine the argument. It is a performance that is so interactive as to qualify as 'vernacular' in my sense; that is, it approaches very closely the dissolution of the audience/performer distinction. As such, I believe it is open to instructive analysis of audience behavior in terms of extended mind or distributed cognition: the participants are 'cognising' through their corporeal interaction, rather than individually expressing ideas formed within each consciousness. Gesture is thought and collective gesture is extended mind. This is hinted in the inspiration for the project: 'Knowledge is not extended from those who consider that they know to those who consider that they do not know . . . Knowledge is built up in the relations between human beings and the world' (Freire, 1998, cited in McGillion, 2013). The 'exotic' nature of this case enables us to perceive what, in more local practices, we tend to take for granted. But if with this case in mind we now turn to some more familiar examples of performance, we can clearly see the operation of the performance dynamics that I am foregrounding. Cognition through collective gesture can be sensed, I believe, in the vernacular performances that I have listed. In church, with the congregation standing, sitting, filing forward to communion, vocalising; the skipping and singing of playground games, the interactive gesturing (audible and visible) in jazz, folk and rock venues.

My argument is that these are musical events which might be more richly understood if we entertain the idea that they are examples of cognition extended into collective gesture, in which the audience/performer binary collapses. We may see these extreme examples of vernacularity as differing only in degree from other live music events, including even the art music concert. Sites of EMT are not positivistic categories, but characterise to a greater or lesser extent all live performance, so that the terms and the dynamics that they imply can be deployed to a greater or lesser extent in the analysis of any non-mediatised performance event.

The juxtaposition of EMT and vernacular music, in the sense articulated here, encourages a heightened scepticism against the constraints of the mind/body model in understanding music cognition and affect. This in turn contests misconceptions about music experience that are invisibly rooted in that binary. In this case, it can reconfirm the importance of live music in an era rather infatuated with mediatisation, and reconstruct our understanding of the relationship between audiences and performers in such events. Of course, the two categories are useful, and even essential for various discourses, ranging from the formation of music policies to quantitative analysis. But the modellings advanced here disturb taken-for-granted paradigms that obscure the extent to which that dichotomy – audience/performer – is in fact a discursive construct that falsifies the dynamic of musical events. EMT also provides a potential path out of the perennial dilemma of music experience, the dissonance between two ways of hearing music as explored by Wardhaugh, which are ultimately based on the mind/body split. It also increases attentiveness to the importance of the body-in-space in music cognition. It underscores the role of the body in laying down musical memory and, as in the arguments mounted by Tribble and Keene, EMT and related models such as cognitive ecology help us to understand the role of live music in the formation of belief and community.[14] These are signposts for journeys that we can't undertake here. To predict in too much detail where they might lead would be the reverse of research. The point is that EMT and live, vernacular music clearly offer ways out of some of the constraints on music analysis and open avenues for further research into the nature of musical cognition in general and the terms of this collection in particular: the relationship between audiences and performers.

## Notes

1  In the preparation of this chapter I acknowledge, in addition to other specific footnoted acknowledgements, the generous assistance of Mark Evans and Liz Giuffre both at that time of Music, Media, Communications and Cultural Studies, Macquarie University, Sydney; Justyna Stasiowska of Poland's Jagiellonian University; and Martin Cloonan of the University of Glasgow.

2  On singing: www.abs.gov.au/AUSSTATS/abs@.nsf/Lookup/4172.0Feature+ Article52010#PARALINK0 (accessed on 16 August 2013). On playing a musical instrument:   www.abs.gov.au/AUSSTATS/abs@.nsf/Lookup/4172.0Feature+ Article12010 (accessed on 16 August 2013).

3  See http://myhillsong.com/ (accessed on 29 June 2015).

4  See for example St. Andrews Cathedral, Sydney: www.sydneycathedral.com/ (accessed on 29 June 2015).

5  Yearbook Australia, 2008 www.abs.gov.au/ausstats/abs@.nsf/7d12b0f6763c 78caca257061001cc588/636F496B2B943F12CA2573D200109DA9?opendocu ment Section 14.39; (accessed on 10 October 2013).

6  www.ncls.org.au/default.aspx?sitemapid=28 (accessed on 15 October 2013).

7  It is significant that among those participating in the ABS survey, above, 'people born overseas (25%) were more likely than those born in Australia (18%) to have participated in religious or spiritual groups or organisations.'

8  I am gratefully indebted to Chris McGillion of Charles Sturt University for this account of Seeds of Life and participatory theatre in Timor; he participated in the project, generously discussed it with me and provided a first draft of his report, from which the following account is abstracted.

9 Ritzer and Jurgensen's useful overview of the history and literature of prosumption focuses on mediatised performances (Ritzer and Jurgenson, 2010).

10 For example, the *Oxford Compact English Dictionary* gives the etymology as 'cognoscere', 'to get to know' (Soames, 2003: 205) while *The Oxford Companion to the Mind* proposes 'gnomon', 'the shadow-casting rod of a sun-dial' (Gregory, 1987: 149).

11 The arguments of Zajonc and LeDoux are summarised in greater detail in Johnson (2008).

12 For a further discussion of the history of this tension, see Wardhaugh (2008).

13 See, for example, Elina Hytönen-Ng's chapter in this volume, where reciprocity is a key factor for musicians' and audience's enjoyment of jazz concerts.

14 Ioannis Tsioulakis' chapter in this volume also confirms that, despite the importance of online interaction between singers and their fans, it is the physical presence of bodies in live evets that is cherished or, sometimes, feared.

# 2 Observing musicians/audience interaction in North Indian classical music performance

*Laura Leante*

The North Indian (or Hindustani) music tradition to which we commonly refer as 'classical' is a form of art music which developed in a courtly environment under aristocratic patronage.[1] Before the twentieth century, it was generally played by a group of mostly hereditary performers for the appreciation of an elite audience of connoisseurs. After the abolition of the courts, during the last century, Hindustani classical music became the domain of the growing Indian middle classes, many of whom still see it as an enriching complement to a good education and from whom the vast majority of consumers and audiences is drawn. Today this tradition is performed in a variety of contexts, ranging from large Western-style public concert halls with a capacity of several hundred people to much smaller (public or private) settings, where musicians and audiences sit on the floor in close proximity to each other, a model which is believed to resemble the older setting of the court.

Musicians' discourse emphasises the value put on this latter context, not least because of the importance that many of them attribute to seeing and interacting with listeners. However, attitudes and feelings towards the wider public vary, as some performers voice a sense of condescension towards the non-expert or 'lay' audiences unable to appreciate the subtleties of their art.

Hindustani classical concerts are conceived as 'presentational': musicians are expected to provide music for a physically separated audience who are there just to listen to them, the forms are closed, the texture is not dense, allowing for an emphasis on the soloist's virtuosity (Turino, 2008: 51–52), to mention but a few of its most immediate features. However, many artists agree on the positive effects that interaction with a knowledgeable, responsive audience can have on the outcome of a concert.

Most of the research carried out to date on interaction in North Indian classical music performance focuses on the relationship between musicians on stage.[2] Literature looking specifically at the relationship between performers and listeners is extremely scarce; exceptions include studies by Silver (1984), Daniel Neuman (1990), and Dard Neuman (2004), which touch upon musicians' interaction with the audience, while Clayton and Leante (2015) examine the interaction between musicians on stage and musicians in the audience.[3] The latter paper draws on seminal sociological work by Erving Goffman (1990), which also provides one of the frames for the interpretation of the performance event that I analyse in this chapter.

Qureshi's pioneering study of *qavvālī*[4] performances (1995) represents the most notable precedent to my methodological approach, which uses observation of video footage of a concert as the basis for analysis. Clayton (2007) also uses video recordings in his study of gesture in the interaction between performer and audience in a concert of *khyāl* (nowadays the most commonly performed genre of vocal Hindustani classical music), with particular attention to the different typologies of hand movement employed by the singer, and to the distinction between 'anticipatory' and 'responsive' forms of audience reaction to the music.[5] This chapter, like Clayton's article, focuses on the analysis of a *khyāl* concert and takes the role of gesture and body movement into account; however, my consideration of gesture is focused on role management in performance.

In the next pages I present recent research into the interaction between performers and audiences in North Indian classical music. In particular, drawing on work by Erving Goffman, Mikhail Bakhtin, Victor Turner and Thomas Turino, I discuss how the study of interaction between musicians on stage and their audiences can shed light on performance and its outcomes, and propose an interpretation of North Indian classical music which recognizes the importance of participation. My discussion will start by delineating musical roles and how these are conventionally understood. I will then move on to the consideration of musicians' views on the importance of interaction with their audiences, and conclude by analysing one such instance of interaction in a performance.

## Performance layout and interaction

In a North Indian classical music concert, participants occupy well-defined positions in the performance space depending on their musical roles. These positions map onto clear hierarchies and are directly related to the degree of movement and interaction that performers are afforded with both fellow performers and listeners.

The soloist (or 'main artist') sits at the centre of the stage,[6] facing the audience; he is the person who leads the event,[7] choosing the musical materials (the *rāg* and the compositions on which he improvises) as well as the structure of the performance. He has the greatest freedom to interact with other musicians and the public, and – if he wants – the greatest freedom to use body movement and gesture, either to support the production of musical sound (especially in the case of singers who often have their hands free) or to facilitate communication with the other participants.

All other performers are accompanists and, as the word suggests, have a musical role subordinate to that of the main artist.[8] At the right of the soloist, at an angle of roughly ninety degrees and facing him, sits the drum player;

among the accompanists, he is the one who is afforded the highest degree of interaction with other musicians and listeners. Throughout the performance (including the introductory section during which he does not play) he is expected to show support to the soloist with hand gestures, nods and verbal expressions of appreciation addressed to both the main artist and the audience. In fact, drum players often explain this form of interaction with the public as a sort of 'duty' that they feel to help the soloist 'convey the message to the audience' (Vishwanath Shirodkar, cited in Clayton, 2007: 81).

In a vocal performance, to the left of the soloist, opposite to the drum player, sits another musician who provides melodic accompaniment on the harmonium or – more rarely – a bowed lute (sarangi). In spite of the position symmetrical to the drummer, this performer usually interacts (and is expected to interact) less with the audience, especially because of the need to closely follow the soloist in the extemporaneous shadowing of his melody. His behaviour is usually much more constrained than that of the drum player, who can also show more flamboyant gestures when granted the space for a solo by the main artist.

At the back of the soloist sit one or more musicians who pluck the *tānpūrā* drone lute and, in the case of a vocal recital, can provide vocal support, as directed by the singer.[9] Their gaze is directed to the main artist through a good part of the concert. These performers' musical status is the lowest among those on stage, as also confirmed by the fact that they are not usually expected to directly interact with the audience, but must maintain a restrained comportment during the performance.

Space in the audience too defines status and the expected degree of freedom of interaction with the performers. This is directly proportional to the proximity to the stage, as those sitting in the front rows are usually connoisseurs (including other musicians) who are more likely to display their appreciation of the concert through gesture, verbal interjections, or by following the rhythmic cycle (by clapping according to its distinctive pattern).

Interaction between performers and audiences is regulated within the structure of the performance. At the beginning of the event this usually takes the form of greeting exchanges[10] between performers and senior musicians or notable people in the audience, or of communication about sound levels with the engineer. Once the concert is under way, during the slow introductory *ālāp* section in which the characteristics of the *rāg* are explored and its mood presented, the main artist's restrained bodily comportment conveys his concentration on the music. While occasional glances at the accompanists and members of the audience are not uncommon in the *ālāp*, interaction with other musicians and the public intensifies over the course of the performance, when compositions are introduced and improvisation develops through an increasingly fast display of virtuosity.

Proper response to the music by listeners who clap correctly or comment at appropriate points of the performance (for example highlighting the *sam*, the first beat of the cycle) provides the musicians with an opportunity to assess the audience's competence and at the same time the members of the public with a means to visibly make a statement of expertise. As Clayton and Leante (2015) point out, interaction with the audience can often also be instrumental to negotiating status and to expressing allegiance and mutual support in performance. My interest here, however, is in interaction as a musician's deliberate strategy to manage a concert and to involve the public in the successful outcome of a performance. Before I turn to the analysis of a specific event, though, I will offer a contextual discussion of musicians' views on audiences and on their attitudes towards them.

## What musicians say about audiences

As noted above, there is general agreement among artists on the value of the expert audience sitting in the front rows: their discourse often implies that the presence of experienced musicians and connoisseurs is a guarantee that the musicians on stage will do their best to maintain the highest standards of performance and not be tempted to just try to please the audience with 'gimmicks'.

Musicians' views, however, vary about the extent to which the degree of competence among the wider audience can affect a concert. Some artists, for instance, choose their repertoire keeping in mind the public that they expect to find at a given venue.[11] This is the case of singer Falguni Mitra, who explains how his first impression of the audience could make him change his original plan and 'decide to present another *rāg*, which would be more intelligible . . . and easily appreciated by those people'.[12] However, he specifies that this would not involve a compromise on his commitment to the quality of the performance, as he would not be 'deviating from [his] own things. It may be a change of *rāg*. It may be change of mood. That's all'.

Similar views, but more focused on the choice of the compositions presented, are expressed by *khyāl* singer Sanjeev Abhyankar: '[I]f I sing something very lyrical oriented in front of an audience who does not understand the language, it's a waste. I have to make a selection accordingly where I perform'. Others, such as sarod player Prattuysh Banerjee, claim that the outcome of a concert is exclusively dependent on the musician's skills: if they make good music the audience will appreciate it and the result will be successful. Thus, the choice of the content or the development of their performance does not depend on the listeners:

I never think . . . 'this audience is not good enough for . . . a serious *rāg*, let's play a light *rāg*'. I will never do that. It does not matter to me at all what the audience is . . . If I cannot [handle the *rāg* well] that is my fault. In a way musicians are definitely responsible. The audience is . . . just one part of the performance.

A similar view is expressed by *khyāl* singer Sanjukta Ghosh, who points out how her focus is just on the music, and that she is used to keeping her eyes 'very much closed' during a performance. Indeed, numerous successful concerts are delivered by artists whose behaviour on stage is introverted and includes minimal interaction with the public. It is not my intention here to suggest that direct communication with or involvement of the listeners is an essential component to the positive outcome of performance. Rather, I am interested in how diverging views can be reflected in different ways of managing a concert through interaction with the audience.

While in fact many performers will agree that the audience's appreciation is ultimately, as Falguni Mitra puts it, 'the acid test of a musician', there are some artists who routinely make interaction with the public integral to their performance. One of these people is Mumbai-based *khyāl* singer Ram Deshpande, who during an interview explained how he believes that a concert is the result of the collective effort of all artists on stage and that this teamwork 'has an effect on the audience'. For him, 'if the artist does not get the blessings of the audience [the event] is meaningless'.[13] He also describes how, during a performance, once he has established the mood of the *rāg* in the *ālāp*, he becomes more 'aware of the audience', and how the concert ultimately relies on a web of interactions between all participants, both on and off stage:

> I try to gauge whether the audience is enjoying the performance or not ... who is listening intently ... I can understand this through their body language. I know which few people really understand my thoughts ... I slowly build rapport with those [people] ... and look at them at the *sam*. The accompanists also give us a response when we look at them. The performance proceeds in this manner, taking continuous response from the audience and the accompanists.

Ram Deshpande's words suggest that he deliberately tries to involve members of the audience, for example by engaging with some of them in focused interaction, granting them 'preferential communication' (Goffman, 1963: 89) at the occurrence of the *sam*, the first beat of the cycle. This allows him to build complicity with the listeners while directing their attention towards key structural moments of the performance. The fact that these are deliberate strategies is further confirmed by his words:

> The audience should get the feeling that we are performing especially for them ... And my experience is that even the person sitting in the last row enjoys the music and communicates with me ... [Performers] have to find some trick so that the audience enjoys the performance.

Does Ram Deshpande's behaviour in performance reflect his statements? How are his strategies deployed and to what extent? I will now move on to the observation of a performance to answer these questions and assess if and how interaction with the audience affects the production of his music.

## Nashik, 13 February 2010

In this section I turn to the close observation of the concert that Ram Deshpande performed a few hours after the interview that I have just discussed.[14] This event, according to all participants to whom I had the opportunity to talk, was an extremely felicitous performance, and in my experience particularly notable for the interaction between musicians on stage and audience.

The concert was organised and recorded as part of a research project whose aims included the study of the interaction between performers and audiences. To facilitate analysis, it was filmed using multiple fixed cameras, including one providing a frontal shot of the stage and one focusing on the audience (see Figure 2.1).[15] On stage Ram Deshpande was accompanied on tabla drum set by Vishwanath Shirodkar and on the harmonium by Anant Lakhe, two artists with whom he is well acquainted. Ram Despandhe's son, Gandhar, sat at the back providing vocal support, and two *tānpūrā* players, Puskaraj Bhagwat and Chaitanya Kelkar, provided further vocal support while playing the drone.

As it is common practice in a *khyāl* performance, on that evening Ram Deshpande performed two *rāgs*, the first longer than the second, followed by a short composition of devotional content. My focus here will be on the first item of the concert, which featured an approximately 60-minute performance of *Mārwā*, an evening *rāg* based on a hexatonic scale, in which the fifth degree is omitted, the second degree is flat, and the fourth degree is sharp. Consistently with other *khyāl* performances, during the introductory free-rhythm *ālāp* section Ram Deshpande's behaviour was more introverted, although on several occasions he glanced at the audience. The interaction with the public increased, as is customary, with the presentation of and improvisation on composed materials, which also involves the active participation of the tabla player who provides the explicit metrical reference. The *ālāp* was followed by three compositions, the second of which was a *tarānā*, a vocal form in which lyrics are replaced by non-lexical syllables. *Tarānās*, like other *khyāl* compositions, are structured in two parts, which are often presented separately with the singer improvising on the first part before introducing the second.

The section of the performance that I focus on here is the beginning of the *tarānā*, in which Ram Deshpande introduces the melody of the first part of the composition, based on the 16-beat rhythmic cycle *tīntāl* in which the main stresses are on the *sam* as well as the fifth and thirteen beats. The clapping pattern characteristic of *tīntāl* includes claps on the *sam*, the fifth and thirteen beats, and a wave on the ninth beat. The melody starts on the tenth beat and is developed over a range of a seventh within one rhythmic cycle.

*Figure 2.1* Frontal shot of the stage and shot of the audience used for analysis

Its main stresses are on the tenth beat (immediately after the wave gesture on the ninth) and on the *sam* (Figure 2.2).

The first ninety seconds of the *tarānā* feature a striking example of a successful strategy deployed by the artists on stage (in particular Ram Deshpande and tabla player Vishwanath Shirodkar) to increasingly involve the audience towards a climactic point of the performance. This excerpt covers twenty-one cycles of *tīntāl* and includes most of the improvisation on the first part of the composition (Table 2.1).

At the beginning of the *tarānā*, Ram Deshpande mostly performs gestures that emphasize the *sam*, first with one hand and then with both; his body gently sways in time with the music. The gestural emphasis on the tenth

*Figure 2.2 Tarānā* – first part of composition

beat becomes evident from cycle 4 as the singer's overall body movements become more marked. By this point, the audience (which at first features only a few people nodding/swaying or marking the beats with their hands or fingers) starts to display a gradual increase in their physical participation in the beats preceding the *sam*.

From cycle 5, the main artist improvises by slightly displacing the melody against the beat, and from cycle 6 the support vocalists start singing the cadential phrase from the tenth beat (which at cycle 7 Ram Deshpande's son emphasises with a visible gesture stretching his arm in the front) to the *sam*. From cycle 9, they join the soloist singing the whole phrase while the tabla player starts a solo. The function of the voices in such moments of the performance is to provide the audience with a simple melodic and metrical reference while the percussionist exhibits his virtuosity and performs complex patterns that might diverge from the explicit stresses of the cycle before landing on the *sam*. From cycle 10, the interplay of gesture and glances between singer and tabla players intensifies, leading Ram Deshpande to vocalise an 'ah!' to show approval of the drummer at cycle 11. By this point, Ram Deshpande has stopped singing, leaving the support vocalists to provide the melodic reference; at cycle 14 he starts clapping the *tīntāl* pattern, through visible gestures which invite the audience to clap along.

Finally, as the end of the tabla solo approaches, at cycle 19 Vishwanath Shirodkar emphasises the tenth beat reaching it through an elaborate threefold cadential rhythmic figure and, raising his arms high away from the instruments with a flamboyant gesture, temporarily suspends playing. The next movement of his arms and torso starts on the fourteenth beat of the cycle and culminates with both hands emphasising the *sam*: rather than playing the drum he points at it and brings his solo to a close with another flamboyant gesture (Figure 2.3). He is joined in performing this deictic gesture by the singer, the singer's son, and one of the *tānpūrā* players. The latter displays his enjoyment and participation at this point with an unrestrained gesture, behaviour which is quite unusual and unexpected from a support musician. The audience too, whose movements had increased steadily over the previous three rhythmic cycles encouraged and 'directed' by Ram Deshpande's clapping, joins in with the gestural display, with many participants stretching out their arms and leaning forward pointing at the *sam* together with them (Figure 2.3).

Table 2.1 Description of interaction during the first twenty-two rhythmic cycles of the *tarānā*

| cycle | singer | | tabla player | other performers | | audience |
|---|---|---|---|---|---|---|
| 1 *(from beat 10)* | Starts singing, glancing at the audience | | Gazes at singer | Apart from singer's son, start accompanying and mostly gaze at singer | | Few people nod/sway and/or mark the beats with their hand or fingers |
| 2 | Marks the *sam* with a hand movement | | Starts accompanying | | | |
| 3 | | Sways and makes gestures to stress beat 10 | | | | |
| 4 | | | | | Harmonium player starts moving head to show appreciation and mark the *sam* | |
| 5 | Marks the *sam* pointing at lap and beat 10 with hand gesture | | Gazes at singer and audience | Support singers join singing cadential formula from beat 10 | | |
| 6 | | | | | | |
| 7 | | Increasingly intensifies gestures on other beats | | | Singer's son emphasises beat 10 with arm movement | |
| 8 | | | | | | |
| 9 | Hand gestures get more restrained | | Starts solo | | | |
| 10 | | Stops singing | | | | Gradual increase in physical display of participation by more people towards the *sam* |
| 11 | Looks at tabla player showing appreciation and smiles at audience | Stresses the *sam* with approving exclamation and hand gesture pointing at tabla player | Makes upward pointing gesture to stress beat 10 | | Singer's son emphasises *sam* with arm movement | |
| 12 | | | | | | |
| 13 | | Shows appreciation of the tabla player with hand gesture | | | Singer's son emphasises *sam* and beat 10 with arm movement | |
| 14 | | | | Support singers sing whole phrase | | |
| 15 | | | | | Singer's son starts clapping | |
| 16 | Claps looking at tabla player and audience | | Appears more focussed on music as complexity of solo increases | | Harmonium player gazes and smiles at audience | Participation further intensifies with more people clapping |
| 17 | | | | | | |
| 18 | | | | | | |
| 19 | Stops clapping after beat 10 | | Emphasises beat 10 performing a cadential formula and raising arms | | | |
| 20 | Emphasises the *sam* by pointing ar the tabla player and smiles as sign of appreciation | | Emphasises the *sam* by pointing at tabla | | Singer's son and one tanpura player emphasise *sam* with hand gesture | Emphasise the *sam* stretching out arms and leaning towards |
| 21 | Behaviour becomes more restrained | | Resume accompanying | | | |
| 22 | Resumes singing | | | | | |

*Figure 2.3* End of tabla solo

In this moment it is as if all are actively participating in the climax of the *sam*, and the fact that the tabla player does not produce an actual sound on his instrument emphasises this sense of collective participation in music making. The *sam* – 'pointed at' by many rather than 'played' by few – highlights a moment in which the boundary between stage and audience temporarily weakens, with the *tānpūrā* player's gesture resembling more the behaviour of a member of the public than his normal role. The sense of enjoyment and fulfilment is marked by a very audible 'ah!' voiced by many members of the audience, and is accompanied by backward sways of their torsos as those who had leant forward return to a straight sitting position at the approach of the *sam*. As the tabla solo is now successfully concluded, all participants resume a more restrained behaviour and the performance continues with Ram Deshpande starting to sing again at cycle 21.

## Discussion

In his study of interaction and in particular of the instance in which members of a leading group manage a temporary relaxation of formal behaviour with another party, Goffman points out how 'such relaxation of distance provides one means by which a feeling of spontaneity and involvement can be generated in the interaction' (1990: 108). Spontaneous involvement is exactly what can be observed in the climax concluding Vishwanath Shirodkar's solo in the *tarānā*. Consistently with what is suggested by Goffman, this involvement is managed by the two performers who have the highest status and freedom to interact with the audience: the tabla player and the singer. I argue that this is facilitated by the artists' close working relationship and long-standing acquaintance which surely contributes to giving them the sense of complicity permeating their performance, and the confidence with which they employ specific strategies to skilfully engage the audience's attention.

I would like to suggest that their behaviour and the interaction that it inspires are deeply related to the felicitous outcome of the concert. In the few seconds leading to the end of the tabla solo, in fact, the participants' engagement with the music is highlighted by a temporary abeyance of the roles which regulate North Indian classical music performance. This moment presents characteristics not dissimilar from those attributed by Bakhtin to carnivals,[16] which 'marked the suspension of all hierarchical rank, privileges, norms and prohibitions' (Bakhtin, 1984: 10), and where 'a special form of free and familiar contact reigned among people who were usually divided' (Bakhtin, 1984: 10). Of course, the carnival and the instance analysed in these pages take place over very different time frames, since the former is more sustained and extended, while the latter is very short, lasting just seconds. However, I suggest that, although brief, the relaxation of boundaries can still have a very intense effect on participants. In fact, where I see Bakhtin's work particularly relevant to my observations is in its focus on the experiential dimension, as 'such free, familiar contacts were *deeply felt*' (Bakhtin, 1984: 10; my italics). As in the concert discussed here where the boundaries between stage and audience are temporarily overcome in a moment of shared music-making, 'carnival ... does not acknowledge any distinction between actors and spectators ... Carnival is not a spectacle seen by the people; they *live* in it' (Bakhtin, 1984: 7, my italics).

It is clear from the footage analysed here that the intensity of the experience of coming together on the *sam* allows participants to share a sense of relief, which is intrinsic in the structure of the music through the resolution offered by the first beat of the cycle. However, I argue that such relief is also enhanced by the effectiveness of the collective involvement which accompanies it. This sense of fulfilment can be better understood in terms of *communitas*, as the 'relation quality of full unmediated communication, even communion, between definite and determinate identities, which arises spontaneously' (Turner 1977: 46).[17] Although the involvement of the audience is encouraged and managed deliberately by Ram Deshpande, it is not pre-planned, but rather results from the artists' ability to seize the momentum offered by the improvised conclusion of the solo, engaging the audience in an unexpectedly intense interaction. The temporary suspension of musical roles and hierarchies creates a genuinely liminal moment in the unfolding of the performance; in this brief temporal lapse, participants are allowed to feel that they can partake of the same experience.

The audience, increasingly engaged in the physical display of their participation through active interaction with the performers, shares a feeling of accomplishment: the tension built up gradually is suddenly released and the performance resumes with participants re-adopting a more restrained behaviour and re-enacting their expected roles. However, it is not simply a case of re-establishing a *status quo*. I argue that what has taken place has a significant impact on the unfolding of the event: the shared enjoyment brought about by the collective interaction allows all to proceed with a renewed sense of appreciation for the music, and the artists, having received 'the blessing of the audience', can enjoy a strengthened confidence in the felicitous development of their performance.[18]

I suggest that these observations invite some reflection on North Indian classical music performance as a presentational event. It could be argued, of course, that occurrences like the one highlighted in these pages are the exceptions that confirm the general rule. In other words, the socio-musical roles and performance boundaries are temporarily suspended only in order to be ultimately reaffirmed and reinforced; they are managed by artists who make decisions on how to direct these moments (which revive the attention of the audience) and never step down from their leading roles. Indeed, this concert would not be too dissimilar from other ones in this tradition where artists (like Sanjukta Ghosh, see above) do not feel that direct involvement of the audience contributes to the quality of the outcome of their performance. However, one cannot underestimate how North Indian classical music is shaped and created in the moment of performance and that the creation of musical sound as well as the overall outcome of the event depend to a large extent on the interactions which take place in that very moment (Napier 2004, 2007; Clayton and Leante, 2015). These interactions mostly involve the artists on stage, but can also significantly include members of the public.

In North Indian classical music performance, clapping to the *tāl*, as Turino points out, is not conceived as 'an essential part of the musical sound'; however, in practice it is more than 'mainly a guide for skilful listening' (Turino, 2008: 52), as suggested in general discourse.[19] I suggest that the practice of clapping to the metric structure embeds the performance with the potential for genuinely participatory moments which can be used strategically by artists, as in the case of the concert analysed in these pages. What is observable in Ram Deshpande's performance, in fact, is not uncommon; it is a particularly striking example of the intensity that such participation can reach.

Hindustani singers often clap to the *tāl* during the solo of an accompanist. This practice fulfils a number of functions: first of all, it allows the soloist to keep a form of visible participation while the accompanist is the creative fulcrum. Second, it allows musicians to encourage the audience to join and gauge its reaction to the performance. Most importantly, especially in the case of a tabla solo, it allows the musicians to guide the audience through a rhythmically complex (and often displacing) virtuosic moment, giving participants a tool to keep their bearings in the music. Although this process is not fully inclusive (in fact it cannot involve the least knowledgeable people who are unfamiliar with the clapping patterns), it brings together audiences whose musical skills are sufficient to follow the metric structure but not to appreciate the subtleties of the solo.

These moments share some structural features and practices with those of the participatory performances described by Turino: the clapping pattern offers an open, cyclical form which invites people with different musical abilities to join in in a non-prearranged manner, affording the opportunity to add to the intensity of the performance experience (2008: 37–43). Ultimately, it gives musicians like Ram Deshpande a chance to influence the positive reception of the music by the audience, implicitly recognizing the value of participation and the sense of togetherness and belonging that it indexes, as an assurance of the successful unfolding of the event.[20]

As it is evident from his interview statement, Ram Deshpande considers interaction with the audience integral to the way in which he approaches and manages the concert. His behaviour in performance confirms that his words are not just an expression of good intentions towards other participants, but are part of the strategies he actually deploys in the process of making music. The tabla solo analysed here offers an example of an instance in which such 'tricks' are used: both he and tabla player Vishwanath Shirodkar encourage the involvement of the listeners who – even if only briefly – actively participate in the performance contributing to the climax through shared gesturality with the artists.[21]

Drawing on Goffman, Clayton and Leante (2015) point out how in Hindustani classical music the definition of 'performance team' should not be limited to musicians on stage. The case investigated seems to confirm such a view: if a 'team is a grouping . . . in relation to an interaction or a series of interactions in which the relevant definition of the situation is maintained' (Goffman 1990: 108), then the grouping which is relevant to the unfolding and the successful performance of the *tarānā* analysed here has to include the audience. Therefore, while there is no doubt that North Indian classical music performance is characterised in its conception by features and practices which can be described as adhering to a strict presentational model, in the study of the actualisation of music-making we need to allow for a model which recognises the importance of instances of participation like the one considered here.

In these pages I have moved from the discussion of musical roles as commonly understood in Hindustani classical music to the consideration of musicians' views of their audiences, and in particular those of artists who see interaction with the audience as key to the successful unfolding of performance. I have then focused on a particular instance of such interaction with the audience managed by *khyāl* singer Ram Deshpande and tabla player Vishwanath Shirodkar. My analysis highlights how the strategies deployed by these artists to involve the listeners go beyond the simple engagement of their sympathy and attention towards key structural moments of the performance. The interaction observed here shows how audiences can become an active part of the process of music production and, through the sense of *communitas* generated among all participants, contribute to the successful outcome of the performance.

## Interviews cited

Sanjeev Abhyankar, 20 November 2013, Pune, India.
Prattyush Banerjee, 28 January 2007, Kolkata, India.
Ram Deshpande, 13 February 2010, Nashik, India.
Sanjukta Ghosh, 29 October 2009, Kolkata, India.
Falguni Mitra, 11 February 2007, Kolkata, India.

## Notes

1 The research on which the analysis presented in this chapter is grounded was carried out with Martin Clayton, to whom I am also grateful for his comments on a first draft of the script. The concert and the interviews discussed here were recorded at different times with Martin Clayton, Mark Doffman, Tarun Nayak, Andrew McGuiness and Simone Tarsitani. I would also like to acknowledge the musicians without whom this work would have not been possible, and in particular: Sanjeev Abhyankar, Manjiri Asanare-Kelkar, Prattyush Banerjee, Ram Deshpande, Sanjukta Ghosh, Falguni Mitra, Vishwanath Shirodkar, Anant Lakhe, Gandhar Deshpande, Puskaraj Bhagwat, and Chaitanya Kelkar. I would like to thank Elena Catalano, Yasmin Dandekar, and Morgan Davies for their help with the processes of interview transcription and translation. This research was supported by the UK's Arts and Humanities Research Council (grants APN19244 and APN19110) and by the British Academy/Leverhulme Trust (grant SG131292).
2 Studies relevant to the present chapter include those by Daniel Neuman (1990), Dard Neuman (2004), and Napier (2004, 2007) which discuss the management of authority between soloist and accompanist, while Moran (2013) addresses nonverbal communication in instrumentalist/tabla player duos. Authority and hierarchy are also discussed by Clayton and Leante (2015), who, building on work by Silver on etiquette (1984), consider deference as a performance strategy.
3 I am extremely grateful to Chloe Alaghband-Zadeh for sharing her ideas on the interaction between audiences and performers, and the contribution of connoisseurship to the shaping of performance in Hindustani classical music.
4 Indian terms are written in their Hindi-derived transliteration for consistency with the musicians' interview statements quoted in these pages. Therefore, for example, the term *rāg* is used instead of the equally common, Sanskrit-derived *rāga*.
5 Richard Osborne's and Barbara Bradby's chapters in this volume also examine video footage as a source of analysis of performer–audience interaction, but also as media that have an impact on future interactions.
6 In a vocal performance, the soloist invariably sits at the centre of the stage; in an instrumental concert, which does not feature an accompanist on a melodic instrument, the space can be managed more flexibly by the soloist and the drum tabla player, with the latter sometimes occupying a slightly more central position than in a vocal recital.
7 For ease of reading, I will refer to the soloist using the masculine pronoun; however, especially in the vocal *khyāl* genre, there are numerous female soloists

who enjoy the same status as their male counterparts. On the contrary, the vast majority of accompanists are male.

8  Clayton and Leante (2015) discuss how this musical role might clash with other – equally important – social roles (especially seniority) which can be deployed in performance, leading to potential frictions. For the management of such frictions see also Napier (2004, 2007) and Neuman (2004).

9  *Tānpūrā* players may provide vocal support if they are students of the singer.

10  For the role of greetings in the context of live performance, see also Barbara Bradby's chapter in this volume.

11  The issue of the choice of repertoire for a given space and audience is also discussed by Hytönen-Ng and O'Donnell and Henderson in this volume.

12  All uncited quotes are from semi-structured interviews, the full list of which is provided at the end of this chapter.

13  The interview with Ram Deshpande quoted in these pages was translated by Yasmin Dandekar.

14  The concert took place in the Dr H. S. Joshi Auditorium, Nashik. Both this event and the interview were organised by Abhijeet Kelkar, to whom I am extremely grateful. The performance was recorded by Martin Clayton, Simone Tarsitani and myself.

15  The employment of audio-visual recording equipment should not suggest in any way that the event was conceived or perceived by participants as taking place in an experimental setting: North Indian classical musicians are used to the presence of recording and filming devices, and the active involvement of the audience in the performance (in fact, higher than in most events) suggests that listeners were not significantly affected by the presence of the cameras (which, in my experience, can in some cases inhibit them). Participants were told at the beginning of the concert that they would be filmed by a team of academics for research purposes, but were not made aware of the specific focus on gesture, movement and interaction of our work.

16  Although Bakhtin refers to European examples in his examination of the carnival phenomenon, Indian culture is not without ritual events in which social roles and boundaries are temporarily suspended (see for example Pandian, 2001).

17  Edith Turner explains how music 'has its living existence in its performance, and its life is synonymous of *communitas*, which will spread to all participants and audiences when they get caught up in it' (Turner, 2012: 43). In a recent study, Ioannis Tsioulakis (2013) has analysed the reciprocal participation between audiences and musicians in jazz music with specific reference to Turner's *communitas*; his work is of relevance to the present chapter also in the discussion of performers' diverging views on audiences (ibid: 207–208).

18  Again, the analogy with carnival is clear, as this is described by Bakhtin emerges as 'the feast of becoming, change, and renewal' (1984: 10).

19  When, a few months after Ram Deshpande's concert, back in the UK, I listened to the audio recordings of that night, I felt that our multi-track audio recordings failed to convey a sense of meaningful conclusion to Vishwanath Shirodkar's tabla solo, which did not feature the canonical drum stroke on the climactic *sam*: the microphones pointing at the artists on stage did not pick up the exclamation of relief expressed by the audience at the end of the solo, which I argue could provide a 'substitute' for the expected emphasis on the first beat of the cycle. It seemed to me that one way to improve the effectiveness of the recording would be to extract the audience's sound from one the cameras' sound files and add it to the mix. A possible development of this study could involve asking a number of Indian musicians to listen to the two versions of the mix of the tabla solo in the *tarānā* (one featuring only the sound from the microphones

on stage, and the other including the sound from the audience) to check my impression with un-biased expert listeners. If the results confirm that the inclusion of the audience sound in the mix conveys a better sense of conclusion to the solo in the *tarānā*, it could be argued that in this particular point of the concert the audience's contribution is integral to music making and the interaction between participants on stage and off stage has become *core* (Turino, 2008: 31–32) to the performance and listening experience.

20  Interestingly, even in Western art music, which Turino rightly indicates as the 'most pronounced form of presentational performance' (2008: 52), analogous moments of structured interaction with the audience have become part of the concluding section of specific events. This is the case, for example, of the performance of Elgar's 'Land of hope and glory' at the Last Night of the Proms, or Strauss' 'Radetzky's march' at the New Year concert in Vienna, where the now-programmatic participation of the audience provides a similar assurance, sealing the success of the event.

21  In this same volume Bruce Johnson discusses gesture with reference to the way in which it provides a cognitive base for communication and to its contribution to the breaking of performers/audience boundaries.

# 3 'One step above the ornamental greenery'

## A survivor's guide to playing to an audience who does not listen

*Mary Louise O'Donnell and Jonathan Henderson*

## Introduction

A user on a guitar forum posted the following comment on a thread entitled 'Playing to an audience that isn't listening':

> At a special lunchtime concert series or some other arts event, sure, people listen better there because that's what they came for. But not at a bar (especially not) a restaurant. There a musician playing instrumentals is basically one step above the ornamental greenery.[1]

Live music is experienced by individuals in a range of social settings including concert halls, churches, arenas and public houses. The conventional understanding of a musician performing to an audience who are in attendance to show their respect for that musician's artistic and/or technical ability excludes a significant number of performers, namely background musicians. A 'background musician' can be defined as an instrumentalist or vocalist who is engaged to perform at a social event or in a social setting to an audience who are not in attendance primarily to hear his or her performance. In fact the 'audience', who are often engaged in other activities including conversation or the consumption of food, is in essence a group of people who become an audience to the musician(s) because they inhabit temporarily the same social space. This type of musical performance can be a solo or ensemble practice and it often, though not exclusively, occurs in social settings where food and/or alcohol is served.

Live background music is an audience-centred mode of creative performance. In these contexts, the performer serves the primary role of entertaining their audience. Some of their audience will be captivated or intrigued by their performance, while others will, consciously or unconsciously, be oblivious to it and perceive it as 'muzak', a term designating pleasant but non-intrusive recorded music played in public spaces. The performer has the agency to actively engage with their audience by performing a repertoire that captures their attention or might be familiar to them; they can also choose to play a predetermined set list, make no effort to establish a connection with those around them, and essentially serve the role of 'muzakian': a musician who performs live but serves the same role as muzak. This chapter seeks to illuminate this type of performance by situating it in the overall context of music-making as a legitimate mode of musical and cultural expression. More specifically, we aim to highlight the unique challenges which musicians providing background music face when they perform, and to delineate the strategies that they employ to forge a relationship with an audience who often do not want to listen.

Background musicians, also known as 'ordinary musicians' (Faulkner and Becker, 2009: 15–16), or 'background atmosphere makers' (Tsioulakis, 2013: 207), are a universal phenomenon. Considering the number of musicians who provide background music in a variety of social settings around the world, it is notable that analyses of the social and cultural significance of their performances rarely feature in extensive research undertaken in the fields of music perception, music psychology and performance analysis. The handful of texts which engage with this type of music-making generally articulate and critically analyse the experience of jazz musicians (Faulkner and Becker, 2009; Tsioulakis, 2013; and Hytönen-Ng, 2013, see also her chapter in this volume). Howard Becker's seminal work (1951) on the often fraught and controlling relationship between 'commercial musicians' (specifically professional dance musicians) working in service occupations and their employers and audiences was the first to address the challenges faced by musicians who serve a background role. In a more recent work, Becker and Robert Faulkner provide a useful ethnographic account of what they term 'ordinary musicians', which they define as 'players competent in a variety of styles, ready to do what is likely to come up in most engagements, interested in jazz and aiming to play it when they can, but in the end doing whatever the world throws their way' (2009: 16). While their text highlights some issues pertinent to our discussion, it focuses primarily on the interaction between jazz musicians in ensemble contexts. Our research is derived from our experience as solo background instrumentalists who play repertoire which includes popular jazz but which consists primarily of classical and popular music.

As this chapter relies heavily on informed observation and our experience as practicing musicians to provide insights into the interaction between musician and audience in live background music settings, it might be of interest to the readers to know something of our musical careers and what prompted this research. We have each played professionally for many years. O'Donnell is a clasically-trained harpist who works as a soloist and with various ensembles in Ireland. She plays Irish and concert harps and her repertoire of background music includes approximately 200 traditional Irish airs and dance tunes, as well as popular classical pieces and contemporary popular music which she has arranged for harp. Henderson worked as a session musician for twenty years in London but now plays guitar at various venues in Dublin and its environs.

On one of these occasions, in September 2010, Henderson and O'Donnell were booked to play at a reception at the Burlington Hotel, Dublin for a group of 150 delegates attending an international conference. O'Donnell was engaged through an agent to play concert harp as delegates arrived for a pre-dinner drinks reception lasting one hour. Although the harp was amplified, the music was not audible to the majority of those present after the first half hour. As O'Donnell later noted, 'they [the event organisers] didn't care what I played or if I could be heard; once they saw a glamorous, young woman with a harp smiling at the delegates, they were happy'. Henderson provided background music throughout the dinner service which lasted approximately two hours. He was positioned on a stage which was later used by a 10-piece swing band. As the evening progressed and more alcohol was consumed, he struggled to be heard above the din of the crowded room. At the end of the evening, we were exhausted and disappointed at the audience reaction but consoled by the prospect of receiving some financial remuneration for what we termed a 'nightmare gig'.

The evening, though unsatisfactory from a creative perspective was the catalyst for our research into the social and cultural contexts of background music performance. In truth, the initial motivation for our research was not academic, it was to identify what communicative and technological strategies we could adopt to cope with a type of music-making that can often leave one creatively unfulfilled, emotionally and physically drained, and with feelings of low self-esteem. Approximately 60 per cent of our combined annual performances consist of background music so it was imperative to critically analyse how we perform in these contexts and how we could improve our musical experience and that of the audience. Over the past five years our fieldwork has consisted of observing each other's performances of background music to people of all ages and cultural backgrounds in restaurants and hotels in Dublin and surrounding counties (Meath, Wicklow, and Kildare). These performances are always solo and instrumental, and the repertoire performed is generally restricted to 'popular' (familiar) music from a variety of genres (classical, popular, jazz, and Irish or 'Celtic'). Our research is ongoing but in the sections that follow we explore some of the main themes which have arisen to date.

## Background music as performance

The concept of an attentive, respectful audience adhering to acceptable codes of behaviour and completely engaged by a musician or group of musicians is a relatively recent phenomenon in the history of the performance of secular music. Although elite groups of musicians have commanded such audience responses through the centuries, for many musicians, this type of audience reaction was rarely, if ever experienced. The background musician, or a musician whose music is relegated to a background role, has existed for centuries. From the Tudor period onwards, palaces and great houses often included a minstrel's gallery in the Great Hall. The nobleman's musicians, who were discreetly located in these raised galleries overlooking the hall, provided music to accompany dining and performed for dancing, plays, and masques (Thurley, 1993: 45–46, 121; Sim, 2011: 28–29). In the seventeenth and early eighteenth centuries, musicians at the court of Louis XIV frequently performed music which was specifically commissioned from various composers to entertain the King and his guests as they dined at elaborate, opulent banquets at Versailles (Heller, 2014: 114–15). In her study of the role and behaviour of the audience during operatic performances in Italy in the eighteenth and nineteenth centuries, Lindsay Michael (2004: 2–3) presented a picture of audiences who were engaged in talking, drinking, and even gambling during performances. Citing Weiss and Taruskin, she noted the utter revulsion of an English visitor in attendance at an opera in Naples in 1765 who commented that '[t]he crowd laughed and talked through the whole performance, without any restraint; and, it may be imagined, that an assembly of so many hundreds conversing together so loudly, must entirely cover the voices of the singers' (2004: 2). In the twentieth and twenty-first centuries biographies and autobiographies of celebrated musicians performing all genres of music are peppered with nightmare experiences of performances in the early stage of their careers in which audiences were unresponsive, rude or just downright terrifying.[2] Although these musicians have transcended these humbling and often humiliating experiences to achieve critical acclaim and financial success, it is noteworthy that sometimes, no matter what calibre of musician is on a stage or in a space in close proximity to them, an audience just does not want to listen.[3]

In January 2010 a guitarist under the username 'gibson311' posted the following comment under the heading 'Playing to an audience that isn't listening' on the website acousticguitarforum.com:

> I played a show in a bar this weekend to a room of about 200 people. I play solo acoustic fingerstyle stuff, a lot of Tommy Emmanuel, Chet Atkins, and other songs in that style. I would say that about 99% of the people there never stopped talking and were paying little if any attention to me. Now I realize that this shouldn't really bother me since they did not come just to see me but I still found it very annoying. I wasn't even nervous when I was playing because it felt as if nobody was listening anyway. It almost makes me feel like it's not worth doing again. There was no pressure which is good, but there was also no rush, and no feeling that people actually enjoyed what I was doing.[4]

To date, there have been over eighty responses to the original post from musicians providing practical advice on how to engage an audience who does not listen and some personal anecdotes about disrespectful audiences and disastrous experiences. Musicians of all ages around the world who provide live background music will, at some point in their careers, have endured similar experiences. A respondent to the post suggested that the accessibility of music means that: 'we're all used to having a soundtrack around us 24/7 [s]o people coming into where you're playing quickly put your music in the same background slot as all the rest of the music which inundates us daily.'[5]

In recent years, digital technologies, the use of mobile internet and social media platforms has transformed the live music experience for all types of music audiences. Extracts from live music performances are streamed online through a variety of websites. We have unlimited, instant access to music from a variety of genres, performed by iconic virtuosic musicians and talented (and often untalented) amateurs. Music is ubiquitous, and as Kassabian notes, 'ubiquitous musics . . . come out of the wall, our televisions, our video games, our computers, and even our clothes' (2013: xii). Yet the musician providing background music still serves some function in twenty-first-century society, even if their performance is often ignored. Whether it is the social prestige of having a musician playing at a family gathering, or the bar manager in a public house identifying that live music can attract a specific type of clientele, live background music in these settings affects to various degrees those who experience it.

With the exception of forums on websites where semi-professional and professional musicians provide anectdotal material based on personal experience, the practice of live background music has not been explored.[6] A possible reason for the dearth of research in this area is that musicians who provide background music are often considered to lack legitimate artistic status by the general public, by academics and by their fellow musicians who regard them as inferior or 'failed' musicians who are content to remain in the background because they struggle in formal performance settings. Most professional musicians crave some form of affirmation whether performing for 20 people in an intimate setting or before an audience of 20,000 people in a state-of-the-art concert arena. Musicians do not train, in some cases for decades, to master their instrument technically and musically in order to provide a background function, or to be ignored. Yet for many musicians, the provision of live background music is an important source of income and an important forum to showcase their musical skills and repertoire. These musicians also serve a crucial social and cultural function providing background music for receptions following ceremonies to mark religious and cultural rites of passage, for example weddings and birthday celebrations, or to enhance the dining experience at restaurants and bistros. The creative interaction and collaboration which often occurs between musician and audience in these settings highlights the importance of this type of performance as a vital dimension of social and cultural interaction.

We propose that background music should be analysed as a performance. In order to do that, however, a broader understanding of performance is necessary to fully comprehend the significance of the interaction between musician(s) and audience in this process. This broad definition of performance was most succinctly articulated by the sociologist Erving Goffman over fifty years ago when he suggested that performance was 'all the activity of a given participant on a given occasion which serves to influence in any way any of the other participants' (1959: 8). Simon Frith's suggestion that 'listening' itself is a performance' (1998: 203) and David Pattie's substitution of the term 'experience' in place of the 'negative term' performance in the context of rock music (2007: 15) are indicative of the increasing acknowledgement of the significance of the audience as active participants in the creative process and not merely as passive figures influenced by a performer/performance. The observations of Frith and Pattie are useful in that they challenge the conventional understanding of performance. Live background music, however, does not fit neatly into the analytical or theoretical frameworks which Frith, Pattie, and others often apply to their discussion of various musical genres. Live background music is unique and more typical of some of the performative genres identified by Richard Schechner and others as 'in between' because they blur the boundaries separating genres (Schechner, 1998: 360). Musicians who provide live background music occupy an uncertain or 'liminal' space during performances as they strive to be more than muzak but not to transcend their background role.

Schechner (2002: 25), one of the pioneers of performance studies, identified eight kinds of performance as occurring 'in everyday life . . . in the arts, in sports and other popular entertainments, in business, in technology, in sex, in ritual – sacred and secular, and in play'. He proposed seven functions of performance: 'to entertain, to make something that is beautiful, to mark or change identity, to make or foster community, to heal, to teach, persuade, or convince, [and] to deal with the sacred and/or the demonic' (ibid: 38). The principal function of live background music is to entertain, but, depending on the musician(s), audience, environment (or context of performance), and repertoire, it can, to varying degrees, also create something beautiful, foster an ephemeral community, mark an important rite of passage, and/or perform a therapeutic role. A successful performance of background music is dependent on the connection between musician, audience, environment, and repertoire; it relies on an integration of all elements. In the following section we will focus on a typical example of live backgound music, in a restaurant where the performer's function is to create an ambience, to enhance the culinary experience for the diners and, ultimately, to encourage them to return to the venue in the future.

## Case study: 'diary of a background musician' (Jonathan Henderson)

As a working musician with over twenty years' experience, I have performed at a variety of musical engagements in concert halls, galleries, hotel lobbies, jazz clubs, on cruise ships, and at outdoor events, including festivals and fairs. The chance to play, perform and earn a living by doing so is of great importance to me and performing during dinner at a restaurant is one of the many forms of musical engagement that is part of my working musical life. Audiences and musicians have mixed reactions to this type of performance. An accomplished flautist and friend once described this type of music making as 'noise pollution'. Some musicians consider work like this to be beneath them, that is until regular 'decent work' becomes scarce and creating 'muzak' becomes a crucial source of income or a useful supplement to teaching. Musicians who work full time earning a living from playing music will consider engaging in most forms of music-making and are prepared to lift up to three times their weight in equipment in order to do their job, set it up themselves, perform, and entertain their audience, no matter how unresponsive they might be (Figure 3.1).[7] The following account relates some observations that I made in a personal diary while playing solo guitar on 9 March 2013 during dinner at the Rococo restaurant at Knightsbrook Hotel, a four star hotel, spa, and golf resort in County Meath, Ireland (Figure 3.2). I have played at this venue on a weekly basis for over three years.

My arrival and consequent setting up of equipment usually provokes a varied response from diners which ranges from indifference, curiosity and humour to horror, probably due to concern that the volume from my speakers will intrude on their conversation. Before a note is played, a table of four diners in close proximity to me request to be relocated. Experience decrees that there is little point in being offended as it indicates that the group of people in front of me, my 'audience', are not here primarily to listen to me. The restaurant can cater for 80–100 diners and approximately forty people have ordered or commenced their meal by the time I arrive. As I go through the routine of setting up, a table of diners catch my eye and I smile back. This gesture is sometimes returned, but other diners often look away embarrassed. A family with two young children are seated at a table in front of the performance area and, before I begin, they approach to inquire what I am doing. While I am tuning they inform me that their dad plays guitar and they know some nursery rhymes. They hum along quietly with my subdued rendition of 'Twinkle Twinkle Little Star' after which they return to their table and their plates of chicken nuggets and chips. Even simple gestures like that can effectively 'break the ice'.

After a quick sound check, I begin with Dave Brubeck's 'Take Five'. This musical gem, although not particularly difficult to play, generally appeals to all ages and musical tastes and quickly grabs the attention of quite a few

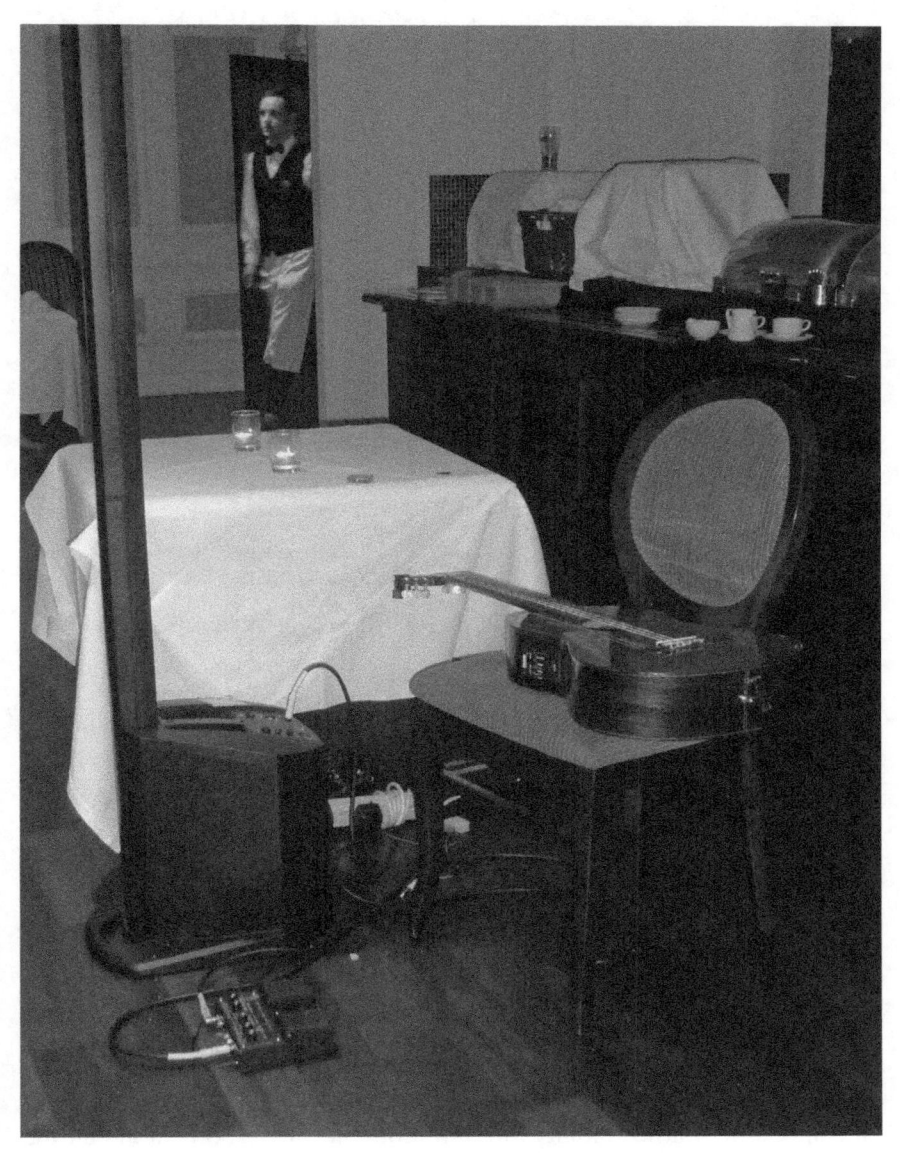

*Figure 3.1* Performance amplification includes a Bose L1 Model II system with B2 bass, and a Dynacord 600 mixer/amplifier

*Figure 3.2*  Rococo restaurant at Knightsbrook Hotel, County Meath, Ireland
(musician's perspective)

people in the room. My audience this evening includes people of all ages and it is important for me to attempt to connect my choice of repertoire with what I imagine their musical tastes might be. I follow 'Take Five' with an instrumental version of Bob Dylan's 'To Make You Feel My Love'. A recording of the song by the British singer/songwriter Adele in 2008 would probably be more familiar to younger members of my audience, but it is a song which has achieved popularity among all age groups. The first set of popular and jazz pieces illicits some response: some smiles, a thumbs up, and even a ripple of applause after 'Moon River'. After my first set, which lasts approximately 45 minutes, I usually take a short break. This evening the manager asks me to delay my break and keep playing. There is a delay getting orders out from the kitchen and the music serves as a distraction to potentially disgruntled customers. I do not mind obliging the manager as he respects my musical ability and intuition and rarely bothers me during a gig. It is refreshing to work in an environment like this as, over the years, I have worked with managerial staff who have not only dictated what repertoire I should play, but frequently reminded me how I was overpaid or how grateful I should be to them to have a gig.

After my break, while preparing to start my next set, a couple leaving the restaurant thank me (Figure 3.3). They were seated in a corner of the

*Figure 3.3* Musician/audience interaction

room where they could not see me and were pleasantly surprised to discover that they had been listening to live as opposed to 'piped music' as they dined. I do not perform on a stage or platform and the positioning of a large cupboard to my left means that I am not visible to a considerable number of diners (Figure 3.4). My performance space is not ideal, in fact it is at odds with the kind of relationship that any musician would like to generate with their audience. This, however, is the space where musicians perform and unless tables are removed, which would have obvious consequences for the customer turnover at the restaurant, there is no other place to set up. The restaurant manager informed me that a diner requested Ennio Morricone's 'Gabriel's Oboe' during my break. I play this piece, along with the theme from the film *Once Upon a Time in the West* (also composed by Morricone), and receive a glass of red wine from the diner in gratitude for my efforts. Being able to draw from a wide repertoire of diverse musical genres is an essential skill when performing live background music and one which I have tried to cultivate over the last two decades. There are moments during the two-hour performance when it seems as if nobody is listening to me play. These are the moments when I play repertoire which appeals to me but might be considered obscure to the 'average spectator'. By this stage of the performance I have made my presence known, entertained and,

*Figure 3.4* Performance space for background music

when appropriate, faded into the background, so playing *Danzas Españolas* by Granados or a self-penned transcription of *Trois Mouvements Perpétuels* by Poulenc are a few moments of musical self-indulgence before the performance ends.

I don't receive a standing ovation, applause or requests for an encore when I finish, but this type of performance does not illicit those kinds of responses. A musician in need of constant affirmation would be advised to avoid this kind of job as, in this setting, they are largely anonymous. My performance is not advertised on the hotel website or anywhere in the hotel, but I play my role in providing a memorable dining experience just like the chefs, servers, ambient lighting, and elaborate floral arrangements. One could argue that prerecorded music piped through the restaurant's sound system would also be effective and would cost the venue less, but a musician performing live is, at the very least, a novelty and the audience can make what they want of the experience. One might ask 'why bother'? I remind myself that I do have a choice: to remain safely anonymous and blend in with the decor or to play the room and try to entertain. There is a challenge in reading an audience and entertaining them, but there is also a deep satisfaction knowing that, although I have not connected with everyone in that room, I have worked hard to justify my presence and my fee, and perhaps more importantly, to ensure more work in the weeks and months ahead.

## Making a connection: background musicians and their audiences

In the above case study, Henderson articulates many of the challenges that a background musician encounters during a typical performance, in particular, the difficulty of communicating or connecting with their audience. In her chapter on the relationship between jazz musicians and their audience in this volume, Hytönen-Ng notes that '[a] performance is always an act of communication'. A successful performance centres on the ability of the performer to establish a connection or 'we-relation' with their audience (ibid.). Establishing a 'we-relation' between a background musician and their audience, however, can be difficult. Background musicians generally perform in a space where there are no backdrops, lighting, sets, or programme notes. The audience often have no knowledge of the musician's biography, training or performance experience and the musician may not be in a position to connect with their audience through verbal communication, for example by welcoming them to the venue or introducing pieces. Typical conventions of performance, such as applause, ovations, or encores, may not be appropriate or even expected at the performance venue, so the musician may not receive any obvious sign of affirmation during or after their performance. The performance of live background music remains in flux as it is dependent on the musician's response to the audience's response, an interaction which is often unpredictable.[8] Musicians frequently employ strategies to sustain audience interest and, sometimes, to revive their own interest during a performance. The practical advice offered in response to gibson311's post mentioned earlier by fellow musicians illuminates many of these simple strategies.[9] It can be summarised as follows:

1 Vary the tempo and volume regularly during the performance
2 Change your physical position even slightly (if possible)
3 Include more popular songs in your repertoire
4 Do not include too much original material or obscure music
5 Add vocals, as instrumentals are often perceived to be muzak
6 Alternate between electric and acoustic guitars (if applicable)

These suggestions could be reduced to one crucial piece of advice for anyone providing background music, namely to try to read their audience and adapt their playing style and repertoire accordingly.

Identifying or adapting to an audience's needs relies on an ability to pick up on various nonverbal cues (Beebe and Beebe, 2012: 100–105). Those who train in media studies, in particular communicators and public speakers, are always conscious of their audience and consideration of their needs is a central part of planning speech length, choice of language, and style of presentation (Beebe and Masterson, 2006: 350–4). An awareness of issues, such as the age profile of the audience and the size and acoustic of the venue, is crucial for a background musician as it will influence where they position themselves, the use and volume level of amplification and their choice of repertoire. Goffman suggests that it is beneficial for a performer if he can 'control' the behaviour of an audience by influencing 'their responsive treatment of him' (1959: 2). In a live background music setting, 'controlling' audience response may involve the musician exaggerating existing personality traits or adopting an alternative persona (makeup, dress style), increased physical movement (gestures, facial expression), adjusting the volume level of amplification to be sympathetic to increased/decreased levels of conversation, or even modifying repertoire choice if the musician observes that a piece played has affected an audience member in a positive or negative way.[10]

Both production and reception of background music vary from venue to venue so the performance rarely adheres to a predetermined set list as is often the norm in concerts/gigs of classical and popular music. Consequently, the choice of repertoire may vary depending on the location of the performance venue or the time of day at which the performance takes place. It is crucial in a live background music seting to perform a broad, diverse repertoire encompassing a variety of genres and styles which will appeal to the widest possible audience. The range of styles performed by Henderson at the restaurant epitomises the diverse repertoire with which most competent background musicians would be familiar. Certain pieces are universal, for example 'Happy Birthday', 'Spring' from the *Four Seasons* (Vivaldi), 'Somewhere Over the Rainbow' (Arlen and Harburg). This type of repertoire crosses cultures, generations, and is, most importantly, easily recognisable. Original material can also be included, but popular music, or music that is 'appealing to the people' or 'grounded in or "of" the people' (Shuker, 1994: 4), is likely to elicit the best response.[11] When the performance has finished, nonverbal and verbal responses generally indicate how the performance was received. Compliments, complimentary gestures such as thumbs up (see earlier Figure 3.3) or applause signify that the musician has connected with some of the audience. On the contrary, lack of feedback or response may result from an inability on the musician's part to read their audience. Complete lack of engagement or response to live background music by everyone in attendance is a rare occurrence, but when it happens it can affect a musician's confidence and mood. Some musicians, however, view the experience more pragmatically as paid practice.[12] Indeed, as Tsioulakis has observed, by focusing on their financial remuneration musicians often 'conceptualize their engagement as *laboring*, an etiquette making their frustration as creative musicians more bearable' (2013: 209).

It is clear from our study thus far that the audience assumes an integral role in the live background music experience and their engagement, or lack thereof, influences the trajectory of the performance. They may converse with others if they choose and can arrive or leave at any point during the performance. Audiences in attendance at venues where there is live background music are rarely an homogeneous group, therefore one cannot identify a 'general audience' but rather different types of audience depending on their level of engagement with the musician(s). In her survey of spectorial engagement at an indie music gig, Wendy Fonarow (2006: 82–153) divided the venue into three zones based on audience behaviour. The audience in zone 1 were engaged with the performance, in zone 2, they were less so, and the people located at (or near) the bar in zone 3 appeared disinterested and distracted by conversation. Although audiences at venues where live background music is performed can choose to move closer to or further away from the musician, generally these venues cannot so easily be divided into physical zones. The audience can, however, be classified similarly according to their level of engagement with the performance as active listeners, passive listeners, and non-engagers.

Beebe and Beebe (2012: 100) suggest that eye contact, facial expressions, movement, posture, and other nonverbal responses reveal how a person feels in the company of those surrounding him or her. In the context of live background music, musicians rely on these forms of nonverbal communication or other unspoken cues to assess audience interest or its absence. Active listeners, although they may not engage with the performance for its entirety, often employ verbal and nonverbal communication to affirm the musician and their choice of repertoire. This can involve a smile or a nod of approval, applause at the end of a piece, or they may approach the musician(s) to compliment them on their rendition of a piece of music, to request a specific piece, or to relate information about their own musical tastes or their level of musical competence. A physical barrier, for example a stage or podium, is often absent from these settings so members of the audience are free to approach and interact with the musician at any point during or after the performance (see earlier Figures 3.3 and 3.4).[13] In her study of theatre audiences, Susan Bennett (1997: 207) noted that when audiences are involved in 'structuring' a theatrical event 'the direct experience of that production feeds back to revise a spectator's expectations, to establish or challenge conventions, and, occasionally, to reform the boundaries of culture'. If a musician performs a specific piece requested by an audience member or repertoire by their favourite artist, the outcome can be a positive experience for both sides and result in a collaboration in the creative process of music-making between musician and audience. Henderson's performance of 'Gabriel's Oboe', which was requested by a member of his audience, is a typical example of a collaboration resulting in the establishment of a connection between performer and audience.

The second level of audience engagement includes passive listeners, in other words those who are simultaneously listening but also engaged in another activity, for example eating, drinking or operating a mobile electronic device. The third level incorporates audience members who are operating electronic devices with the use of earphones or those who are engaged in conversation with others and have no interest in the performance. Much research has been carried out into the importance of the face, hands, and feet in nonverbal communication (Ekman and Friesen, 1975; Ekman, 2003; Quilliam, 2008). Passive listeners and non-engagers are more likely not to make eye contact with the musician, lower their head, shift their posture frequently by, for example, slumping their shoulders or crossing their arms and position themselves away from the musician or with their back to them. Nonverbal cues such as these are a rich source of information for the musician who can read them, decide on which (if any) audience members they can establish a connection with, in order to refocus their attention and repertoire accordingly.

## Coda

This chapter confirms the centrality of the audience in background live music-making and it exemplifies how their acknowledgment or dismissal of the musician(s) shapes the performance. It highlights some of the challenges faced by these musicians, in particular the inability to fully explore and express their artistic creativity. Some musicians find this type of performance degrading and demoralising, and this is understandable because musicians hope that their musicality and technical ability will be appreciated by their audience. The practical dimension of eking out a living in a competitive field, however, results in musicians being pragmatic and entrepreneurial. Musicians who perform background music occupy a liminal space somewhere between formal performance and recorded music. Most of the settings where musicians perform live background music do not actually require a live performance, but there is usually an economic or holistic reason for engaging them. Their presence needs to be felt, particularly since the people who surround them are their sole audience and the restaurant owner or venue manager has made a choice to hire a musician to present music for them. They also need to be conscious that they serve a background role and should not impinge on the intimacy of a family dining together or a couple sharing a drink in a bar.

Background musicians, if they choose, can engage an audience and draw them by using musical, communicative, and technological skills. If they are successful, then this can have a positive formative influence on the resulting music-making experience. The audience can also have unrestricted engagement with the music and musician if they choose, but they can also resist or even reject the performer. In this type of music-making, the audience response is in fact the means through which the status of the musician is asserted or challenged. It is up to the musician to embrace the challenge; if they refuse, then they will forever remain 'one step above the ornamental greenery'.

# Notes

1 www.acousticguitarforum.com/forums/archive/index.php/t-174258.html (accessed on 3 February 2014).

2 Some bizarre examples of these experiences were included in an article by Paul Lester for the *Guardian* in 2011, see www.theguardian.com/music/2011/aug/04/musicians-worst-gigs (accessed on 8 February, 2014). See also Hytönen-Ng's chapter in this volume for an account of musicians' negative experiences of the audience.

3 The virtuoso American violinist Joshua Bell was filmed in 2007 busking at a metro station in Washington DC as part of an experiment to analyse the reaction of commuters. A detailed account of Bell's performance and the largely apathetic response it engendered from commuters was discussed at length by Gene Weingarten in the *Washington Post*, see www.washingtonpost.com/wp-dyn/content/article/2007/04/04/AR2007040401721.html (accessed on 2 October, 2014). For some footage of Bell's performance, see www.youtube.com/watch?v=hnOPu0_YWhw (accessed on 2 October, 2014).

4 www.acousticguitarforum.com/forums/archive/index.php/t-174258.html (accessed on 3 February, 2014).

5 Ibid.

6 See, for example, http://musicianspage.com/forums/ (accessed on 26 June, 2015), http://forums.allaboutjazz.com/archive/index.php/t-730.html (accessed on 26 June, 2015) and http://theunofficialmartinguitarforum.yuku.com/reply/536432/Rude-audience-members#.UtvKpNLFK70 (accessed on 26 June, 2015).

7 For amplification at background music gigs, I bring two Electro-Voice speakers on stands or a more compact Bose L1 Model II system with B2 bass, a Dynacord 600 mixer/amplifier, three guitar stands, a Maton steel-string acoustic guitar, traditional nylon Spanish guitar, Godin electro-acoustic guitar with midi facility and two vocal microphones (in case a member of my audience decides that they would like to sing).

8 See Bruce Johnson's and Laura Leante's contributions to this volume for thorough discussions of how continuous responses between performers and audiences shape the performance interaction.

9 www.acousticguitarforum.com/forums/archive/index.php/t-174258.html (accessed on 3 February 2014).

10 See Faulkner and Becker (2009: 139–164) for an analysis of the processes involved in choosing repertoire and negotiating set lists between ensemble performers of background music.

11 Roy Shuker's broad definition of popular music, which includes rock/pop music and classical music that has been popularised and commercialised, characterises the majority of the repertoire which a musician will perform in a live background music setting.

12 In her study of the importance of the audience in jazz performances, Elina Hytönen-Ng (2013: 107–109, 122) noted that lack of appreciation by an audience or a negative audience response can often effect musicians psychologically (self-esteem) and physically (technique).

13 Richard Schechner (1985: 119) describes the physical space, which often incorporates a stage, as the 'time/space/spectator/performer aggregate'. The boundary between spectator and performer (audience and musician) may be less obvious or nonexistent in a live background music setting and the absence of a stage or podium may result in a diminution of respect for the musician who is now at the same level as their audience, as opposed to occupying an elevated position on stage.

# Part 2
# Live relationships
## Negotiations of performance

# 4 Contemporary British jazz musicians' relationship with the audience

## Renditions of we-relations and intersubjectivity

*Elina Hytönen-Ng*

## Introduction

> It's little past eight o'clock on a Friday night in July. I'm looking for a venue in downtown Poole. I'm late. I walk into a pub and head downstairs entering the venue, luckily just as the performance begins. I'm surprised to find the small windowless venue with an arched roof rammed with people. I calculate that there are roughly forty people in the room, varying from elderly men to young male students. Not that many women.
>
> The band is set up at the back of the room, and I can see them well, even though I am situated at the other end. The rest of the audience is sitting close to the performers, so close that the musicians could touch the front row if they held out their hands. During the build-up, the audience has been talking with excitement, but once the performance starts people quiet down and the atmosphere in the room intensifies. There is a sense of concentration. People are here to listen.
>
> (Field notes, July 2012)

When an insightful observer enters a venue and reflects on the events taking place, it is clear that a public performance is influenced by two groups: the audience and the musicians, both of whom have expectations and wishes from one another. Both parties have ideas of how the performance would progress in addition to what they should receive from it. Both have the need to reach out to one another and establish a relationship. It is this complicated interaction and relationship between the audience and the musicians in the context of contemporary British jazz that is the focus here.

This chapter examines the way in which British jazz musicians conceptualise their relationship with their audiences, by emphasising how this relationship is constructed in the musicians' discussions. This includes themes such as how the relationship with the audience is made meaningful through the musicians' speech and actions; how these discussions highlight negotiations made with the audience; how these negotiations are shaped by power struggles in performance; and how boundaries between the audience and the musicians are being built, maintained or deconstructed.

In order to grasp the musicians' perspective, this paper uses the theoretical framework of Alfred Schutz's phenomenological sociology. Broadly speaking, phenomenological research aims to capture the first-hand experience of a certain phenomenon, described as it occurred. The researcher tries to capture as closely as possible the way in which the phenomenon is experienced within the context, and then attempts to extrapolate the essence of the phenomenon (Giorgi and Giorgi, 2003: 26–27; Ihde, 2007: 26). Schutz has pointed out that researchers have the tendency to concentrate too much on idealisations and formalisations of the social life-world. This problem can be overcome by reference to the subjective point of view (Schutz, 1976: 6–7). It is therefore important that the researcher pays attention to the actions and feelings of the actor at the centre of this social world. Following this argument, this article focuses on the people at the centre of a certain social world, the musicians, by examining their activities, perspectives, and emotions. I will also try to grasp what induces the participants to adopt certain attitudes towards their social environment. According to Schutz (1976: 6–7), this allows us to analyse the production of meanings that a social phenomenon has for the participants.

The research material used in this chapter is composed of direct observation of performances and interviews with professional jazz musicians. The interviews have been analysed by using discursive psychology,[1] a form of discourse analysis. Observation of performance venues was done mainly around London with a few additions outside the metropolis. Between 2006 and 2012 altogether 37 venues were observed, and from 2009 to 2012 eleven musicians were interviewed.

The observations and the musicians interviewed are all part of what I would call the contemporary jazz scene in Britain. The musicians mainly performed modern jazz, but they also did occasional traditional jazz performances if finances demanded it. All the musicians participating in the research were white and the gender balance tilted towards men, following the norm among jazz musicians internationally.[2]

## Creating a connection with the audience

A performance is always an act of communication imbued with power dynamics. The performers have different means of getting their message across to the audience and establishing the kind of communicative relationship that they prefer. The musicians, therefore, have each developed their own distinctive strategies of how to deal with the audience and their expectations of the event. In this effort, they tend to employ two kinds of strategies: either ignoring the audience or trying to create a working relationship with them. In the former case the musician is relying on the music to do the communicative part while the musician himself has no need to communicate in any additional ways, such as through verbal commentary. The former strategy can also mean that the musician does not want to engage with the audience in any way, possibly because he feels that the audience is hostile towards him. In the latter case, the musician is aiming to create a connection with the people attending. This connection can be formed by using verbal, physical and visual means. These are often intertwined but the most common is using verbal communication.[3]

One of the ways of creating a connection with the audience at the beginning of the performance is the musician welcoming them to the gig. One of the musicians interviewed stated that there are many alternatives for audiences today, so coming to the gig is an effort in itself and the musician should acknowledge this. The respect can be shown in a variety of ways; even dressing up smartly can be seen as such evidence. As this example demonstrates, the connection and the respect that the musicians have towards the audience is often communicated in subtle ways and it can go unnoticed.

By using the analytical lens of phenomenology, it can be detected that the connection with the audience is what makes the performance a meaningful experience for both parties. During the process of establishing this connection, the musician communicates his ideas to the audience through the use of auditory – including verbal – physical, emotional and musical resources. These strategies can sometimes be too abstract or sophisticated for the audience to understand, causing the musician to feel that he can only be understood by other musicians (see Hytönen-Ng, 2013). Past experiences have therefore taught most of the musicians whom I interviewed or observed to establish connection in a more direct manner.

Telling jokes and humorous stories seems to be a popular way to engage with the audience. This can be described as one of the strategies in which musicians indulge when providing entertainment. As it has been pointed out, humour seems to create bonds between people, but it can also ridicule something or someone (Billig, 2005; Vinton, 1989). It could be suggested that the use of humour engages the audience by creating oppositions. The audience has to then decide if they are on the musician's side or on the opposition, but in both cases they can participate in the joke either by laughing at someone or laughing at themselves. In most of the cases that I observed, I perceived the audience to be on the same side as the musician. In such a situation the musician comes mentally close to the audience while the jokes create an invisible tie between them. This allows both parties to relax with the secure feeling that one is among friends, even if this idea is an illusion.

One of the musicians pointed out that through dry humour he was able to involve the partners of audience members, who had come to the gig unwillingly. This group of people can be viewed as the 'opposition' group. Addressing these audience members directly integrates them within the performance, thus making it more enjoyable for them and increasing the likelihood that they will stay longer.

> It's a terrible thing to say this, but you see people who've been dragged along, who didn't really want to come. And it's usually wives and girlfriends who don't want be there a lot of the time, you know. And I say: 'Look, it's only two hours of this. We're going to get through it, you know. We're gonna get two hours of jazz, but we're gonna get through this. Okay?' And you can see them sort of [relax] . . . Because you've hit exactly on what they're thinking, they start laughing.

Assuring them that any uncomfortable situation is temporary is supposed to make the experience easier for the audience members who did not come by their own volition. Through humour the musician acknowledges the presence of these participants, the 'opposition', and makes them feel that they have been seen, which allows them to perhaps enjoy the rest of the performance. Humour is nonetheless not directed only towards the unwilling audience members. It involves the jazz fans as well, who can, through these jokes, gently laugh with their reluctant partners. By using humour, the musician is then clearly creating two groups in the audience – the jazz fans and the non-fans (opposition) – and working on both allows them to have a shared experience through laughter, even though the reasons behind this laughter might be different for each of the groups.

The quote could be interpreted as potentially sexist, since it gives the impression that the audience members who are attending the performance of their own will and interest are exclusively male. Females are presented in the musician's comment as disinterested, but also easily entertained. This critique, however, should take into account that most of the audience for modern jazz in Britain is indeed composed of men while women are a rarity. This gender imbalance varies depending on the genre of jazz, as traditional jazz performances are more likely to have an audience composed of older men while more modern contemporary jazz performances have a younger and more balanced audience.

The musician's comment can also be interpreted along the lines of shared communal experiences and intersubjectivity. The musician is claiming that he understands how this reluctant part of the audience feels. As inter-subjectivity would allow us to imagine ourselves in the shoes of another, the musician suggests that for the sake of our loved ones we have all been in circumstances where we have had to endure a situation or event that we do not enjoy; having to attend the opera, to see a movie featuring an actor whom we dislike or to attend a rugby game. This intersubjective element is cultivated by the musician in order to facilitate a satisfying experience of the performance, for as many members of the audience as possible.

Other musicians also highlight the idea of creating a shared experience for the participants. It is considered as part of the performance that the audience is taken on a journey and the musician invokes different feelings within them. To a degree, this is also expected by the audience when they pay for the performance. Fulfilling the expectation of a mental journey could be considered a sign of a successful performance which would, in turn, encourage the audience to come back and listen to that musician again.

The musician is thus using the intersubjective aspect of the musical experience to reach out to the audience. He, as an active participant, shares experiences of the world around him and, through these experiences, he is then able to expand outside the realm of his individual experience. This allows the audience to imagine that their private experience, that may include excitement, arousal and other emotional states, is shared with others but without becoming public, which could make the individual feel vulnerable. The situation is therefore intimate but simultaneously safe for everyone.

Engaging the audience with the performance could also be created by explaining some details about the chosen repertoire. The explanations can include, for example, opening up historical facts about the song: who wrote it, when, and what does the name refer to. Sharing such details can also include more personal accounts such as talking about the meaning of a certain song to the musician or where it was heard for the first time. If the song is the musician's own composition, the introductory speech might include details about what inspired it. Such introductions produce shared knowledge and familiarity with the repertoire, which then direct the audience's experience of the coming song, thus creating a deeper and more lasting impression. The introductory practice also allows the musician to create an illusion of closeness for the audience, not just with the musician himself but also with the pieces being performed.

Using Schutz's ideas, the verbal communication and introductory speeches described above are means of creating socially approved knowledge, which Schutz sees as distinct from socially derived knowledge. Socially approved knowledge, even when based on the individual's immediate experiences, receives additional weight if it is accepted by the other members of the group to which the individual belongs. The individual therefore believes that his or her own experiences are indubitably valid if other members of the group, whom the individual considers as competent, corroborate the experience though their own experiences or through mere trust (Schutz, 1976: 133). The musician validates the audience's experience with his explanations while he is also creating a structure within which the audience is to interpret their individual experience.

The content of the discussions with the audience are chosen according to the audience and the location. From what I was able to observe, musicians are more likely to tell cruder jokes in the countryside than in London. Whether this was to do with the musician's expectations of the educational level or class values outside the metropolis, it is difficult to say for sure. The early part of the performance is, therefore, marked by a constant evaluation, where musicians read the audience to ascertain what kind of behaviour and jokes are appropriate. This leads into a cycle of reading, re-reading, antici-pation, and reaction. Adapting Schutz's (1976: 160) idea of 'conversation of gestures', it can be stated that the musician is reading the audience's reactions to his actions from their gestures and expressions and adapts his future choices based on the interpretations that he made.[4]

## Intimacy with the audience

Musicians tend to have an internal need to communicate with the audience. This is what brings them out of their practice rooms and in front of the audience, turning the music into a profession instead of a hobby. This need is enhanced by a meaningful interaction created with the audience. The physical and emotional closeness, a sense of intimacy that the musician has with the audience, mark and shape this interaction. Some musicians consider 'closeness' so important that they ask for the tables to be moved closer to the stage. This enhances the feeling of functional connection, allowing the musician to choose people from the audience to whom he can play, while it also provides a stronger sense of intimacy between them. Some musicians, as is often the case with singers, might use this opportunity to blur or break the barrier between the stage and the audience, and extend the performance space into the audience territory by walking off the stage and venturing among the spectators during the performance. It has also been pointed out that the audience prefers venues where they have direct access to the performer, where the artist is close at hand (Brand et al., 2012: 642).

Another important part of this closeness relies on the musicians' ability to create intimacy with the audience. One of the interviewees described how, while attending a performance as an audience member, the sense of meaningful encounter with a certain musician and music is created by being able to hear the saxophone keys rattling as well as seeing and hearing the instrumentalist breathe. These aspects are part of the music, the ethos of jazz, which according to him is after all an 'intimate music'. Even though this sense of intimacy is affected by several factors (see Hytönen-Ng, 2013: 111–128), it is evident through the analysis of the interviews that intimacy is maximised by physical proximity between the musician and the audience. It is the physical closeness that gives essence to the process of sharing. As Eric Clarke (2011) has pointed out, it is the secrets that are whispered, while the physical proximity associated with whispering is also linked with authenticity. The music becomes real and genuine when we hear it in shared time and space, and witness the effort that it takes to produce those sounds.

Schutz points out the need to distinguish between face-to-face and intimate relationships. In a face-to-face relationship, the participants share space and time so that the other's expressions and gestures are 'immediately observable as symptoms of his thoughts' (Schutz, 1976: 109). The sharing of common space also means that the other person's thoughts can be grasped in a vivid presence that Schutz calls the 'pure we-relationship'. Intimacy, on the other hand refers to mutual knowing and knowledge of the participants engaged in face-to-face interaction. This can be brought back to the idea of sharing 'the naked soul' as well as the common space and time. Intimacy, according to Schutz, is an emotion heavily reliant on knowledge (Schutz, 1976: 109–110, 113). Hearing the music close up, feeling it move through our bodies, makes the experience intimate. We know the music because we have felt it physically. Through the sharing of common space, the audience breathes with the musician and witnesses in close proximity the performer's vitality pass through the instrument. This, according to my hypothesis, is what makes the audience's musical experience intimate.

This level of closeness is not always easy or enjoyable for the performer, since often being accessible to the audience can be straining, resulting in negative feelings. In small venues musicians do not necessarily have a separate back stage area, which leaves them sharing the space with the audience, during breaks and after the performance. This might be a good reason for the musician to find other types of performance venues. One of the musicians interviewed pointed out that, towards the middle of his career, the legendary saxophonist Sonny Rollins stopped doing club performances and limited himself to concert halls. Rollins found that in club performance there was no escape from the audience. I have not been able to verify whether this story was true or not, but the circulation of such narratives offers an interesting view into the discourses among musicians. The story indicates that being available at the club makes a musician vulnerable if they do not know how to protect themselves.

Occasionally, musicians' encounters with the audience are also marked by negative feedback. Even though musicians recognise that, as paying customers, audience members can rightfully express their disappointment, stating opinions about previous performances might be considered irrelevant for the event taking place now. One of the musicians stated that he tried to work the audience, to make a good connection, in order to avoid these kinds of circumstances. There are, nonetheless, situations when the musician would want to escape the audience and rest in a back room.

The grievance over receiving negative comments from the audience is even more pronounced when observing events such as the Norwich Jazz Party. As part of the event people have started giving grades to the bands or performances. Whoever introduced this procedure remains unknown to my interviewee:

> People actually mark their programs. 'Seven out of ten for that one.' And then they'll come up and say: 'Yesterday you got a six, a seven and a nine.' [The musician:] 'Thank you, thank you very much.' . . . They [the audience] tell you stuff like: 'Oh! You've had that jacket a couple of years now! . . . You've put a little weight on. Lost a bit of hair, haven't you?' I say: 'Unlike you I'm not immune to the aging process, you know.' Bizarre, isn't it.

As this example indicates, the audience is actively engaged in the performance and the creation of the event even if it is with a critical mind-set. This might mean that the feedback does not take the forms that the artist is expecting. The performer has to be prepared for all kinds of feedback that does not relate to the music at all. Similarly, Brand and colleagues (2012: 641, 643) also reported situations where the audience came up to comment on the music or programme choices made by the musician. Brand et al. noted that unhelpful comments from the audience were often greeted with 'a refusal to accept this intrusion' and could cause the musician to 'alter their playing, their physical position or even speaking out to alter their audience's behaviour' (2012: 641).

While artists are not necessarily offended by such comments or take them too personally, the encounters are still remembered years afterwards. The stories point out that audiences do not view the artists in the same way as they view other people. Being a public figure, the artist is often expected to maintain an idealised image by remaining the same and not ageing. The audience can treat the musician as if he is a close friend to whom one can say all sorts of things in a very blunt way. They might remember meetings with the artist from years before that the musician himself has long forgotten. As the musician above continued, members of the audience might venture up towards him and say that they've last seen him in a venue somewhere in 1979. This perhaps unwanted closeness for the musician, aims to shift the power relationship between him and the audience members. These forms of intimacy can therefore be viewed as part of the power play where negotiations are being made.

However, the audience's intention to engage with the musicians in very concrete ways does not always result in negative forms of communication. The musicians also see this as a way of creating desired publicity. At times, these types of interaction can also be regulated by the organisers, as one of my female interviewees pointed out. In a particular venue she was expected to entertain the audience members during the band's break, while the rest of the musicians were being sent out to the backstage area (Hytönen-Ng, 2014: 117–118). The way that the musician then interacts with the audience might not always be down to their own choices or something that comes out naturally. Creating contact with the audience is, therefore, something that performers have to learn.

Following Schutz's (1976: 110–111) ideas, the audience creates a 'we-relation' with the musician when they first see him perform. This is associated with the generated feeling of intimacy. Even though the we-relation is intermittently occurring during the performances, it can be re-established when the person meets the artist again, in a sense continuing from where it last broke off. The relationship, however, can be one-sided, as it only exists within the audience member's idealised view of the musician. This level of intimacy might be partly maintained and constructed through the musician's recordings, and, nowadays, through YouTube and other videos,[5] that the audience can listen to and watch at home while waiting for future live performances. The musician can, therefore, be an auditory and visual part of an individual's everyday life.

## Indifference in the performance

The musicians pointed out that the audience often sees the music as secondary.[6] People visit venues in order to spend time with their friends and socialise. In these situations, attention is not on the music or what is happening on stage, and music becomes a mere background affair. This creates feelings of frustration for the musicians, as they have prepared for a performance that now goes unnoticed.

> But then I guess different things can come into it, like what the audience is like. What kind of people show up to the gig, you know, because some places might be nice room[s] to play in but . . . The audience might be, you know, they might not listen, they might talk or whatever. Like for instance the [name of venue] on a Saturday night is . . . You know, it's great club and it's a nice room to play in but sometimes it can be a nightmare because the people, the audience just talk and talk and talk.

The musician expects the audience to listen to the music. The audience's behaviour, for example talking loudly, can distract the musician from the music, impairing the actual performance. The musician is not able to concentrate to his fullest capacity or it could be that it takes extra effort to get the audience to engage. In instances like these, the we-relation never becomes established, since the audience is not prepared for, or interested in it. The musician is left on his own trying to create this connection, which in effect causes feelings of disappointment. He is reaching out, but not being met half way.

Outside the interviews, I was also told how offended a musician felt when he had brought his girlfriend with another friend to listen to one of his gigs and they were talking throughout the performance. The social aspect of a gig was different for the audience than what the musician was expecting. In this example, the girlfriend seems to want to spend time with her friend at the same time as the musician, who has prepared for the performance, is expecting her to behave like a jazz fan and direct her attention to the music. This phenomenon of betrayed expectations and the failure to generate a we-relationship, often leads musicians to completely ignore the audience and their desires.

Musicians also state that there are situations where the event organisers, or venue owners, want to provide jazz in clubs that the audience frequents for different reasons. The organisers might want to raise the profile of the place or attract a different kind of audience, but the existing clientele is reluctant to embrace such changes (see Tsioulakis, 2013). This can create situations where the audience seems indifferent towards the musicians and the music being played, or the venue itself might be too small or otherwise unsuitable for the performance. One interviewee described a gig on a Saturday night in Soho, London, in a place where people came to drink. Even though the venue was extremely small, the organisers had booked a quartet.

> It was Saturday night in Soho. If they [audience] want to listen to jazz they go to Ronnie Scott's or PizzaExpress and they go to this place to drink and to get drunk so it was just a waste of time. That was pretty horrible. Just people shouting, pushing past you and really drunk. Nobody, nobody cares, nobody's listening. That just felt like a waste of time, just wanted to go home [laughs] . . . They're rather like a hostile audience, they'd rather you weren't there. They just want you to shut up.

The musician points out that the audience knows what they want and where to find it. It is situations like these that make the musicians ignore the audience and concentrate on playing for one another (see Hytönen-Ng, 2013: 109). Through a 'conversation of gestures', in this case even very physical gestures such as pushing, the musicians are able to read the audience's attitude and determine that they would prefer that the music would stop. During the research project it was also pointed out that the worst audience is the one that has not paid to hear the music. The interviewed musician pointed out that it does not matter if the fee is just a few pounds, but even a minimal fee desists a certain type of audience who is not really interested in the music itself.[7]

## Requests as part of the performance

As the previous sections demonstrate, the performance is a joint creation, but also a negotiation in which the musician as well as the audience participates. The audience has an important role in the creation of the event, the atmosphere, and the content of the performance. The audience's opinion on what is acceptable affects the options that the musicians have. If the audience is not happy with what the musicians are providing, those that are attuned with musical desires are unlikely to come back. Therefore, the audience's perception of what is good has a strong impact on the musician's work, and this influences the choices of repertoires being presented. The musician has to take into account the type of jazz that the audience is expecting to hear. The chosen songs cannot represent solely the musician's preferences but have to correspond to the audience's expectations. There are different strategies in how the musicians respond to these expectations:

> If I went into certain venues and played some of the stuff I've played, they'd probably leave at the interval ... They [the audience] have a very clear idea of what jazz is, and it's usually based around when they stopped buying records ... Cannonball Adderley used to say three for them, two for you, three for them. So, if you structure a set of eight songs, do three that they're happy with, three that they're very happy with at the end and two for you in the middle.

As this quote demonstrates, the live performance can be considered as a series of negotiations between the musician and the audience. The musician has to consider what the audience wants and how much he is permitted to please himself. The balance is regularly maintained. At certain points during the performance, the musician considers how happy the audience is, and how many songs can the musician afford to play for himself (see also Falkner and Becker, 2009: 135–164). Should the musician find himself unsuccessful in this endeavour, the chances of the audience protesting through their behaviour is enough to make the situation uncomfortable. Furthermore, the audience may take more evasive actions, for example talk during performance or leave early.

Another interesting point that is raised from the previous quote about Cannonball Adderley and the earlier comment that referred to Sonny Rollins, is the musicians' tendency to refer to the example of famous artists in explaining their own behaviour. This demonstrates that the musicians are validating their own actions by referring to the conduct of other well-known musicians as well as pinpointing that these discussions and negotiations are timeless and recurring themes within the jazz scene. In the previous quote, the musician can also be interpreted to draw on a famous example as a discursive strategy to elevate himself by comparing his actions to those of legendary musical figures.

The audience also tries to influence the performance by requesting songs and acknowledgements. It is quite usual for audience members to ask musicians to play a particular song or to make special requests, such as congratulating someone on their birthday. Some musicians find this annoying and consequently, after a polite decline, the requests are rarely played. According to testimonies, requests seem to make the performer feel as a 'second-class' musician or a 'cocktail pianist'.

Suggesting songs can be interpreted as intentional controlling and an effort to turn the we-relationship on its head. As one musician stated, she feels like a jukebox when the audience is making several requests. When the audience wants to choose the songs, the musician's own choices are diminished and the anticipated effect of the performance is partly compromised. The musician usually made an estimate about the target audience and the venue beforehand, and constructed the set list based on this. The intended storyline created by the songs is then disrupted by the unexpected requests. This often created the feeling that the musician's own set list is not valued or trusted.

However, there are times when musicians purposefully ask the audience for requests. This is a strategy used when the musician might feel that he is not reaching the audience in the way that he wants. In effect, it is a way of trying to create the we-relationship by pointing out to the audience that the performance is a joint creation. The musicians can only do this once they have the confidence that they are familiar with a varied repertoire over different styles. This strategy has its own risks and might backfire if the audience asks for songs with which the musicians are not familiar. Having to turn the audience down several times because they do not know the requested song understandably does not give the desirable impression about the musician's competence level.

The strategy of asking what the audience wants to hear has also been used at performances where contact with the audience has already been working well. During the performance in Poole described at the beginning of the chapter, the musicians asked the audience to choose a song, as well as the style and the tempo in which to play it. The audience's response was very enthusiastic. Experiments such as these show the musicians' talent and wide repertoire, but also make the audience feel that they have an immediate impact on the performance.

Other types of requests that the audience often makes are to ask the musicians to acknowledge someone's birthday or anniversary between the songs. Such acknowledgements are perhaps even more difficult to handle than requests of songs. The musicians do not want to dismiss the audience and make them feel that they were not heard, but simultaneously they worry about their own power over the content of the performance being diminished. One of the interviewees notes that he rarely acknowledges such requests as it reminded him of working at a holiday camp. He tends to 'forget' the requests intentionally or, alternatively, he dedicates a particular song to the person without mentioning the birthday. He feels that if he is to acknowledge all possible requests he would start 'getting into being a dreadful entertainer' while he wants to retain 'some kind of dignity'. The actions chosen by the musician are aimed at maintaining his own sense of self-worth. The musician considers the kinds of actions with which he is happy and acts accordingly. These comments echo Merriam and Mack's argument that, due to the nature of his or her occupation, the jazz musician is 'faced with a dilemma regarding the nature of her/his art and, in one's own view, in expected to be both a creative artist and a commercial entertainer' (Merriam and Mack, 1960: 213). These two roles are contradictory and often lead to confusion regarding the musician's status.

The situations where an individual audience member wants to be acknowledged for something are perceived in a two-fold way. While the requests and acknowledgements are important for that particular audience member, the action itself is meaningless for the other participants. Thus, the musician has to also consider that these kinds of acknowledgements cannot be carried out for everyone present at the performance. Even though these requests might not affect the planned narrative, the musician is no longer in control of the overall performance, but the audience begins to have a larger impact on the end result.

A female singer also pointed out a situation where the audience makes even more personal requests than acknowledgements for birthdays.

> [During a break a] guy asked me if I could propose on his behalf from the stage to his girlfriend which was just really weird. I just thought that maybe he wanted the mic which would have been fine, but the message was clear, he wanted me to ask her. And it was such a stressful moment because, you know, she's . . . They were sitting right in front of the stage, you know, really close. And she was obviously genuinely shocked [by the proposal] and didn't, you know . . . and then probably really embarrassed . . . And coming, it's a bit weird coming from a singer she doesn't know. So the first things she said was 'Oh no!' Like this really loud and I was: 'On my god!' And I was like: 'Please say yes!' . . . First I thought, this has backfired [laughs]. She doesn't want to marry him and it's a disaster.

In the described situation the audience member is handing over the control and conduct of an important life event to the singer. Perhaps he was afraid to ask, but in the given situation he is making the proposal a very public event and wants to include the whole audience in this significant event. The proposal becomes a performance. He nonetheless seems unaware of the ambivalence of the situation, whereby a woman is asked to propose on his behalf to another woman.

These kinds of requests are not unheard of in other circles as well. Similar requests have apparently been made to other musicians to the extent that Jamie Cullum's website once noted that they do not take personal requests, song requests or arrange for marriage proposals before, during or after concerts. The existence of the statement would suggest that the audience makes such requests often enough.[8]

By making requests of such personal nature, the audience members create a connection between the performer and the audience. It also closely ties the performance into a personal memory, and makes the audience members feel that the performer is part of their life more closely than in reality. These actions therefore diminish the barrier between the audience and the performer, uplifting the role of the audience. The audience becomes an active participant, who does not just listen but participates in the creation of the event, and manipulates it for their own desires. Through these requests the audience tries to involve the musician, as well as perhaps a particular venue, in their significant and intimate life events. This demands the creation of intimacy and the establishment of a we-relation with the musician.[9]

## Conclusions

It is often said that live performances encapsulate the essence of authenticity in modern jazz, while jazz fans tend to agree that the 'real' or 'genuine' jazz experience cannot be captured on recordings. These vinyl pressings, cassette tapes, CD burnings, or digital recordings catch the music in a single moment, resulting in music that is frozen in time (Laing, 1991; Thornton, 1995; see also Osborne's chapter in this book); it remains the same every time it is played. Jazz traditionally shapes its performative features in live performances as its essential traits revolve around the use of improvisation. It is through improvisation that jazz musicians' skills in generating new material adhering to or breaking the limitations of tradition become apparent.

Beyond the quality of music, what happens in a live performance is more than the music unfolding in front of the audience. The experience of a live performance is jointly created by the audience, the venue and the musicians (see also Brand et al., 2012). Thus, the situation is unique and virtually unrepeatable each time. The live performance is also where the musicians and audience's relationship takes an interactive form, and allows both of these parties to witness the presence of one another. Live performance therefore offers the chance to deepen the relationship that has been or is being formed between them, which, in the best case scenario, creates a we-relationship.

Paradoxically, one informant stated that he had noticed that musicians who are not that bothered with the audience interaction or who do not make compromises, are often musically more successful. As an example of this I was told stories about the pianist Keith Jarrett, who was very well-known for his conduct towards the audience. The interviewee noted that Jarrett once shouted at the audience when someone coughed in the middle of his performance. These stories seem to demonstrate an appreciation towards the fact that the audience does not affect the content of performances by Jarrett and other successful musicians, while at the same time the audience seems to value these eccentric performers and find their music more interesting.[10] In response to this, musicians often prefer to ignore the audience and actively reinforce this separation (Tsioulakis, 2013).

The musicians have two strategies in facing the audience: turning inwards or outwards. This division is visible within the jazz scene in the United Kingdom. Some musicians are quite externally active, looking for ways of constructing the connection with the audience. Others turn inwards avoiding even eye contact with the audience. It is nonetheless evident, based on the observed gigs, that the audience's responses to the performance were clearly enhanced by musicians' interaction. Jokes and other stories seem to be an important part of the performance that enhance the connection between the audience and the musician. The expectations of the scene also direct the musician to perform in a certain way. When the musician acts in the socially approved way he stands a better 'chance, by such actions, of coming to terms with everyone who accepts the same system of relevance' (Schutz, 1976: 237). The musician is likely to become more successful as the audience can understand his actions and relate to them.

At the same time the audience is actively seeking ways of constructing a we-relation with the performer. In order to make this relation more intimate, the audience addresses the musician by making requests asking for particular songs that they themselves like or have a special connection to. The audience members are in these situations trying to affect the direction of the performance, but also involve a musician – or a place – in one's significant life events. Such actions have a multi-layered and often unpredictable impact on the performance.

On the other hand, the audience's intentions and hopes with regards to the performance can be fragmented and inconsistent. Some of the audience members have come to the performance to spend time with friends, others are there to listen to the music, while some are also engaging in important life events along with the music. In contrast, the musicians have a more unidirectional aim in the performance. This can involve the idea of sharing with the audience and the creation of intimacy. Despite all the preparations and planning done beforehand, the interaction with the audience can deeply influence the direction and the end result of the performance. It is also clear that the musician's work with the audience is not just limited to the duration of the official performance, but starts before the gig when the audience comes in and continues until the moment when the last member of the audience leaves the venue.

Both parties are therefore actively constructing the we-relation, through auditory, visual, and emotional interactions, even though the relation might be different from one party to the other. The audience can view the musician in a very intimate way, asking to share life events such as birthdays, anniversaries, and engagements, in effect making the musician's life intertwined with the life of the audience members. Within this intermittent and partly unrequited we-relation that has been established in the audience's mind, the musician remains to some respect unchangeable, fixed in time, until he is witnessed again in another live performance.

For the musician this we-relation is a temporary construction, existing in most cases only during the performance, while the fixed relationship is created more with the whole scene rather than with individual audience members. As the musician faces different audience members in his daily life, the encounters are most of the time less memorable in their content. The musician is unlikely to remember the individuals with whom he has created this temporary but intimate we-relation with, whereas the musician is remembered by the audience. The fixed we-relationship can therefore be considered as illusionary since in-between the live performances it exists only in the audience's mind, while the musician is creating similar temporary relations with others. Approaching the phenomenon from a phenome-nological perspective it can be stated that musicians use intersubjectivity as tool for creating the we-relation and the feeling of community with the audience. At times this intersubjectivity can be illusionary but it none-theless engages the audience in the performance. To a certain degree, inter-subjectivity is always illusionary, as it is only an understanding of how the subject would feel if they were in the object's shoes. In other words, it is based on a feeling of empathy that is not necessarily reciprocated or shared.

Following Schutz's (1976) thoughts we can conclude that the individual musician or audience member identifies with their counterpart's experiences and actions within the common we-relation. The face-to-face interaction taking place at a live performance makes this relation concrete, direct and vivid as individuals influence each other during this co-presence through visual and auditive gestures, and behavioural cues. At the same time, a larger we-relation of the scene, which surpasses but is composed of the individual members, is created through this face-to-face interaction. It is within this we-relation that the jazz scene itself is created, and what makes devoted fans to choose live performances over recorded music.

The live performance offers us multiple perspectives and possibilities. One that has been excluded from this article, but which could provide a fruitful way of looking at jazz musicians' interaction in performance, is seeing the performance itself as a struggle for power. This struggle can be detected in the discursive undertones taking place in the music scene, and in musicians' speech specifically, of which this article has given mere indications. In a balanced performance, the power struggles are subtle and difficult to detect. In the opposite case, both parties can try to forcefully influence one another, reach their own aims through different means, in turn creating a situation where only one or neither of the parties enjoy the end result. This can cause the audience to dislike the performance and the musicians to turn inwards. It is often in relation to the audiences' expectation to involve the performer and the performance into their significant life events that the power struggle becomes more pronounced.

## Notes

1 In discursive psychology, I have followed Edwards and Potter's (1992: 2) definition that the method focuses on 'the action orientation of talk and writing'. The social actions and interaction work is perceived to be done within the discourse itself. Discursive constructions are to be examined in the context where they occur and they are seen as situated and occasioned constructions that make sense when they are being perceived in the light of what these discursive descriptions accomplish (Edwards and Potter, 1992: 2–3).

2 I will be using the masculine form in the text in accordance to the musicians' gender, as most of the participants were men (see also Faulkner and Becker, 2009: 3). In the case of the single female respondent, her gender is pointed out by the text as it is significant in that particular context. Even though men also tend to be a majority in the audience, I have here chosen to use gender neutral pronouns when describing this more diverse demographic.

3  For a discussion of the role of verbal utterances from the stage to the audience and back during live concerts, see also Barbara Bradby's chapter in this volume.

4  See Bruce Johnson's chapter in this volume for an in-depth examination of 'gestures' in performance.

5  For a more detailed discussion on the interaction and intermediary role of television and video on performances see Richard Osborne's contribution in this volume.

6  Some aspects of this topic have also been discussed in my previous work (Hytönen-Ng, 2013: 103–108). The musicians' experience of playing background music have also been discussed extensively by O'Donnell and Henderson (in this volume).

7  See also O'Donnell and Henderson's contribution in this volume for a discussion of performance with a non-attentive audience.

8  The website has since then been updated and the statement disappeared.

9  The audience's strategies of creating personal encounters with the artist is also discussed by Barbara Bradby in this volume.

10  This is connected to the idea of avoiding the principle of 'selling out' and artistic prostitution while musicians prefer to follow their own vision (Brand et al., 2012: 365; Gordon, 2006: 156; Hytönen-Ng, 2013: 103). Similar discussions can be found both in jazz and in classical music. Whether this is financially feasible could depend on the musician's status in the scene.

# 5 Performer-audience interaction in live concerts
## Ritual or conversation?

*Barbara Bradby*

### Response cries and talking to oneself

> Walking back from the local chemist's, I spot an old friend about to step onto the pedestrian crossing that I am half way across. As we approach, I smile and say, 'Hi, Bill!' He does not react or apparently see me, and as I get ready to repeat the greeting louder, I see that he has earphones in and is listening to music. I therefore wave my hand in his line of vision as I shout more loudly, 'Hi, Bill!'. But by that time we are nearly across each other and I don't make an effort to stop him to chat, especially as he is by now on the pedestrian crossing and the traffic lights aren't even red. Just as he is nearly past, he sees me and acknowledges me with, 'Hi, Barbara!' but we don't stop. My smile as I walk on is one of relief.

By the time I am back at my desk, I have seen that the interaction nicely exemplifies Goffman's analysis of 'talking to one's self', in his article on 'Response Cries' (Goffman, 1981a [1978]). There is a social prohibition on talking to oneself in public, such that if caught doing it, we can engage in a number of social repair mechanisms to make it appear that this was not what we were doing. This explains my anxiety to get my greeting heard/seen and returned, since otherwise I would be seen by others in the vicinity as talking to myself, hence mad. At the same time, Bill's self-absorption in his music in a public place was unheard of at the time that Goffman wrote his article in 1978, but nowadays, the visible feature of his little black earphones can excuse his apparent refusal to act sociably and return my greeting.

The endeavour to get one's greeting noticed is an interactional part also of many live music events as in 'Hello, Dublin!', or other place-based greetings amplified across a stadium. And how often have we heard greetings phrases being *repeated* by the performer if s/he is not happy with the response received from the audience? Typically, this occurs with the follow-up to the actual greeting, 'Are you having a good time?', where the performers try to build a crescendo of enthusiasm from the audience by repeatedly asking this question. Of course, this is itself a risky strategy, which can fail if the audience is reluctant to join in and ignores the performer, or if the performer's repetition is rejected as too redolent of a 'showbiz' ritual that is inappropriate to the context of different musical genres.

Audiences too, seek to get their greetings noticed by the performer and achieve a response. This is the case of the diehard fan who goes to the gig in the persistent hope of getting noticed by the star. In the literature on popular music audiences, so-called 'Beatlemania' has a foundational place (see also Osborne's chapter in this volume). Yet it has usually been analysed without questioning the Freudian legacy of the labelling of the girl fans' behaviour as 'hysteria' or 'mania'. While Ehrenreich *et al.* (1992) give this a feminist twist in seeing it rather as a direct rebellion against the sexual repression of the 1950s, I argue that from the interactional point of view there is more going on. It is the girls' refusal to respect the social rituals of personal space – what Goffman calls, citing Durkheim, the 'sacredness of the person' – that gets them labelled mad, in a way not dissimilar to Goffman's mental ward inmates (Goffman, 1967 [1956]: 47; Durkheim, 1965 [1915]: 273ff). However, I argue that this refusal to comply with the 'avoidance rituals' of personal space (Goffman, 1967 [1956]: 73) stems here from a competitive *interactional* desire to have one's greeting heard, above the clamour of other voices. The girls scream louder, not just out of the usual attribution of hormonal energy to their mindless bodies, but out of frustration that they cannot get their greeting heard by their friend. In cases like the encounter on the zebra crossing, one shouts louder and louder in order to elicit that return greeting and so persuade the 'gathering' (Goffman, 1963) that one is, in fact, *sane*. In the case of teen fans of boybands, this is to no avail: s/he who shouts (or ratder to an iher, he who shouts, and she who screams, in the usual verbal attributions) louder and loumaginary friend and receives no response, is easily labelled as mad or hysterical. The attribution is social and situational, though, not biological and psychoanalytic.

In writing of these interactional needs to get one's greeting heard and returned, which could be glossed as achieving a 'response' to one's 'summons' (Schegloff, 1968), I am, on the face of it, deviating from what Goffman meant by 'response cries' (Goffman, 1981a [1978]). Goffman was writing of the 'out louds', such as 'Ooops', 'Ouch', or expletives, that are uttered apparently to oneself, but often in public 'gatherings', and he was concerned to show in this way that there are situations of 'talk' which are social and interactional, but not part of 'conversations'. Despite these differences, I argue that applause in popular music concerts includes an element of just such 'response cries'. Indeed, it is the non-conversational yelps and yeahs, whistles and whoops that are a mark of the distinction of the popular music audience from the audience for a classical concert. Clearly there is much continuity between applause practices at popular music events and the conventions of classical applause – particularly the basis in hand-clapping. Nevertheless, the vocalic whoops and yeahs are distinctive to the popular music context and help to create the feeling of informality that is a mark of the successful popular event, in implied opposition to the formality of tradition and classical music. Verbal shouts, such as 'Bravo' and 'Encore', even the simpler 'More', are common to both contexts, if generally louder and more enthusiastic in the popular concert. Their function is more clearly interactive, however, as they appeal to the performers for encores and returns to the stage.

The vocalic shouts and screams of applause at the popular music concert have something in common with Goffman's 'response cries' in that they are utterances in public which are overheard by the others with whom one is co-present. However, these cries are not merely, or even primarily, emitted for the self and surrounding bystanders, but are also directed to the performer on stage. Applause is itself interactional, part of a rudimentary 'conversation' between performer and audience: most basically, applause and 'response cries' serve simply to establish that the singer/performer is not talking to him/herself – that there is in fact a social interaction going on.

I explore this idea here in relation first to some further pieces of writing by Goffman. The next section looks at the difference between recordings and live performances in light of his article on 'The Lecture' (1981b), while the following one puts forward a theory of interaction between performer and audience drawing on his 'On Face-Work' (1967 [1955]) and 'The Nature of Deference and Demeanor' (1967 [1956]). My reading of Goffman owes much to Randall Collins' (2004) defence of Goffman as consistently Durkheimian in taking 'the situation' as his starting point, against the charge of Schegloff (1988) that his focus on ritual and on 'face' betrays a continuing concern with individual psychology. However, I endorse Schegloff's further criticism of Goffman for his failure to examine examples and recordings of actual talk and interaction – rather than the imagined or 'typical' interaction to which Goffman continually and persuasively appeals – and particularly for his failure to study the 'ordinary conversation' which is the focus of Conversation Analysis (Schegloff, 1988). It was this failure that allowed Goffman to avoid really focusing on the 'system' or 'the traffic' underlying interaction and to resist the findings of his ex-students who developed Conversation Analysis (Goffman, 1981c), a resistance that Schegloff implies is Oedipal, citing Sacks' interpretation of the Oedipus myth (Schegloff, 1988: 91).

In this chapter, I attempt to combine Goffman's intuitional brilliance around public situations, with the more exacting findings of Conversation Analysis (CA). To this end, I use both observations and narrative accounts, but also actual recordings of talk and interaction in popular concert situations, and I argue that CA's fundamental analytical insights of turn-taking and sequential organisation, found by conversation analysts in 'ordinary conversation' but argued *against* by Goffman (1981c), can also be productively applied to interactions in popular concerts. In this way, I aim to explore *how* rituals are re-created and collective emotion generated in the social situation of the live concert (Collins, 2004).[1]

# 'They were so much better live': the infusion and illusion of liveness

One Friday night in December 2013, a friend of my daughter's told me that she had just been to the most 'amazing' concert by Haim. She told me excitedly how friends of hers had been going, how they managed to find one ticket online at the last minute and she got it. What particularly struck me was that she emphasised that 'they were so much better live'. They were all such great musicians and put on such a good act, 'you felt like crying the whole way through' and 'it was like watching something big about to happen'. Though she loves their album and knows it well, 'the album pales in comparison', she said.

In his lecture/article on 'The Lecture', Goffman (1981b) identifies and explores a tension between the lecture as 'text' and as 'social event', and argues that despite the precarious understanding that audiences are involved in the text of the lecture,

> In fact, . . . audiences become involved in spite of the text not because of it; they skip along, dipping in and out of the lecturer's argument, waiting for the lecturer's special effects which actually capture them, and topple them momentarily into what is being said.
>
> (Goffman, 1981b: 165)

Audiences, he argues,

> attend because a lecture is more than text transmission; indeed, as suggested, they may feel that listening to text transmission is the price they have to pay for listening to the text transmitter. They attend – in part – because of something that is infused into the text on the occasion of the text's transmission, an infusion that ties the text into the occasion.
>
> (ibid: 186)

I argue that Goffman's framework of the lecture as social situation is applicable in both its outline and detail to the popular concert, where a similar tension exists between audience focus on 'the music' and on 'the event', and between the reproduction of recordings as 'text', and the infusion of liveness in performance.

In order to 'get at these interactional issues', Goffman argues that we must look at how the lecturer handles himself so as to change 'footing' and distance himself from his 'textual self' (ibid: 173–4). He finds three basic ways in which the lecturer infuses liveness into both text and occasion – namely, 'keyings', 'text brackets' and 'parenthetical elaborations' – each of which, I shall argue, is directly relevant also to the analysis of 'liveness' in live concerts. A fourth concept of unintentional 'noise' is also vital to the experience of music as authentically 'live', while his pointing to 'topicality tokens' as a key mechanism in establishing the footing as one of live interaction, turns out to be highly relevant to the analysis of recordings of talk in concerts, and even to song set-lists (Bradby, 2008).

In the context of a lecture, 'keyings' are a musical metaphor for voicings such as ironising a passage, or, alternatively, reading with passion, which give the audience a feeling of live access to the speaker: 'In sensing that these vocally tinted lines could not be delivered this way in print, hearers sense they have special access to the mind of the author, that live listening provides the kind of contact that reading doesn't' (Goffman, 1981b: 175). Applying Goffman's concept to live concerts, 'keyings' becomes a useful shorthand for all those ways in which audiences feel that performers have given them something in the musical performance that 'could not be delivered this way' on a recording. Such 'keyings' can be found to figure in many written reviews of concerts, as a focus of attention and praise, and my observation would be that this becomes more relevant as performers achieve canonical, or 'classic' status, not least because in these cases the 'text' of their recordings is so well-known. Audiences both want to hear the classic, early songs of performers like Bob Dylan or Van Morrison, but they also delight in hearing them in different 'keyings'. I illustrate this below in three extracts from reviews of these performers' concerts in 2012–13. The first is from the online 'Cleveland Scene Magazine' and reviews a Dylan concert in Akron, Ohio in April 2013. 'Keyings' of well-known recordings here provide a focus for reflection and description in the writing, and are a means of valuing and praising the performance:

> Dylan brightened up a bit and switched to piano for rearranged renditions of the beautiful ballads 'Tangled Up in Blue' and 'Visions of Johanna', the latter of which found him standing up from the piano stool at song's end to bring it to a climactic close. His voice sounded sharp, too, and lost the gravelly sound that characterized it on the majority of the set's 16 songs.
>
> The set highlight was the closer, a rearranged version of 'All Along the Watch Tower' that benefited from a bit of lap steel guitar. Dylan let his five-piece backing band jam on the tune and seemed to enjoy performing the song. He returned for a single-song encore before taking a bow and leaving without saying a word to the audience. But that didn't matter. The performance enthralled the capacity crowd . . .
>
> (Niesel, 2013)

The second extract is a review from the British *Daily Telegraph*, of a concert in Glasgow in November 2013. It is more humorous and ironic in tone, suggesting that Dylan changes his songs almost beyond recognition from their recorded versions, but uses such 'keyings' as the motif for the review which ends, like the concert described, on a climax of praise of Dylan's master-status:

> Agreeing to attend a Bob Dylan concert is like volunteering to step inside a boxing ring: without the right preparation one is likely going to get hurt.
>
> Be prepared not to recognise even his most familiar songs . . . 'Things Have Changed' is fast and frantic, 'What Good Am I?' – filled with doubt on record – sounds almost jaunty . . . By lacing 'Simple Twist of Fate' and 'Tangled up in Blue' in steel guitar and setting them to a country rock rhythm Dylan was doing the musical equivalent of attaching a false moustache and plastic nose to them.
>
> A blast of harmonica and acoustic guitar began what I could have sworn was going to be 'Just like a Woman' but which astonishingly turned out to be 'Blowing in the Wind'.
>
> And just as one is about to lose faith Dylan provides a reminder of his undimmed genius: a venomous 'Pay in Blood' and a stunning 'Forgetful Heart' where Dylan's ragged voice is set against Donnie Herron's delicate violin – which was simply mesmerising.
>
> Tonight was a reminder of why Dylan remains the master.
>
> (Manzoor, 2013)

My final example of 'keyings' in a concert review comes from an online review of Van Morrison's 'homecoming' concert in Belfast, in February 2012. The review is phrased rhetorically against the 'trepidation' and 'horror stories' of Morrison's live performances:

> Yet Morrison arrives on stage to the opening bars of 'Brown Eyed Girl', his most famous song, and it appears that we've got him on a good day after all. The jazzy version of the popular standard features a saxophone solo from Morrison and an instrumental section in the middle. It's an upbeat opener . . . 'Crazy Love' brings them back. There are cheers, whistles and mass singalongs, which are never easy at a Van Morrison gig. Morrison's free reinterpretation of his own arrangements makes karaoke very difficult. It is worth keeping quiet, though, to hear the singer's fresh takes of his more well-known songs.
>
> 'Talk is Cheap' and 'Why Must I Have to Explain' sound particularly heart-felt from a man who works hard to keep his private life out of the press. They might also be an answer, of sorts, to the accusations of taciturnity and his less than engaging on-stage persona.[2]

In the case of these notoriously taciturn performers, the challenge for the audience is in part to realise that privileged access to the mind of the performer of which Goffman speaks, through reading their musical 'keyings' in such ways. The highlighting of 'fresh takes' in the above review of

Van Morrison is particularly reminiscent of Goffman's analysis of 'fresh talk' as vital to the infusion of 'liveness' into the lecture, even though he cautions as to its illusory status: 'It might be noted that fresh talk itself is something of an illusion of itself, never being as fresh as it seems' (1981b: 172). Goffman brings to mind occasions when he himself has repeated an apparently 'fresh' anecdote because of its aptness, and warns us that 'these inspired moments will often be ones to most suspect' (ibid: 179). Likewise, as audiences at live concerts, we may know rationally that performers are playing the same 'fresh takes' night after night on their current tour, but still be captivated by the illusion and the privileged access it appears to give us.

The ambiguous nature of 'fresh talk' in live performances becomes more central in looking at 'text brackets' and digressions – Goffman's second and third forms of 'distance-altering alignment' on the part of lecturers. The introductions and closings that bracket the text of a lecture usually involve 'fresh talk' (as opposed to memorising or reading out loud), as is also often the case at live concerts, if only in terms of greetings and farewells from performer to audience. The absence of such talk almost always becomes a talking point, with audience reactions ranging from bewilderment to annoyance. Even the two reviews above written from the 'fan' standpoint in full knowledge that one does not expect talk from these particular performers, both feel the need to excuse this absence, with the specialness of musical 'keyings' being used as a kind of compensatory discourse. [3] This 'accountability' of the absence of talk shows the ritual nature of such interactional changed footing in presenting known material in 'live' format.

However, in live concerts, 'text brackets' generally occur not only around the concert as a whole, but also around each song of the performance. Each song may be introduced, and its ending marked in some way, by changes of footing into 'fresh talk'. In Goffman's analysis of the lecture, his third example of distance-altering is the digression, or 'text-parenthetical elaboration' (ibid: 178), as an example of which he specifically refers to talk between songs at pop concerts: 'Between songs, pop singers in recital commonly switch into direct address, providing out-of-frame comments as a bridge between offerings, presenting themselves in their 'own' name instead of characters in sung dramas' (ibid: 179). While Goffman here succinctly analyses a crucial part of what makes any musical performance 'live' – it could be seen as prescient of the importance of 'own name' performance within the direct address of hip-hop, for instance – nevertheless, his analysis suffers from failing to look at actual examples of talk, and so (con)fuses his two categories in this statement about the pop concert.

If we instead look at actual pieces of talk between songs, it is clear that some take the form of 'text brackets' *around* the song, while others involve talk that might be seen as a digression from the 'text' of the songs, and so bracketed *by* it. To illustrate this, Extract Version 1 (below) presents my first draft of a transcription of between-song talk by the lead singer of a local Dublin 'indie' band, who were opening the show for an international act in the Olympia Theatre in 2007. The Olympia is a fairly small, traditional nineteenth-century variety theatre, used both for theatre and live popular music in central Dublin. I was standing half-way back in what would have been the 'stalls' area of the usual three tiers, the seating having been removed for the gig. The downstairs auditorium was fairly empty, people were drifting in and out from the bar at the back of the stalls, but there appeared to be a small group of fans or friends of the band standing to my left and nearer to the stage. The most enthusiastic applause was coming from this area. In the extract below, the lead singer is addressing the crowd through his voice microphone from the raised theatre stage.

### *Extract version 1: Dublin support band: between song talk, first draft of transcription notes*

(the numbers below refer to minutes and seconds on the recording)

00.30 – First song [[singer a bit flat, not all words distinguishable]], female backing singers audible towards end, oo-oo-oo-ooh
03.50 – Applause starts over last chord, clapping and some yelps
03.54 – [[over applause]] Thanks a million folks. [[applause audible]] How's it goin'. [[applause, then drops back, small audience still]] This is our first time playing the Olympia, I've kind of been waiting for this since I was about, thirteen, so, it's a really big deal [[yelps]] Backstage, [[speech punctuated with pauses]] I'm finding endless scenes from Spinal Tap, I got lost about six times, This is called [Name of Song] [[pause, audience talking audible, strums a few chords on guitar, then goes into intro]]
05.00 – Second song [[singer starts a bit out of tune again]]

For the purposes of illustrating Goffman's categories, I now simplify these notes and transcription by eliminating the audience's applause, focusing solely on the singer's talk. In extract version 2, performer-talk can then be represented in numbered lines as follows.

### *Extract version 2: performer's between-song talk transcribed as a series of lines*

1   Thanks a million folks
2   How's it goin'
3   This is our first time playing the Olympia,
4   I've kind of been waiting for this since I was about, thirteen,
5   so, it's a really big deal
6   Backstage, I'm finding endless scenes from Spinal Tap,
7   I got lost about six times,
8   This is called [Song Name]

Here, line 1 – the singer's first piece of talk after he finishes playing/singing – functions as a closing 'text-bracket' around the previous song, as he thanks the audience for their applause and attention. He then performs an 'opening' to the concert as a whole at line 2, in the form of a 'personal' and intimate, colloquial greeting to the audience.[4] Lines 3–7 are, in Goffman's terms, a digression or 'text-parenthetical elaboration'.[5] Finally, line 8 is the opening bracket to the next song, and refers forward in the performance.

In this way, this short piece of actual talk reveals several functions of between-song 'fresh talk'. There is both 'song-bracketing' and 'song-bracketed' talk: the song-bracketing talk works as opening and closing to each song; while the talk that is bracketed by the song is a digression into personal, 'own name' talk. There is also an opening 'bracket' to the concert as a whole. The fact that these functions can be discerned and separated out suggests that Goffman's various forms of 'distance-altering alignment' vis-a-vis a 'text' do have validity for looking at live concerts. Furthermore, we can follow Goffman in being suspicious of the 'freshness' of this talk, a suspicion that he derived from personal experience of his own repetitions in lectures. In the case of a band, where similar shows are being presented night after night in different venues, audiences may well be suspicious of the scripted nature of 'fresh talk', and even more so once widespread uploads of recordings of live concerts became available on YouTube.

However, my over-simplification in extracting the performer's talk from the interactional applause and 'response cries' of the audience has encouraged me to follow Goffman in speculating and generalising; for instance, I have just written, 'audiences may well be suspicious'. In the next section, I try to remedy this sort of generalised speculation by reworking my first, rough transcription, to see whether we can find evidence of audience members themselves understanding this talk as either genuinely 'fresh', or as illusorily 'suspect'. Goffman may be right in maintaining the ambiguity of 'fresh talk' as both infusion and illusion of liveness: but I hope to show that the analysis of different members' orientations to the talk, to interactional turn-taking, and to the social 'situation' as a whole is the only way to determine whether this is so and how it is accomplished. However, before this, I bring in a further ingredient of Goffman's work that predates both 'Response Cries' and 'The Lecture'. I return to his theory of 'Face-Work', where we find a more genuinely interactional account of the small-scale gathering, one which I believe can help us to understand what is going on in concert situations.

## Applause and thanks: maintaining face, or losing it, as an outcome of sequential organisation in the live concert

Writing in the middle of the twentieth century, Goffman saw 'face' as something that is produced in social interaction: 'The term face may be defined as the positive social value a person effectively claims for himself by the line others assume he has taken during a particular contact' (Goffman, 'On Face-Work' (1967 [1955], p. 5). As such, face involves work so as to maintain it, or avoid losing it, and this maintenance of face is a joint product also of self and others: 'A person may be said to "maintain face" when the line he effectively takes presents an image of him that is internally consistent, that is supported by judgments and evidence conveyed by other participants' (ibid., p. 6). The situation of the 'live' concert is complicated by our living in the age of mechanical, or digital, reproduction (Benjamin, 1968). The live performance must 'live up to' the recorded performances of the star or band, with which most of the audience are already familiar. If this is not attained, we may assume that the band, group, or star loses face, because their perceived 'line' is not consistent.[6] However, we have already seen in the concert reviews that in certain genres or contexts live musical mastery trumps studio sophistication. At the other end of the rock-pop spectrum, there are concerts where it is well-known that the performers are miming, or 'lip-syncing' to recordings of the songs. While most music critics would decry this aesthetic, it does not necessarily deter the fans of boy bands or girl groups, possibly because they indeed expect to hear the song as recorded, but also because, if my approach is right, 'going to see' a live band is conceived of as going to a personal encounter (see also Hytönen-Ng's chapter in this volume). Despite the large-scale gathering, individuals see this as their small-scale chance to meet their star. This is not simply a delusion of grandeur and the effect of cults of celebrity or the loss of the individual in the fantasy of mass culture so often decried (Jenson, 1992). It is rather because, regardless of genre, the interaction between crowd and performer at a concert, at least in some ways, works like a face-to-face interaction. The ambiguous expression 'going to see', so commonly used about our attendance at concerts of all types, bears this out, as do numerous fan accounts of what it means to them to make eye contact with the star.[7]

In traditional musical performances, where a smaller gathering comes face to face with the performers, it is commonplace to find audience displays and reactions being responded to by the performers, and ethnomusicology has begun to document this, albeit through the notion of 'ritual'.[8] However, it is harder to find analysis of performer–audience interactions in modern concert settings. Alex Ross (2005) provides an interesting history of applause in classical concerts, but says nothing about performers' immediate reactions to the applause.[9] In the sphere of popular music, Emma Webster's critical analysis of 'the ritual of the encore' looks for explanations of encore practice beyond the interactions between audience and performers, hence exposing the 'ritual' as rather empty (Webster, 2012). Mark Duffett's research on heckling at live concerts is closer to an interactionist account, arguing that heckling can alter the balance of power that is normally attributed by the audience to the star (Duffett, 2009). At a generalised level, Wendy Fonarow's contention that the bodily participation of the indie rock audience tells a story of 'African expression in a Protestant world' begs precisely the question of the relationship of traditional 'face to face' gatherings to the modern setting of live music (Fonarow, 2006: 175ff). Even in the popular sphere, I would argue, such settings inherit the social demarcations of the classical concert hall or theatre, with a marked and hierarchical separation of performers and audience, whether through the stage/auditorium division, or through the use of technology and amplification. My proposal is that close analysis of interaction between audience and performers can help disentangle how much is scripted ritual and how much is the open-ended interaction that we know from ordinary conversation.

In this spirit, I turn my attention to the 'ordinary' rituals of live concerts, in particular the exchange of applause and thanks that one could say form the underlying, expected, ritual economy of all live music-making. In line with Goffman (1967 [1955]), the musician/performer cannot give themselves 'face' – only the audience can do that for them. Hence, at its most basic, the necessity of live performance, and hence, the mutual face-building as performers congratulate and applaud audiences in various ways. More mundanely, our expeditions to 'see' the persons of our favoured recording artists need to confirm for us that they can project a 'line' through their personal interactions that is consistent with what we already know about them from their recordings and other sources.

It seems clear that it is not just by empirical chance that most live concerts do indeed end by according the performers face and with the performers acknowledging the warmth of the audience's own action in applauding by thanking them equally warmly. I argue that such mutual face-building at public concerts is a kind of 'preferred response' (Pomerantz, 1984), similar to that pointed to in relation to political speeches by Steven Clayman (1993). Clayman shows empirically that a crowd will engage in positive applause almost simultaneously and without delay (Atkinson, 1984), whereas if booing happens, there is pausing, as members of the audience wait to see whether others are joining in this 'disaffiliative response' (Clayman, 1993: 116–117). Since in the sequential organisation of ordinary conversation, 'preferred responses' follow instantly, while dispreferred ones are preceded by a pause (ibid: 125; Pomerantz, 1984), Clayman therefore argues that applause is the preferred response in the interaction between political speaker and audience (Clayman, 1993: 126).

However, the meaning of applause in live concerts is complex and subtle, since, especially in popular music events, if applause sounds 'routine', as in 'we're giving the accepted, or preferred response, so as not to embarrass ourselves or the performer', this can be interpreted as indicating a mediocre or disappointing performance. Applause must sound genuine and have an element of spontaneity and emotion in it, if it is to avoid being construed in this 'routine' or 'polite' way. The social situation 'prefers' applause to booing, perhaps, but that applause has also to be more than *just* applause.

Take the case of the 'support act'. Often this may be a newcomer to the scene, a band that is only slowly paying its dues on the hierarchy of venues and audiences. The audience has almost always come *not* to hear them but the main act, and may be annoyed that their ticket money and time is being wasted on an inferior act. They may time their arrival to miss the support act, walk in half way through, or stand around at the bar talking through it. These are observations that I made on the occasion when I recorded the talk that we have looked at in Extract Versions 1 and 2. One way or another, the support act often has to work harder for audience attention.

To look at all this further, I present Extract Version 3, which is transcribed more in accordance with the conventions of Conversation Analysis, though it differs in transcribing on a scale of time intervals (seconds and fractions of seconds), which accord with those on the screenshots of the Audacity sound files that follow the transcript. Together these two visualisations of an audio event help to show how music, applause and talk from the stage are sequenced as interactions. For instance, the transcript shows the last chord as being played at 3.47, held for around four seconds, and the first whoop and clap of applause occurring over this still reverberating chord, at 3.51. This first applause is visible on the Audacity file at 3.50.5, from where it can be seen that the applause grows in intensity and volume up till 3.58.5, after which there is a remarkable drop on the sound file, representing the audience silence *before* the singer goes into his personal story at 3.59.[10]

Enlarging the view on the Audacity file, we can look at these eight seconds of clapping, and find that while the clapping has lulled before the singer's first 'Thanks a million folks', which occurs between 3.52.6 and 3.53.5, it rises visibly after that for about two seconds (3.53.5–3.55.5). Listening to the recording, or viewing its transcription, then, this rise in the applause – a few more cheers and whoops, others join in, and so on – can be understood as a *response* to the singer's talk and its form of thanks. It is therefore a form of 'sequential organisation' of action.

### Extract version 3: Performer's talk as an interaction with audience applause, response cries and heckling

*Table 5.1* Key to extract version 3

---

Numbers in left-hand column = minutes, seconds, and percentages of a second, on the original recording
Roman typeface = singer's musical actions and spoken words
*Italic typeface* = audience applause, 'response cries', spoken interventions
**Bold**/***bold*** = spoken words of either singer or audience
Word underlined = emphasis
[[action]] = my description of what is going on or heard
[.] = short pause in speech
[.25] = pause of 0.25 of a second
⌈word
⌊*word* = simultaneous utterances

---

3:47  final chord of song [[holds about four seconds]]

3:48

3:49

3:50  *a whoop and first claps audible*

3:51  *a bit more clapping*

3:52  *a couple of faint cheers, ay sound, [[could be yay, yay]]*

3:52.5–3:53.5  Thanks a million folks

3:54  *clapping [[thicker than previous]]*

3:55  *clapping*

3:55.3 – 3:55.75  How's it goin'

3:56  *clapping*

3:57  *clapping*

3:58  *whoo! [[whoop audible]]*

3:59  [[clapping stops abruptly]] So this is our first time playing

4:00  the Olympia, and I'

4:01  've kind of been waitin for thi

4:02  s: [0:5] since I was a

4:03  bout thirteen,

4:04  *whoo* so it's a really big de

4:05  al [.] 4.05.4 *[[male voice]] Come on down and watch y'self*

4:06  *piss then* 4:06.25 *[[female voice]] whoo* n back

4:06.8  ⌐stage
    └*whoo*

4:07  [0.5] 4:07.5  ⌐I'm finding there's end
    └*eee*

4:08  less scenes from Spinal Ta

4:09  p [.] [[guitar note]]

4:10  [.] I got lost a

4:11  bout six times

4:12  [2:5]

4:13  [[guitar note reverbing in background, being tuned, octave below previous one]]

4:14

4:15  This is called Name of Song

4:16  [[little bit of guitar audible then only audience voices, long pause on stage]]

4:18

4:20

4:22–23 [[bang as of something dropping, then sounds of tapping on wood]]

4:24

4.25

4.26

4.27

4.28

4:28.5  **zzh** [[lead singer sniffs loudly near mic]]
4.29
4.30
4.31
4:32       [[warm up chords from stage, top two guitar strings still out of tune]]
4.33
4.34
4:35–4.36  [[strums up a chord in second inversion]]
4:37       [[Intro to song on same chord]]

**Screen shots of Audacity sound file of extract version 3**

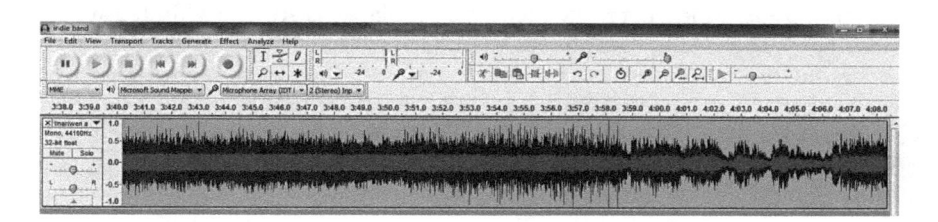

*Figure 5.1*  3.40–4.08 (screenshot of Audacity file)

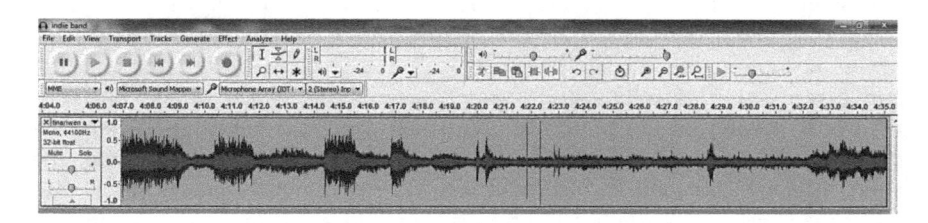

*Figure 5.2*  4.07–4.35 (screenshot of Audacity file)

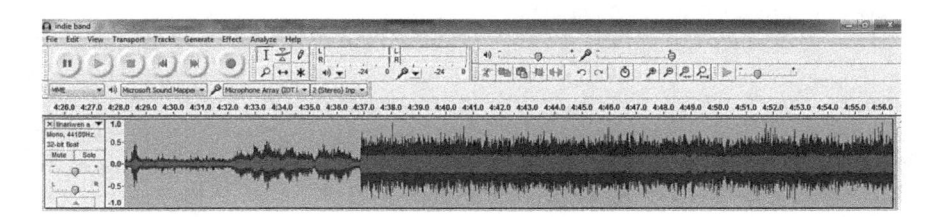

*Figure 5.3*  4.28–4.56 (screenshot of Audacity file)

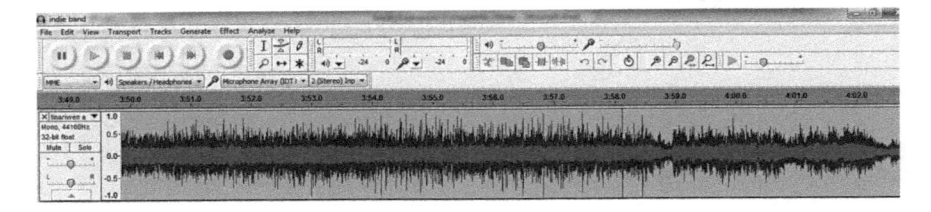

*Figure 5.4* Enlargement of 3.50–4.02 (screenshot of Audacity file)

The ubiquitous thanks given by musicians to their audiences can be understood in three principal ways: as thanking the audience for their applause, as thanking them for being attentive and listening to the song just played, or as thanking them for coming, for being there at all. In the 'local' situation under study here, the (acoustic) applause is still very limited when the singer voices his (amplified) thanks, and the thanks are heard as addressed to the audience as a whole, not to the small segment of the audience that has started applauding. He voices his thanks immediately after the last chord has finished reverberating. We therefore understand the thanks, as primarily, in the immediate situation, 'thank you for listening'. There may be overtones of 'thank you for coming', and this may be picked up in the rise in applause that follows, as those who are his friends or fans increase their clapping and emit a few whoops in the immediate aftermath of the thanks.

However, the primary functional understanding of thanking us for paying attention, which is found again and again in live recordings, allows us to make an interesting parallel between Harvey Sacks' (1995) analysis of conversational story-telling and the performance of songs. Effectively, the telling of a story in conversation means allowing the teller an 'extended turn'. Similarly with the singing of a song or performing of a number in concert: the performers are allowed an 'extended turn' during which the audience is relatively silent and attentive and does not in general applaud, unless 'turn-relevant places' are indicated by the musicians as inviting applause in the course of the number, as occurs in genres which feature instrumental solos and virtuosity.

The dropping of the applause at 3.59 immediately before the singer starts to tell his personal story is another instance of Sacks' insight and analytical finding, that in order to tell a story in conversation one must first secure the permission and attention of one's audience, or partner in conversation (Sacks, 1995). That this is indeed going on is indicated by the rapid and almost complete drop in audience applause at 3.59, so that the singer launches into his 'fresh talk' with an attentive audience. Without a video recording it is not possible to see precisely how this was done, but we can assume that there is some body language as the singer indicates that he is about to speak, to which the audience is responding – perhaps to do with approaching his mouth to the microphone. Again, this drop in the applause, effectively giving the singer permission for an extended turn over the microphone, indicates that there are some fundamental similarities between concert interaction and conversation, as regards the rules of turn-taking and sequential organisation (Sacks et al., 1974).

In this very brief and preliminary exploration of these routine, taken-for-granted aspects of a concert, I hope to have shown that there are features of interaction, turn-taking and sequential organisation involved between the actions of performer on stage and the audience attending him. In terms of the theory of 'face-work', this local examination of how applause is started and stopped in relation to understandings of what the other party to the interaction is doing, bears out the idea that the performer takes applause as evidence that he is being attributed face and a consistent line, while the audience takes the performer's thanks as evidence that he appreciates their immediate attentiveness and applause, and more broadly, their being there.

Finally, a read of the transcript will show that a heckle was revealed (at 4.05.4) by slowing down the recording, which I had not perceived myself as a member of the audience, and had not transcribed on my first draft transcription (version 1 above). In a sense, then, this heckle was not part of my own audience experience that night, nor even of listening back to my recording at normal speed. Nevertheless, it was obviously heard by those around the heckler in the audience, and my intuition is that the singer heard it (whether or not he picked up the actual words), because of the way he immediately continued talking into the microphone so as to be heard to actively 'ignore' and dismiss the heckle.[11]

The heckle occurs at a 'turn-relevant transition point' where the singer pauses after the words 'big deal'. However, we all know that performers on stage (musicians, actors, and similarly to teachers) are allowed to pause without the audience filling in the gap as if it were a real conversation. The heckler is breaking the rules of turn-taking for the stage-performance 'situation' by applying the rules of 'ordinary conversation' here. In terms of the theory of liveness we have derived from Goffman, then, the heckler is actively exploding the 'illusion of fresh talk'. The singer's talk is not really conversation, as it purports to be, with its greetings, colloquial expressions of thanks, local references to the venue, and the appeal to the teenage self of those in the audience. The heckler's conversational 'reply' to the singer's 'big deal' statement shows up the unreality of the 'conversation' precisely by treating it as if it were one.

What is more, the content of the heckle, 'Come on down and watch y'self piss then', itself refers to coming down from the 'frontstage' position for which the singer has just said that he has been waiting for half a lifetime, and so invites a levelling of the social roles with which the singer is claiming difficulty. It also on the surface denigrates the performance, though it is impossible to know if the heckler was, like myself, unhappy about the out-of-tune performance, or a friend of the singer engaging in homosocial 'banter'.

The two audible whoops from a female voice, or voices, soon after this heckle, seem intended to encourage the singer not to be deflected by the heckle and hence represent audible competition for the singer's attention. Earlier, I stated my hunch that competition for the attention of the performers on stage was part of the interactional sense that we must make of 'Beatlemania', where the fans have so often been seen as irrational because of their making the music inaudible with their shouting.[12] Here we see a less dramatic form of competition for interaction with the singer on stage, with the female voice playing a 'supportive' role to the male voice's ostensibly 'adversarial' role (Herring, 1996; Whelan, 2008: 157ff).

And here I arrive at my conclusion as regards the two broadly contrasting theories and approaches with which I have been working in this chapter, namely Goffman's interaction ritual, and Conversation Analysis. Goffman's approach can in turn be subdivided into two. His account of the 'infusion of liveness' into a script in live performance clearly helps to illuminate the way in which the singer here engages in between-song fresh talk. But such an account presents a peculiarly one-sided view of the interaction, replicating and reinforcing the hierarchy of rights to speak given by the stage and amplification. As such, Goffman's 'infusion of liveness' approach fails to capture the precariousness of successful live performance, the fact that all the keyings and topical references in the world may still produce a flat lecture or a mediocre musical performance, because all depends on how the audience understands and responds to these infusions. The second approach that I have borrowed from Goffman, namely his theory of face-work, is more encompassing of the whole interaction, because it does not assume that face is always maintained. Face has to be worked at and is clearly something that is commonly 'lost'. In the example discussed here of the heckle inserted in mock response to the singer's claim of the 'big deal', the performer is indeed in danger of losing face. The naming of the performance as the 'pissing' of the singer/guitarist is potentially deflating of the face he has garnered so far with the audience. His hurrying on with his talk after this interruption is evidence that he heard the heckle (or was aware that someone was heckling), while the amplified talk from the stage limits any possibility of local laughter at the heckle catching on and producing a wider 'disaffilia-tive response' from the audience (Clayman, 1993). Though the singer appeared to have a small group of friends and fans near the front of the audience that night, it is not a foregone conclusion that this group of applauders in a large venue is going to save and maintain his face. The topic of his talk revolves around his nervousness, invoking the thirteen-year-old looking ahead to this 'big deal', and the slightly incoherent grammar of the phrases after the heckle may, indeed, be an enactment of nerves.

While face-work provides a pertinent framing for analysis, this is hardly surprising, given that Goffman's metaphors are taken from drama and other large-scale encounters, and used to explain small-scale encounters. I here reverse this and use the small-scale metaphors to explain the large ones. However, my second, broad approach, which moves into the area of Conversation Analysis and looks at how applause/thanks and other interactions are organised sequentially with reference to the actions of the other, renders a general theory such as 'face-work' somewhat redundant. In this particular, local situation, we understand 'nervousness' in the singer's talk when we hear how the heckler responded on the night, and how the female whoops responded in turn to the heckle, inviting the singer to ignore the heckler and encouraging him to continue. In other words, nervousness is jointly constructed in the interaction and understanding of the parties to this exchange. The different responses of men and women in the audience at this point, as well as the fact that my recorder picked them up but my own ears did not, reminds us that there is not one 'audience experience', but potentially many. Again, this cannot be encompassed by a theory that looks only at one side of the exchange, namely at the infusion of liveness into the script by the performer.

I conclude that both, or all three, approaches are useful, not least because there is potentially more than one 'situation' at play. I did manage to have a brief conversation on the phone with the performer after making this recording of his concert-talk, and he admitted to me that he used much the same 'between-song talk' at different gigs. Goffman's point about the need to sustain the illusion of fresh-talk was therefore relevant to his own preparation of his act, which is of course rehearsed and, effectively, scripted. However, how it works out on the night always contains more than an element of unpredictability. This is the difference an audience makes. There is interaction, indeed multiple interactions, going on. And, as we have seen, it is always possible that people will interrupt stage talk with heckling and effectively deflate it by turning it into ordinary conversation. However, underlying both the infusion of liveness into a script, and the need to work at and maintain face on the part of both performer and audience, are the interactional necessities around applause and thanks, and the undoubted situational preference for the maintenance of face.

## Notes

1 Mark Duffett's chapter in this volume also comments on issues of 'ritual' and collective emotion, in relation to the development of fandom during and following live events.
2 Anonymous review at 'Belfast Music' website, 7/02/12, www.belfastmusic.org/article/4748/music-review-van-morrison (accessed 29 June 2015).
3 My own view from watching online recordings of Dylan and Van Morrison live is that both do provide brief moments of changed footing, particularly through body-language, such as bowing, or just standing facing the audience.

Nevertheless, I defer to multiple audience perceptions that they do not. One of Simon Hoggart's last columns in the *Guardian* before his death records his slight disappointment after going to his first Dylan concert at the age of 67, and he writes that Dylan did not talk to the audience at all: 'a simple "Hello, Kensington Gore" would have been nice' (Hoggart, 2013).

4  Prior to the first song, the whole performance had been introduced by an 'over-the-top' circus-type 'roll up' call to the audience, made by an MC character.

5  Parenthetically to this formal analysis, it can hardly escape our notice that this emotional statement of 'my life so far, leading up to this night' is put in beautifully Goffmanesque 'frontstage/backstage' terms (Goffman, 1959).

6  As Hillegonda Rietveld's chapter in this volume illustrates, issues of authenticity and liveness might even emerge in relation to DJs, even though their performance relies on pre-recorded music.

7  As an example, a fan review of a Girls Aloud concert at the O2 in London on 21 May 2008, writes, 'OMG last night was the most amazing night I have ever had. The entrance was fantastic too! I was so close as well and when the girls sang Whole Lotta History, Nicola looked down at me and waved!' (collected from Girls Aloud *MySpace* blog).

8  Qureshi, for instance, provides a detailed transcription and analysis of audience responses at two Sufi Qawwali performances in Delhi, in the form of bodily swaying, ecstatic arousal, and pinning money onto the musician, and how the performers elicit and respond musically to this audience appreciation (1995 [1976]: 143ff.). See also Veblen's rich description of performer–audience interaction during the recording of Stephen Folan's dancing to Séamus Ennis's playing of 'The Copperplate Reel' as recorded by Alan Lomax in Connemara in 1951 (Veblen, 2014: 152ff.)

9  Cottrell (2004) supplies a few experiential examples of how classical performers orchestrate applause, and particularly (what follows is my gloss) the respectful pause-before-applause that is indicative of superlative performance or a transcendental musical experience in classical contexts.

10  My references to 'applause' here must be qualified by my subjective position in the auditorium. As already signalled, I was hearing, first, the applause of a group of enthusiastic fans who were nearer to the stage than I was, and further to the left. This applause was joined, a few seconds later, by people clapping close to where I was standing. Rather than seeing this subjectivity as an atomisation of the concert into discrete and incommensurable experiences, I focus rather on the interaction of affiliation, as different sections of the crowd join in the applause started by the fans. Despite different subject positionings within this 'wave' of affiliation, its growth would be discernible from different points in the crowd and, importantly, from the subject position of the performer on stage.

11  Again, my understanding here follows Conversation Analysis in attributing 'members' understandings' to the analyst also.

12  See Osborne, this volume, for a discussion of the televisual construction of the 'mania' of female Beatles fans in the 1960s. And see Bradby (2011) for an analysis of the conversational structure of interaction between performers and audiences at a Beatles concert, where I show that the fans do *not* drown out the talk from the stage, but on the contrary, listen attentively, and demonstrate through applause their understanding of what is being said.

# 6 Refiguring Maltese heritage through musical performance

## Audience complicity and the role of venues in Etnika's stage shows

*Andrew Pace*

## Introduction

Maltese traditional music is a topic that has received little scholarly attention outside of a small but dedicated Maltese academic community. However, over the past fifteen years, their publications and involvement in organising public performances have raised considerable awareness of traditional music among the Maltese general public.[1] Their efforts came at a critical time as by the end of the twentieth century the rich variety of instruments and instrumental music that had once existed in Malta had significantly reduced, and most of the older musicians who knew how to craft and play them had passed on. Performances of instrumental music had been largely confined to heritage contexts such as carnival, the Mnarja festival[2] and folklore troupes. The only form of music that thrives today as part of a continuous folk tradition is *għana*, usually encountered in the *spirtu pront* form of sung debates between pairs of singers with guitar accompaniment. This tradition continues in bars, homes and garages in Malta and across the Maltese diaspora, and, despite fluctuations in popularity over the years, it remains in a healthy state today.

The aforementioned heritage context underpinned the development of public performances of Maltese traditional music during the 1990s–2000s revival with the emergence of national folk festivals in 1998 (Festival Nazzjonali tal-Għana) and 2008 (Għanafest), folklore troupes such as the Menhir Qala Folk Group (2003– ), and musical ensembles such as Etnika (1999–2008, 2014– ), the Ġukulari Ensemble (2002– ), and to an extent Nafra (2004– ).[3] This was not, however, a grassroots revival initiated by traditional musicians themselves, but one orchestrated largely by an academic community who recognised that traditional forms of music were being lost through neglect and a lack of local support. The ensemble on which I will focus is Etnika. Having disbanded a few years prior to beginning my research on them, and after the fervour of the revival period had somewhat dissipated, I am afforded a more reflective perspective on their achievements and local impact. Primarily drawing upon Pierre Nora's theory of 'sites of memory' (1989) and directing attention to the capacity of place as a highly affective stimulus for recalling and shaping memory (Casey, 2000; Tuan, 1990), I detail how Etnika's choice of performance venues and their methods of presentation within those spaces was as significant to their success as was their use of revived melodies and instruments in a modern, 'world music' context. I contend that although Etnika's performances appeared wholly presentational in nature (following Thomas Turino's (2008) definition), their success was greatly attributable to their audience's complicity in constructing and consuming a heritage product.

## Etnika, 1999–2008

The Maltese ensemble Etnika was formed in 1999 as a project to revive traditional Maltese instruments and their music through 'interesting compositions and arrangements which evaluate the heritage and present it within a modern and contemporary framework' (Zahra, interview with the author). Before Etnika, the Maltese general public primarily knew their traditional music as the vocal duelling of *għana spirtu pront*,[4] but Etnika sought to draw attention to far lesser known Maltese instrumental music. By the late 1990s there were very few musicians still alive who could either play or make traditional instruments such as the *żaqq* bagpipe, the *tanbur* drum, the *flejguta* flute, the *żummara* reed pipe, or the *żafżafa* friction drum, and the remaining instruments themselves were often found in a poor state or in need of rebuilding. This led the four core band members, composer Ruben Zahra, instrument maker Ġużi Gatt, researcher Steve Borg, and musicologist Andrew Alamango,[5] to work closely with the handful of living traditional performers and to search through paper, sound and television archives for source material.[6] The reconstructed instruments, melodies and rhythms were then placed into new musical textures that brought to the foreground the instruments that played this material as well as, often, the traditional musicians themselves. Prominently presenting the 'living heritage' (Alamango, 2000) of the physical instruments, their repertoire and their unique sonorities were an important component of Etnika's live performance aesthetic.

Thus, from the outset Etnika's intentions were threefold: they wished to reconstruct local instruments, revive the music associated with them and place the results in a context that spoke to a contemporary audience. A few days before their first performance in 2000, Alamango clearly stated the band's intentions and motivations in the English-language newspaper *The Sunday Times of Malta*, setting the tone of rhetoric they would continue to employ over the following years:

> The break in oral tradition of this instrumental folk music has led to a loss in musical heritage . . . The results of research and documenta-tion yield a forgotten heritage in music waiting to be rediscovered,

reinterpreted and revived on a contemporary platform ... The recognition of these melodies and instruments is a consolidation of our local identity, through the association with our roots, yet placed within a contemporary context. Only through such an 'upgrading' process will any art form or folk tradition survive and thrive as a cultural expression.

(Alamango, 2000)

Etnika's inaugural concert in August 2000 was to a packed audience at the University of Malta as part of the university's public concert series, 'Evenings on Campus'. A CD of their repertoire, Nafra, was launched simultaneously. Zahra's recontextualisation of traditional instruments and melodies into a jazz-tinged contemporary classical setting that comprised voice, piano, percussion and wind instrumentation was generally well received, although some reviewers called for a separate CD of traditional Maltese music without the modern interpretations (Owen, 2000). However, Etnika's aesthetic was not simply to revive the instruments or their music as museum artefacts, but to bring them back 'alive' so that the instruments could communicate with a contemporary audience (Zahra, interview with the author).

Soon after this first performance, Zahra departed Malta to continue his composition studies abroad. From this point on Alamango took the lead and began to develop Etnika in new directions, continuing to evolve the band over the next eight years while maintaining their original aesthetic. From 2001 Etnika 'mark two' became more outward-looking, taking inspiration from the wider Mediterranean and fusing Maltese elements with world music, flamenco, jazz and gypsy styles. This musical multiculturalism was mirrored in their increasingly elaborate stage shows that began to foreground Maltese flamenco dancer Francesca Grima and Serbian percussionist Andre Vujicic, two new additions to the core band. An increase in percussive elements, including rhythms, modalities and timbres alien to the Maltese tradition, marked Etnika as a self-styled Mediterranean world music band (Alamango, personal correspondence).[7] However, the Maltese elements were still visible and audible in their performances: the duo of *żaqq* and *tanbur* musicians, the *flejguta* and *żummara* melodies, Maltese lullabies and children's songs, and the spectacular collaboration of *għana* singers. These, along with Etnika's exclusive use of the Maltese language in their lyrics, were important markers of Malteseness to local and international audiences. However, in an ironic twist, the audience's relative familiarity with the jazz and world music elements of Etnika's music contrasted with their general ignorance of local Maltese styles, thereby rendering the Maltese components as the more alien. As a result, a Maltese musical identity was seemingly formed through the recognition of difference, rather than of familiarity.[8]

In the introduction to his volume on Mediterranean music, Goffredo Plastino points to the reflective dialogue that exists between local and global musical realities that ultimately determine local developments:

> Local music cultures are revisited, redeveloped, relaunched via the acquisition of other repertories, whether global, Mediterranean or local. The dialogue is between that which is at hand and familiar and that which is perceived as distant (though sometimes not that far off) but similar, or in some way assimilable.
>
> (Plastino, 2003a: 28)

There are parallels to this in Etnika's determination to reconstitute Maltese traditional music into a modern context – in their case, fusing traditional Maltese elements into a pan-Mediterranean soundscape. In doing so they simultaneously achieved two goals: they translated and transformed traditional Maltese music to appeal to a wide audience (both local and international), and they also instantly upgraded it into a Mediterranean world music soundscape. What both of these points achieve is continuity; continuity with a Maltese past and continuity with a Mediterranean past. Mirroring a trend in Maltese society at the time, Etnika were seeking roots, but were looking at ways of incorporating these roots into a modern context. In the years preceding its EU accession in 2004, many local debates emerged about Malta's position within Europe. Nationalist fervour and a questioning of Maltese identity were undoubtedly catalysts in the traditional music revival of which Etnika was a figurehead, its members becoming a mouthpiece for the resurgence of interest in defining Maltese cultural identity and heritage, and in confirming musical and cultural links between Malta and its European neighbours. During their many performances outside of Malta, Etnika were positioned by the Maltese government and national cultural institutions as international ambassadors for Maltese culture, a designation that sometimes sat uncomfortably with the band.[9] Furthermore, Etnika's musical collaborators from the traditional Maltese music communities were lauded as national cultural icons.

The audiences for Etnika's annual showcase events in Malta (which averaged 700–900 a night) comprised largely urban Maltese 'captivated' by music which they felt represented Maltese heritage (Alamango, interview with the author). Contemporary reviews of these shows in the popular media were very positive, with performances being viewed as highlights of the Maltese cultural calendar. Etnika certainly championed Maltese culture, but their success required their audience to be complicit with their particular stylised rendering of music, history and culture. Alamango has stated that it had always been a Maltese audience that Etnika targeted, not a tourist market, and that tourists in fact made up a relatively small proportion of the audience for their annual stage shows (Alamango, interview with the author). Although Etnika's Maltese audience encompassed a wide age range, according to Alamango the audience comprised few from the traditional music communities whose music and instruments were being transformed by the band (Alamango, interview with the author). Etnika's musical appeal seemed to speak to those urban Maltese who yearned for a romanticised revival of music, identity and culture – indeed, the same milieu of people who orchestrated the revival itself – rather than those who were in fact already practising members of traditional music in Malta.[10]

## EtnikaFé: performances of reconstruction in spaces of decay

Etnika's choice of venues and their affective influence on the audience's role in constructing and reinforcing a particular conception of Maltese identity is my focus for the remainder of this chapter. Etnika's annual stage shows, known as EtnikaFé, were typically held in Malta each summer over three nights.[11] These shows consisted of increasingly elaborate musical and staging concepts, each year reinventing their sound and styling while continuing to incorporate 'authentic' local and international musicians. These stage shows were the primary means for an audience to engage with the band as, in their seven-year 'mark two' formation, they released only one CD album of material, *Żifna*, in 2003.[12] Experiencing Etnika was realised almost exclusively via physical attendance of their performances.

Table 6.1 outlines each of these annual showcase events.[13] Their locations are all situated in Valletta, Malta's capital city, except for the 2002 show in Mdina, the medieval capital. Although Etnika did benefit from government and commercial sponsorship and promotion, each location was ultimately chosen by the band.

All of these locations are highly symbolic places tied closely to the grand narrative of Malta's post-medieval and pre-independence history, effectively the history of its occupying powers: the largely Spanish, Italian, French and German Knights of Malta, 1530–1798, the brief French occupation, 1798–1800, and the British colonial period, 1800–1964. Many buildings from these eras remain standing and in use, and are aggressively defended by all sectors of the population when plans for destruction or modernisation are raised. Architecture, both ancient and modern, is a core facet of Maltese heritage that contributes significantly to the tourist industry economy. However, these sites play an important role in Malta's ambivalent cultural memory, many being places where an official, elite history intersects with a more localised, indigenous one. The ruins of the Opera House and the

*Table 6.1* List of Etnika's annual showcase events

| Year | Title | Location |
| --- | --- | --- |
| 2001 | EtnikaFé | Opera House ruins, Valletta |
| 2002 | EtnikaFé | Vilhena Palace, Mdina |
| 2003 | EtnikaFé Bumbum | Fort St. Elmo, Valletta |
| 2004 | The Giant Dream | St. John's Ditch, Valletta |
| 2005 | Żażu Klabb: Kabaré Malti | Barrakka Lift, Valletta |
| 2007 | EtnikaFé | Opera House ruins, Valletta |

Barrakka Lift in particular are highly charged sites with long, contentious histories. Alamango has declared that the band at the time were not consciously aware of these controversies when choosing to utilise such spaces; rather, they were locations they found interesting, suitable, and available for use (Alamango, personal correspondence). It is, however, hard to believe that Etnika were not familiar with the wider debates surrounding these spaces. For example, a 2001 newspaper interview with the band suggests that the Opera House ruins were specifically chosen as the first performance location in an attempt to contribute to the revival of Valletta. In the interview Alamango added that the lives of street musicians in the city had, in the distant past, been made difficult by British laws banning such public performances (Galea Debono, 2001). Perhaps it was fitting, then, for the first EtnikaFé concert to be staged in the Opera House that had been a British addition to the cityscape.

This most controversial of social spaces, the ruins of the Opera House situated just inside Valletta's city gate, Etnika used first in 2001 and again in 2007. Designed by the British and opened in 1866, it was heavily damaged in a German bombing raid in 1942. After the war the site was largely levelled for safety, leaving the ruins to be used as a car park. Ever since the 1950s there have been numerous plans to rebuild the Opera House, but heated arguments and conflicting interests have prevented the site's development for over sixty years. However, as of 2013 the venue has once again become a performance space, this time an open air theatre designed by Italian architect Renzo Piano. The redevelopment of the site has been a hugely contentious issue for the Maltese owing to its historic association in social memory with the glories of the Vallettan past and of European urbanity. As it existed pre-war, recalled in the memories of elderly locals today, its architectural beauty and supposedly perfect acoustics – better than anywhere else in Europe, according to some (Mitchell, 2002: 54) – was a source, and focus, of local and national pride. Jon Mitchell, in his ethnography of Valletta's community in the 1990s, found in the minds of locals a parallel between the eminence of the past and the decline of the present mirrored in the ruins of the building:

> This image of quality contributes to the sense of pride and nostalgia for a lost glory of both monumental and cultural quality. Its disappearance is associated with a decline in the quality of not only Valletta's cultural life, but also that of Malta as a whole. The Opera House was never properly replaced, and its ruins stand as a monument to this decline.
>
> (ibid.)

Renzo Piano and the Maltese government commented along similar lines after the 2008 redevelopment plans were unveiled: 'After more than 60 years of controversy, the ruins of the demolished opera have undeniably reached the status of monument, irrevocable witness of history and the dignity of collective memory' (Stagno-Navarra, 2009). The absence of an opera house has been as much a part of the Vallettan cityscape and social-scape as did the building as it stood pre-war. The ruins have increasingly taken on a romanticised history and become a monument both to Maltese history and to the heated debates of this contested space. Etnika's decision to use the ruins of the Opera House as a backdrop for their first and last showcase performances was thus quite an acute one, as their performances attempted to revive and rebuild glories of the past by revisiting music that once had great social significance, but which had since fallen into disuse, decay and ruin. Enacting this musical transformation within a contested, ruinous space was a powerful statement.

The eighteenth-century courtyard of Vilhena Palace, Mdina, that served as the location for Etnika's 2002 performance was another space of past glory, but one which had been revitalised just weeks earlier in a 100,000 Euro makeover.[14] The Bumbum show of 2003 was at Fort St. Elmo, a military complex built in Valletta by the Knights of Malta in the sixteenth century, used in the present day as a police training academy and war museum. Parts of it still remain in disrepair. The Giant's Dream, the 2004 folk-opera stylising Etnika's rediscovery of the *żaqq* bagpipe, was performed in St John's Ditch at the base of the fortifications surrounding the city, fifty feet below the walkway to the entrance to Valletta. This derelict space was a car park and often utilised by fly-tippers. In 2005 Żażu Klabb: Kabaré Malti was located on the Lascaris Wharf waterfront area of Valletta, in the space next to the old Barrakka Lift. The lift, built in 1905 to transport people and goods directly from the waterfront into the city 190 feet above, was closed in 1973, dismantled in 1983 and rebuilt in 2012.[15] The lift itself has been a popular symbol in local memory, having been memorialised in popular songs and literature since its closure and removal.

Alamango has stated that the 2005 Żażu Klabb show (Figures 6.1 and 6.2) actively took advantage of the nostalgia the band and their audience felt toward its performance space (Alamango, interview with the author). Etnika attempted to capture the vibrancy of Valletta's port life of a century ago through music, theatre and cabaret, their performance replete with brass bands, dancing sailors, elaborate costumes, port soundscapes and set pieces in an on-stage café. The event began with the performers – some twenty or more – slowly parading noisily down the historic, long, zig-zag stairway on the outer wall of the city that served as the backdrop to the show, before making their way through the audience and up onto the stage. By opening their performance in the streets high above the audience and processing down the staircase toward the stage, Etnika appeared to be symbolically transferring the considerable nostalgia felt for the city above to the disused space below, bearing the spirit of the city toward the re-imagined old wharves and thereby legitimating the latter space as an equal stakeholder in Valletta's rich social history. Etnika and their audience were engaging with

*Figure 6.1* Etnika's Żażu Klabb show, 2005. (Copyright Darrin Zammit Lupi, courtesy Andrew Alamango.)

*Figure 6.2* Toni Camilleri *it-Tommi* with Andrew Alamango, 2005. (Copyright Darrin Zammit Lupi, courtesy Andrew Alamango.)

what Svetlana Boym would term 'restorative nostalgia', reconstituting a lost past by 'reconstructing emblems and rituals of home' (Boym, 2001: 49) through the band's reconstruction of music and instruments and via the performance itself restoring functionality to a once neglected space. Yet, this was simultaneously a 'reflective nostalgia' that thrived in the very act of longing, dwelling on the ambivalences of 'longing and belonging' (ibid.) demonstrated by the historical fiction of Etnika's show, of its reinvented music and its hyperreal theatrical visuals. Before the performance had even begun, in the minds of the audience Etnika had fixed the stage as the space where complex convergences of nostalgia were to be made tangible.

## Performance locations as *lieux de mémoire*

To further analyse the significance behind such theatrical use of space in the minds of the audience, particularly as found in Etnika's 2005 show, it is useful to draw upon the work of Pierre Nora. Nora proposes sites of memory (*lieux de mémoire*) existing where real environments of memory (*milieux de mémoire*) no longer exist (Nora, 1989). Environments of memory are manifested in those activities rooted in a functional community; a living experience of memory. Sites of memory exist where direct relationships to the continuity of those memories have been broken. Such sites can be physical places such as buildings, monuments and archives, specific objects, or concepts such as public commemorations and rituals. These sites of memory are artificial historical (re)creations based on the recognition of a lack of 'real' environments of memory due to a rupture in the continuity of memory. Nora attributes this rupture to the rapid 'acceleration of history' of the modern world through the industrialisation of European society, the breakdown in influence of traditional institutions of power, and the loss of peasant culture and their environments of memory, effectively eliciting 'an accelerated precipitation of all things into an ever more swiftly retreating past' (Nora, 2002: 4; see also Nora, 1989). This, Nora further argues, has 'shattered the unity of historical time, that fine, straightforward linearity which traditionally bound the present and the future to the past' (Nora, 2002: 4). Since the linearity of past-present-future has been ruptured, and discontinuity with the past indicates an uncertainty towards the future, Nora posits the present as having been given autonomy over composing both the past and the future (ibid.: 5). Thus Nora suggests that sites of memory, *lieux de mémoire*, encourage artificial and deliberately fabricated remembrances of the past in order to make sense of the present,

> where consciousness of a break with the past is bound up with the sense that memory has been torn – but torn in such a way as to pose the problem of the embodiment of memory in certain sites where a sense of historical continuity persists.
>
> (Nora, 1989: 7)

Many of Etnika's performance environments are sites of elite histories which retain historical continuity, specifically the Opera House, Vilhena Palace and Fort St. Elmo.[16] These locations reverberate with rich historical narratives that tie them to the history of occupying powers, a history that has become important in defining wider Maltese heritage and culture.[17] However, these can be viewed as *lieux de mémoire* in a dichotomous way: they are sites of a celebrated elite Maltese history, but they are also sites from which non-elite, subaltern Maltese histories have been excluded. Malta's indigenous 'peasant' history, for want of a better term, is little documented and is not a part of the official narratives that constitute these spaces and their elite historical continuities. However, in placing the music of this social class into such environments from which they were once excluded, Etnika simultaneously promoted indigenous Maltese culture into the popular consciousness by grafting it onto already visible spaces, and made a political statement that suggested that this music and its performers are just as much a part of Malta's historical narrative – as human sites of memory themselves – as are the locations.

This ties in neatly with Nora's assertion of the increasing democratisation of history and the rise of collective memory, a phenomenon in which the 'minority memories' of individuals within marginalised groups ('for whom rehabilitating their past is part and parcel of reaffirming their identity') are foreground, thereby acquiring for memory all the 'privileges and prestige of a popular protest movement' against the authority of those who write 'History' (Nora, 2002: 5). Bearing in mind Malta's contemporary concerns with nationalism, the EU, identity and heritage, Anthony Cohen's evaluation of the significance of the methods with which to symbolise the past is also valuable to consider here: 'The manner in which the past is invoked is strongly indicative of the kinds of circumstances which makes such a 'past reference' salient. It is a selective construction of the past which resonates with contemporary influences' (Cohen, 1985: 99). Etnika's actions fit with Nora and Cohen's theories precisely due to the collaboration of a sympathetic audience. It is the audience who 'make' Etnika's performances, as it is the audience who are ultimately (re)constructing memories of their past in order to make sense of their present and future. Etnika provide the conditions and space within which various historical discontinuities can be focused and negotiated, relying on the complicity of the audience to confirm a collective 'memory' of what traditional Maltese music is, even if that memory is artificially created in the moment by Etnika and consumed by the audience in a presentational manner.

Alamango has commented that some fans did not in fact understand the transformative nature of Etnika's revival project, often mistaking modern elements for traditional ones (Alamango, interview with the author). He felt that this revealed a deep-seated yearning among the audience to identify with their past, to feel emotion toward their own local music, for something they could dance to (ibid.). For the audience it did not seem to matter so much which elements were traditional and which were modern or even foreign; what mattered was that there *was* a Maltese element with which they could connect. After the 2003 show one audience member commented:

> Proud to be Maltese – that is the feeling I experienced during the EtnikaFé Bum Bum show of July 31, in the magical surroundings of Fort St Elmo. . . . Etnika is something that Malta should be proud of. Not only is the group made up of excellent musicians, all still very young, but they also manage to integrate our dying traditions into something exciting, vibrant and attractive both for locals and tourists. [. . .] I wish to thank and congratulate Etnika for the sensational evening and the emotions they managed to provoke in the crowd.
>
> (Cassar, 2003)

Such a statement depicts Etnika as presenting or reflecting back to their Maltese audience existing sentiments towards their past and their present. Etnika reinforced this instantaneous memory creation and consumption by blending their musical rediscoveries with rediscoveries of place. The Opera House as a functioning opera house would not have been as powerful a statement as an opera house in ruins, a place that symbolised a lost heritage and neglect, elements that are mirrored in Maltese sentiments towards their own neglected instrumental music. Perhaps their music, like the building, was not lost but simply left to decay over time either through indifference or disagreement over the nature of its restoration. The Barrakka Lift, St John's Ditch, Fort St Elmo: these are all spaces that suggest neglect, loss, decay, of glorious times gone by, storing great potency in social memory as places that 'once were'. These *lieux de mémoire* were simultaneously physically decaying and fading from modern memory as no longer functional, useful environments. A Maltese audience was eager to fill these spaces with something new, but which also referenced tradition in order to maintain a legitimate historical continuity of some form. Extrapolating from Nora, Etnika and their audience were attempting to slow the acceleration of these places from vestigial memories into an unreachable, monumental history, perhaps in an attempt to restore or recreate them once more as relevant, living *milieux de mémoire*.

## Reconstructing memory through performance

These points resonate with Yi-Fu Tuan's study of 'topophilia', of our 'affective ties with the material environment' (Tuan, 1990: 93), in that it is often in a crystallising moment through sensory stimuli when feelings towards a space can suddenly be realised, thus coupling sentiment with place. Such latent emotional responses are revealed through the use of space, although they are not necessarily directly triggered by it: 'environment may not be the direct cause of topophilia but environment provides the sensory stimuli' (Tuan, 1990: 113). The importance of place in the evocation of emotion can be tied to Edward Casey's phenomenological approach to space and place through memory and remembering:[18]

> It is the stabilizing persistence of place as a container of experiences that contributes so powerfully to its intrinsic memorability. An alert and alive memory connects spontaneously with place finding in it features that favor and parallel its own activities. We might even say that memory is naturally place-oriented or at least place supported.
>
> (Casey 2000: 186)

Place is a highly affective stimulus for recalling and shaping memory, and is particularly powerful in Etnika's case where many of the performance spaces have long-standing, complex relationships with local Maltese. In line with Christopher Small's theory of musicking (1998), the audience is as much a part of the performance as the musicians on the stage or, as I have illustrated, the performance location itself.[19] Although Etnika's performances were presentational and not participatory in the terms of Turino's classification (2008: 23–65), it was nevertheless the audience's recognition of the band's manipulation of space and memorability during musical performance that provided those crystallising moments of recognition that contributed to Etnika's enormous local success.

Indeed, this tangible release of emotion during their performances was noted and described by Etnika as 'collective catharsis' both for the band and their audience (Vujicic in Spiteri, 2003), placing Etnika very much on the same field as their audience. By recognising their audience's emotional investment in their performance, Etnika were seemingly conscious of a deep-seated identity conflict between pride and shame that the Maltese 'grapple to come to terms with' (Spiteri, 2003). Paul Sant Cassia traces this anxiety over Maltese identity to at least the seventeenth century, suggesting that the lack of historical interest in and documentation of indigenous Maltese music has resulted in its limited variety today, in turn exacerbating the present-day perception of a heritage lost through neglect (Sant Cassia, 2000: 286–288). Vujicic discerns that the recreation and restoration of a Maltese identity is evidenced in the live, two-way feedback between the band and their audience: 'The emotion at a concert is palpable . . . because most people recognise that the music is giving voice to their identity' (Vujicic in Spiteri, 2003). Etnika seemed to be aware that they were serving their audience by providing a cathartic space in which they could both negotiate these concerns through immersive performances that drew together a series of local discontinuities of music, place and history.

## Conclusion

The decaying venues in which Etnika presented their performances were contested urban spaces towards which they and their audience harboured pre-existing sentiments of nostalgia. In these controversial *lieux de mémoire*, memories secreted within the walls and cracks of ruinous buildings awaited people re-entering them to temporarily dislodge and reactivate these memories and enliven their spaces once more. Yet these were reconstructed memories of the same nature as Etnika's reconstructed melodies: these historic spaces and traditional musics were not rebuilt as they once were, but rather reassembled as the band and their audience desired them to be in the present, as vibrant statements of a contemporary Maltese and Mediterranean identity that recognised the value of the past to the present. The success of Etnika's performances required the active complicity of their audience to recognise and engage with these sentiments of reinvention on an individual level within the collective environment that was constructed and controlled by the band, tapping into an emotional undercurrent of issues surrounding nationalism, nostalgia, and the parallels between monumental and cultural neglect. By placing musical traditions linked with the lower classes in spaces that often conjured associations of elite histories and colonial administration, Etnika encouraged their audience to refigure notions of Maltese heritage.

These questions of identity were prominent in the popular consciousness at a time when Malta was considering its political and cultural position in Europe, and so perhaps it is little wonder that questions of Malteseness might be negotiated in spaces associated with foreignness. Etnika's use of such conspicuous venues reflected a mutual frustration that they and their audience felt over the neglect of their past: the neglect of physical spaces once administrative powers had withdrawn from using them, and the historical neglect of indigenous Maltese culture. By utilising socially charged spaces within their performative mise-en-scène, Etnika revived and reconstructed the histories of these spaces through their transformation of traditional Maltese music. It was a symbiotic relationship: Etnika borrowed the nostalgia felt towards these contested physical spaces and grafted it onto their music by association, thereby legitimating their musical reinventions and the values for which they stood. A complicit, active audience was a critical component in this adroit rendering of music, space, heritage, nostalgia and collective memory.

## Postscript

In 2014 Etnika reformed and began working on new material. A promotional video released in September 2014 shows a private performance filmed in the remodelled Opera House in Valletta.[20] The legacy of these spaces continues.

## Notes

1 Popular print publications by such contributors are: Alamango, 2010; Borg Cardona, 2002, 2007, 2014; Mifsud Chircop, 2004; Pullicino and Camilleri, 1998; Ragonesi, 1999; Zahra 2006. A number of additional articles by some of these (and other) scholars have also appeared in journals and local newspapers.

2 Mnarja is the national Maltese festival of SS Peter and Paul, celebrated annually on the 28th and 29th June in the woodland area of Buskett, during which traditional forms of music-making have occurred for centuries.

3 Nafra is an ensemble that Ruben Zahra established to continue the contemporary art music settings of Maltese melodies and instruments that he began with Etnika in 1999 to 2000. Nafra is not a 'heritage product' and their music is not usually performed in such a context, but Zahra's use of traditional instruments such as the *żaqq* bagpipe is still highly symbolic of Maltese heritage.

4 Even though *għana* has been broadcast on the national Rediffusion radio network since the 1930s, on Maltese television stations Xandir Malta (later PBS Malta) and Super One since the 1980s (largely through the efforts of Charles Coleiro), and at Ġorġ Mifsud Chircop's annual Festival Nazzjonali tal-Għana (National Folk Music Festival) (1998–2007), it was not until Ruben Zahra's annual Għanafest music festival (2008– ) that *għana* was embraced by a broader local and international audience. Even into the 1990s *għana* was still a stigmatised activity with which the Maltese middle classes rarely associated themselves.

5 The core Etnika ensemble were often supplemented by a number of additional musicians for their performances – for example, their first concert in 2000 involved thirteen musicians.

6 See Borg (2000) for more on Etnika's research methodology.

7 For further studies of this particular form of Mediterranean world music, see Pace (2011) and Plastino (2003b).

8 See Pace (2011) for a more in-depth study of this issue.

9 For a depiction of Etnika's status as cultural ambassadors and their support from government officials, see Zammit (2004).

10 Some of these urban individuals have been referred to as '*Melitensia* people'. *Melitensia* designates artefacts that relate to Maltese history and culture – typically books, manuscripts, ornaments, paintings, and furniture. Collecting and/or engaging with these materials suggests a financial as well as an intimate, personal investment in Maltese history and culture. Paul Sant Cassia's article (1999) on the consumption of Maltese history and the local perception of private collections of *Melitensia* is particularly interesting in this light.

11 Etnika played regularly as a reduced ensemble at other times of the year in Malta and around Europe and the Mediterranean, but these were smaller concerts not always reflective of their showcase events.

12 This CD sold in the region of 2500 to 3000 copies. In addition to the CD album, two DVDs were produced: the 2003 *Bumbum* concert with a documentary detailing the Etnika project, and a live DVD of the 2005 *Żażu Klabb* show. Unfortunately these DVDs were not easy to acquire at the time or in the present.

13 In 2006 Etnika took a break from their summer shows, instead performing a smaller event during the February carnival in Gozo. This was a carnivalesque musical play and not an official EtnikaFé event.

14 See Galea Debono (2002).

15 For a succinct pictorial history of the Barrakka Lift, visit https://vassallohistory. wordpress.com/the-barrakka-lift/ (accessed 3 November 2014).

16 The Barrakka Lift area on Lascaris Wharf stands alone as a performance venue that has firm links to the Maltese lower classes rather than of elite histories.

However, like St John's Ditch it is also a space outside of the walled city proper, yet in abutting the bastions it nevertheless absorbs some of its elite associations.

17 Jeremy Boissevain notes that the Maltese often construe architectural heritage as belonging to 'them, not us' – 'the Knights, the British, *il-gvern* (the government), even the tourists' (Boissevain, 2000: 11).

18 I am grateful to Mikaela Minga for suggesting this relationship (see Minga, 2013: 51).

19 See also Bruce Johnson's discussion of gesture and corporeality in this volume, as ways of understanding the crucial contribution of audiences in shaping performance.

20 www.youtube.com/watch?v=jFgzX6NFJqw (accessed 28 October 2014).

# Part 3
# Technological mediations
The virtual and the material

# 7 Authenticity and liveness in digital DJ performance

*Hillegonda C. Rietveld*

## Introduction

Within the context of electronic dance music events, the DJ (Disc Jockey) can be understood as a musician who manipulates music recordings, synchronizing and blending these into a soundtrack – a musical journey for an audience of dancers, participants, listeners, and bystanders (Brewster and Broughton, 2006; Fikentscher, 1997; 2000; 2003; 2013; Lawrence, 2003). [1] Fikentscher defines 'the club deejay [as] a pioneering force transforming the relationship between music as defined by performance and music conceptualized as authoritative text' (2003: 290). Furthermore, Katz (2012: 33) describes performative hip-hop DJs as *turntablists*, 'who treat their turntables more like musical instruments than playback devices'. In this way, the DJ operates as a type of curator as well as performing producer (Fikentscher, 2001; Rietveld, 2011; 2013a).

Butler (2014) differentiates between traditional DJs, who assemble a soundtrack from being distinctly vinyl-based (and therefore analogue), and the laptop performer who, in effect, brings a miniaturized version of the digital studio to the stage. However, as DJ practices have turned digital not only in terms of CDs and digital mixers but, more radically, by engaging with the fluid affordance of production software, the distinctions between music production, remixing, DJ-ing and music performance are more difficult to maintain. Within the practices of the *digital DJ*, a musicianship is emerging that invites a reassessment of the relationship between audience and performer. It will thereby be argued that an authentic experience of live performance can be generated not only through the spectacle of performance but, importantly, through the embodied engagement by and between all participants of an electronic dance music event.

## DJ technology

The digital DJ uses a range of hardware and software that each implies different performative, creative and sonic affordances or potentials. Many digital DJ technologies tend to emulate vinyl-playing turntables, DJ tools that historically may be regarded a residual media in the realm of hip-hop, disco and electronic dance music (Rietveld, 2007). Such *skeuomorphism* (in this case the digital emulation of vinyl playing turntables) is to be expected as it enables the continuation of established creative and performative practices. Yet, this does not fully take advantage of the current potential of digital music technology. To understand some of the debates and concerns regarding the digital DJ, the discussion will first provide a brief overview of the development from the vinyl turntable and the CD player to digital mixers and software-based DJ technologies.

DJ-specific vinyl record playing turntable is an adaptation of the record player that was first made commercially available on the market by Technics in 1972. This enabled musical solutions, not only because the disk could be moved forward and backward to line up a recording (slip-cueing) ready to segue into the audio mix with another recording, but also because it enabled turntablist techniques, such as back-spinning and scratching. As Katz explains, turntablists are not only performative DJs but create 'wholly new music through their complex manipulation of recorded sound' (2012: 4). Specific to the turntable-vinyl combination is the tactile relationship to an analogue recording where, unlike digital files, the visible and touchable grooves in the vinyl record represent the sound that they reproduce. During the 1970s, DJs started to edit and remix recordings to suit the requirements of their crowds, bringing these to the dance floor in a variety of formats including test pressings, dub plates and audiotape, heralding the emergence of the DJ-producer (Fikentscher, 2001). This practice could be extended during performances with special effects units and with additional live musicians. During the 1980s, underground electro and house music DJs also explored the additional use of the electronic drum machine to enhance the beat.

Contrasting to analogue recordings, digital files differ in that they are based on numerical conversion rather than on analogue representation. Although untouchable in an immediate sense, these numerical values can be tweaked and altered, almost like putty, offering extensive creative possibilities. Digital manipulation of recordings was possible through the use of samplers since the mid-1980s; initially, these could only record very brief sound bites to be entered into an audio recording. The sampler seems to have partly been developed from digital delay effects, a sound engineering device that could enable audio insertions within the process of multi-track recording and mixing (Porcello, 1991). Sampling was also a component in the development of digital synthesizing technology. As soon as the cost and physical size of such equipment made samplers affordable and transportable, they were adopted by DJs to reshape recordings during their performance as well as in their (remix) production work. The low sample bit rate and short sample time resulted in a crude but effective aesthetic during the 1980s electronic dance music genres, including electro and house music in New York and Chicago respectively. Thus, the roles of DJs and producers started to merge within an interactive performance framework, adapting their music in response to the dancefloor. To understand audience expectations within this context, the discussion will next address residual techniques in music performance that have developed within the creative practices of DJ-producers.

## Residual techniques

Over the years, sampling technology has developed into sophisticated components of the DJ's kit, not only for special effects and as part of mixing consoles, but also as a function in the CD player, the CDJ, specifically made for performative DJs. First explored by Pioneer during the early 1990s, by the early twenty-first century CDJs had become commercially popular, enjoying an uptake in the era of digital music files and rewritable CDs (Gwertzman, 2004). Hereby the latter took on the function of the earlier dub plates and audiotape. A CDJ can be understood as a digital turntable with a jog wheel on top of the unit, which can be handled similarly to a turntable through what seems direct touch, yet as a digital interface such interaction is digitally mediated. This Human Interface Device (HID) enables the manipulation of music recordings on CD in a turntablist manner; this however is only a simulation, since the CD keeps spinning. The advantage of CDJs is first that it is easier for the DJ to travel with a wide selection of music files, aiding their popularity with international DJs who, although creative with the audio spectrum equalizing controls (EQs) on the mixer, use the turntable in a relatively traditional manner.

CDJs offer more than a simulated turntable experience though, in terms of digital sound processing, such as the creation of digital sound samples on the spot, enabling stuttering, looping and rhythmic repetition. This can be further enhanced by connecting the CDJ directly via digital cable to a DJ mixer with digital processing components, enabling extensive creative potential in the manipulation of recordings. An example of how, using this type of DJ set-up, distinct recordings can be morphed into a cohesive musical journey, can be found in a DJ performance by Japanese DJ-producer Goth-Trad (Takeaki Maruyama) for Boiler Room in January 2015, at the regular Tokyo-based club night Back to Chill.[2] Although he is also known to perform his own music with a range of electronic instruments and audio processors, on this occasion he DJs with a Pioneer set-up of two CDJs and a digital 4-channel DJM 900NXS mixing console, with a built-in 24bit/96kHz sound card. A range of recordings are played, including examples of Goth-Trad's latest productions, that share a nihilistic edge dominated by bone-shaking deep bass and industrial sound, sprinkled with screams and hints of Japanese percussive instruments (bells, wood blocks). The tracks shift within a calm, self-contained *Adagio* tempo, between 87 and 66 BPM (beats per minute), with the odd track at around 144 BPM, which, due to the context, can be perceived as halved, at 72 BPM.

If human voices are present, they are processed almost out of existence. The overall genre could be identified as dubstep; yet, unpicking the material in the mix, a range of genres can be distinguished that, each on their own, belong to sound cultures as contrasting as dub reggae and sludge metal. The result is a trademark soundscape: a deeply textured dark and digitally warped labyrinthine sonic space, kept cohesive through constant attention to the EQ settings, framed within a head nodding meditative pace.

Software-based DJ tools, mostly used in conjunction with laptops, tend to emulate conventional DJ set-ups, either visually on the computer screen or haptically, via a vinyl-based interface played on a turntable. An example of the former is Virtual DJ, which visualizes several spinning disks onscreen that simulate a traditional CD or Vinyl DJ set up, while the software is also able to process sound and to VJ (Visual Jockey) an additional video show. The vinyl-based digital interface, by contrast, is used with vinyl emulation software or Digital Vinyl System (DVS). DVS enables playback of digitally stored files to be physically handled by vinyl records that have a digital time-code engraved on them. In effect, the conventional DJ turntable is transformed into a HID between the DJ and the computer-stored digital audio files. Popular examples of DVS are Final Scratch, first sold in 2001, Serato's Scratch Live, and, currently, Traktor Scratch Pro.[3] The DVS has proven to be a popular interface within music scenes that place high (sub)cultural capital (Thornton, 1995) on vinyl records and dub plates, while the turntable itself is a performative and haptic device that many DJs are used to. However, digital audio files can also be manipulated using CDJs, or handled with a MIDI-controller and other HIDs, making it possible for a mix of formats to be used during a DJ session.

For example, during a session by New York DJ duo Masters at Work (MAW: 'Little Louis' Vega and Kenny 'Dope' Gonzales) for Boiler Room in London, August 2014, each have three CDJ players at their disposal, which seem to be there more for the visual effect than necessity.[4] Although each takes turns to spin in tracks with the CD players, Kenny Dope keeps an eye on audio files displayed on a computer screen as they play a series of known dance club classics, many of which are their own remixes and productions. This particular set remains blended at a fairly consistent *Allegro* pace, of around 128 BPM (resembling an average heartbeat during exercise) until a distinct break in the set, which moves blending classic dance club to a selection of slower (around 112 BPM) funk and disco recordings.

Louis Vega manipulates the EQs using a rotary mixer and handheld headphone, a residual set of tools from the analogue days of the New York underground dance scene. Such EQ manipulation, or 'filtering', can be used to emphasize specific elements in the recording through the volume amplification or reduction of a specific frequency range, such as a particular vocal, instrument or bassline, which can invite the crowd to participate by singing 'missing' vocal lines, for example. Other DJs from this American underground dance scene, for example Ron Trent, Joe Claussell or Theo

Parrish, can be more extreme in their filter techniques, obliterating recordings and skillfully disorienting dancers, bringing back music coherence just in time to maintain attention, fine-tuning their dialogue with the crowd through peaks and troughs of textures. Although this filter technique developed within an analogue setting, it set the scene for the creative manipulation of recordings within digital DJ settings.

So far, the discussion addressed how the DJ enters into a producer's role on stage. Vice versa, however, producers enter the arena of DJ-ing, using equipment that resembles tools from the music studio, adding a different dimension to performative potential of the digital DJ. In turn, the resulting variations of hybridity in DJ performance practices can challenge audience expectations.

## Performing DJ-producer

Moving away from residual turntable set-ups, a different entry point into digital DJ-ing is made via the Digital Audio Workstation (DAW), software that allows prepared sections of recorded music and sounds to be uploaded and placed into specific arrangements during music composition and during performance. A good example is Ableton Live, which like other digital DJ tools was also first commercially available in 2001. Initiated by Gehrhard Behles and Robert Henke (Butler, 2014) and developed in Berlin, it is similar to other studio-based digital composition software, or Virtual Studio Technology (VST). It is compatible with other creative digital media art tools, such as Max/MSP, and hosts a wide array of VST plug-ins, from samplers and synthesizers to special effects. Yet, it simultaneously makes improvisation possible during performance, in terms of programming, arrangement and sound processing. As a performance tool, the on-screen interface is compacted for single screen use with pop-up windows in two views: arrangement view and session view, with the latter particularly used for performance purposes. Although compatible with a range of MIDI controllers, Ableton Live works most effectively with multi-functional and intuitive performative human interface hardware, such as the flat visual grid of multifunctional square LED buttons of AKAI 's APC40, Novation's Launchpad and Ableton's own hardware interface, Push.

The combination of interactive performative hardware and creative software takes the performance of the digital DJ into an engaging and creative, yet blurry, territory of studio-based pre-production and improvisation that occurs live on stage. The studio-based producer can make a relatively easy transition into the realm of the performative DJ, while the DJ reaches further into the realm of music production. For example, although he performs with a range formats and audio media, for studio production Goth-Trad uses Ableton Live with a MIDI keyboard (Asanuma, 2014). A mix of analogue and digital music technologies is also possible, such as DJ-Producer Paula Temple's set-up, which she explains on Ableton's website:

> Macbook Pro with Ableton Live 9, Push (for live and remix elements), Allen and Heath Xone K2 (for digital DJing), Technics 1210 turntables (for vinyl non-digital Djing). This way, I can test out my new music ideas and perform something exclusive for every gig, play other artists' promos that have not been released on vinyl, and still play some of my older records I love.
>
> (Temple, 2013)

A more detailed example can be found in the observation of a performance by DJ-producer Henrik Schwarz for the Boiler Room, in Berlin, on 6 December 2012.[5] The camera faces Schwarz, so it is not possible to see the screen of his Apple laptop; however, sources elsewhere confirm that Schwarz uses Ableton Live,[6] stating at a Red Bull Event that 'I don't prepare anything for a set. Everything I have ever done live is still in Ableton, I save it all' (*Amsterdam Editor*, 2013).

Tracks and musical fragments are mixed in a deep blend of contemporary techno with an archive of funk and jazz recordings. Samples of soul and highlife vocals appear in between large sections of instrumental music, enabling Schwarz to 'speak' to his audience. The recordings are mixed with his own music programming, in particular the drums that are evidenced by the consistent use of recurring drum pads, especially the emulation of Roland TR-909 or Roland TR-808 snare and high-hat sounds, at a consistent pace of around 123 BPM. Repetition of specific musical segments enhance to the overall groove. The musical components are treated with special effects that add not only virtual space through resonance and echo, but also alter the EQ and waveforms of the sound. Rather than relying solely on software plug-ins for specific sound processing that would be invisible to the audience during performance, these special effects are also produced through hardware effects and, rather than utilizing a mere keyboard and mouse interface with the laptop, they are manipulated and controlled through hardware interfaces, such as a small DJ mixing console and a Novation Launchpad (characterized by multifunctional square push buttons) enabling a visibly kinetic performance.

Schwarz makes an explicit visible connection to his music, not only through the use of HIDs, but also through his expressive facial and body language, bouncing to the groove as he engages with the screen, selecting recordings and adjusting effects. Like many other DJs and digital performers, he does not make eye contact with his audience during the gig, neither to the dancers behind and around him nor to the camera, but his facial expressions seem synchronized with his creative decision-making and manipulation of digital audio devices. Importantly, he embodies the musical output as heard by the audience, including miming most of the lyrics, some of which include his own vocal recordings, such as from his recording with Japanese artist Kuniyuki, 'Once Again' (2010, Mule Music) that can be heard at the end of his set.

Although Schwarz stresses the importance of improvisation, he does keep tight control over the way in which his set sounds:

> I always start my set with more or less the same intro. In 15 min. I do a little soundcheck, listen to the sound of the room and adjust my sounds accordingly. I rather not work with presets. It might be easier, but it doesn't sound as good.
>
> (Amsterdam Editor, 2013)

Schwarz' facial expressions seem to indicate an intense decision-making process during the performance, yet some viewers still suspect that Schwarz delivers an entirely pre-programmed set, and therefore accuse this as being an 'inauthentic' performance, a type of miming.[7] Such debate regarding technologized performance, in which risk and unpredictability of interaction and live presence are valued, requires further unpicking.

## Audience expectations

As has also been argued by Cascone (2002) in the context of laptop-based music performance, the audience experience of authenticity in digital music performance is central to understanding the success of the performance of a digital DJ. A music recording is *acousmatic*, as sound is separated from its visible originating source. The absence of the performer in recordings can lead to a fetishization of a material object or subject that seems to stand in its place. Vinyl has long played this role for the collector, now replaced by ubiquitous designer MP3 players. Furthermore, the performing DJ can take on the role of embodying absence during DJ shows, like a god magically breathing life into otherwise 'dead' recordings (Middleton, 2006). From the perspective of a live performance, electronic music is even more abstract, since it is created, recorded and produced in studio settings in a way that cannot be reproduced in unmediated form. In the case of the DJ-producer, the two roles of recording artist and performing DJ may well coincide. This enhanced role can be exploited in a lucrative business of the spectacular DJ, who not only sonically dominates an electronic dance music event but is effectively staged and marketed in a visually dominant manner (Rietveld, 2013b).

Auslander (2008) argues that in the age of studio-produced music, live music performance is often expected to mimic the recorded event. He borrows Jean Baudrillard's concept of 'mediatization' to make sense of performance that is technologically reproduced and circulated, showing that the virtual and the real have become indistinguishable, and argues that, 'the historical relationship between liveness and mediatization must be seen as a relation of dependence and imbrication rather than opposition' (Auslander, 2008: 56).[8] He further states that, 'audience perception (is) likely to be most influenced by the dominant media of the time . . . interactions among media, and between live and mediatized forms, needs to be understood in relation to a concept of dominant media' (Auslander, 2011: 194). Following this argument in the context of the DJ, the recorded and distributed DJ mix, remix or music production would create a specific audience expectation. As DJs are marketed and mediated within a range of visual media, from magazines to videos, a shift has taken place in the role of the DJ from interactive music selector to stage performer. The shift towards the visual stage performance was particularly noticeable for marketable higher-paid DJ-producers at music festivals and dance clubs during the early 1990s.

A well-known example is French DJ-producer David Guetta, who was filmed raising his arms to share the celebratory atmosphere of Belgium's *Tomorrowland* Festival in 2012, with seemingly all volume sliders down on his mixer, while the music continued to play (Abbott, 2012; Attias, 2013). Critics wondered if Guetta actually DJ-ed at all. Given that Guetta entered the DJ profession as music producer, such detail may not be too high on his list of priorities, especially when playing to a crowd of thousands with synchronized fireworks, where advance planning is all-important. In such circumstances, perhaps the notion of a digital music performer rather than of a digital DJ may be more appropriate. However, Guetta is marketed as a DJ, with the specific audience expectations that this roles entails, which includes not only Auslander's notion of mediatized 'liveness', but also the idea of interactive presence, as part of a participatory dialogue.

## Participation

In contrast to Auslander's argument regarding the 'mediatization' and thereby 'hyperreality' of contemporary music performance, Steve Dixon (2007) argues that 'live presence' in (digital) performance invites communal interaction, activating the audience and thereby bringing liveness into a performance.[9] Interaction between the digital DJ and the audience, then, may be crucial in producing a sense of authentic performance. In his discussion of attitudes towards analogue and digital DJ styles, Attias (2013) notes the importance of 'risk' in how audiences judge a DJ-set, in particular when synchronizing, through beat-matching, two or more recordings in the mix. However, digital DJs benefit from beat-matching functions such as the sync (synchronization) button that minimizes the possibility of making mistakes during a layering segue between recordings. This means that the technical turntable skill to align the tempo of recordings, which gained an almost obsessive popularity during the 1990s with techno and house music DJs and fans, is now less central to digital DJ performance. However, beat-matching is still regarded as a crucial skill for DJs who use turntables for playing analogue vinyl recordings. Instead, live remixing is emphasized, for example, through the re/combination of recording fragments and a percussive use of special effects. In addition, Fikentscher (2013) argues that the music program, meaning the selection of the 'right' record at a specific moment in the sequence of the DJ performance, has returned in importance in the era of digital DJ technologies. Hereby, a creative approach to the arrangement of available music elements actively contributes to a sense of live presence, comparable to jazz improvisation performances (see Berliner, 1997; Hytönen-Ng, 2013; Tsioulakis, 2013). In such cases of taking risk and in programming a DJ set, a live feedback loop between dancers and the DJ seems crucial to the audience experience of authenticity. Feedback between DJ and dancers can take on a range of sensory aspects from 'feeling the vibe', based on dance movement, audible responses, increase and decrease of heat. However, in a visually dominated culture, this interaction seems often interpreted visually, in terms of a marketable spectacle (Rietveld, 2013b).

Butler (2014) notes that many of his respondents seem to associate the laptop more with administrative activities such as checking email than with music performance. This can be illustrated further by a DJ-training blog, where in DJ Sean Gallagher (2012) comments that,

> The challenge . . . is that DJs are now even more boring to watch. Lots were fixated on the mixer and the decks to begin with. While this was boring itself its [sic] not as boring as watching someone click a mouse on their laptop . . . If you just stand there pressing the Sync key between loading tracks, that's not really a show.

Indeed, there is a visual disconnection between the minimal physical finger movements that the digital equipment requires and the dynamics of electronic dance music, or what sound artist Cascone calls a lack of 'gestural theatre' (quoted in Turner, 2001). According to Butler (2014: 66) the digital DJ compensates for such an audio-visual discrepancy through 'a coupling of aural and visual signals through the medium of movement', because 'nerve cells . . . fire not only when an individual performs a certain action but also when he or she observes that action performed by someone else'.[10] Hence, the addition of hardware interfaces and effects to a computerized live set-up, as is noted in the performance of Henrik Schwarz, not only helps the digital DJ to perform in a tactile and kinetic manner, but also to make their shows visually more engaging.

There is also a trend for DJs to 'tweak' effect and EQ controllers, to process sound from a wide range of sources. In all three examples discussed above, Goth-Trad, Masters at Work and Henrik Schwarz, this is an ongoing practice throughout the performance in order to produce a cohesive sound-scape, to deconstruct or emphasize aspects of a music production and to ensure a strong audio delivery. However, in the case of laptop and CDJ performances, these actions may seem the main evidence of live performance.

This has led to some critical ridicule, especially of well-paid DJs, as illustrated in videos such as 'What DJs Do These Days . . .'.[11] This clip shows DJs Sander van Doorn, Laidback Luke and Steve Aoki seemingly doing little else than raising their hands in the air, nodding their heads to the beat, playing air guitar and twisting the occasional audio controller, accompanied by satirical comment boxes to point out their 'knob turning' antics.

Although visually such actions do not seem to directly connect with the music, Butler (2014: 106) proposes that such ongoing audio adjustments perform a type of 'listener orientation', a 'dual consciousness' in which the DJ is both producing and consuming the music. The DJ is thereby a participant in the event within an active feedback loop with a 'performing audience' (ibid: 112), a point that resonates with Ferreira's (2008) argument regarding the collective experience of a DJ performance.

Ferreira (2008) argues that the embodiment of recorded music takes place not in the DJ but on the dance floor, as participants dance to the music and thereby bring it to life. In this model, although the DJ makes decisions about what to play and when, the dancers, as performance participants, make important contributions to this creative process by, in a sense, voting with their feet. Unlike a seated audience that may politely remain in their place, at a DJ-led dance event one can choose to engage and disengage. Therefore, the DJ and dancers are locked into a type of seduction game, a dialogue in which the reputation of the DJ depends on the interest of the dancers. In such circumstances, the musical skills of the DJ to interact and improvise with the crowd are crucial. Through the manipulations of a range of aspects including the music, the dance space and the imbibing of 'body technologies' (Rietveld, 1998), a core of participating dancers 'work' towards a peak experience within the event, where the different elements of a dance event fall into place (Pini, 2001: 176). This includes synchronicity with the performing DJ (St John, 2009). Such interaction can be based on sonic dominance, rather than on visual performance. For example, a study of DJ-led Jamaican sound-system events by Henriques (2011) shows an emphasis on the immersive auditory experience of dancing to recorded music, in which the musical vibe of the dance floor is emphasized. A DJ performance, whether digital or not, can therefore be audibly live in an improvised sense in response to the crowd, as part of a stimulating (rather than simulated) dialogue.

## Conclusion

In summary, on the one hand, risk and improvisation are heralded as measures of authentic DJ performance, creating a sense of live presence. On the other hand, authenticity may be based on the mediatization of the production work of the DJ, whereby the performance is compared by the audience with the pre-existing production of the performer. To achieve an 'authentic' sense of presence within the performance of a digital DJ, participation by all relevant actors seems key. This may be the result of the ability of the DJ to interact with the crowd, sometimes through the music alone, through sonic immersion, but also through a visual connection between the musical dynamics and the actions of the DJ and of other performers, in dialogue with the audience. In this way, the DJ can appear to be part of, and yet separate from the audience, while as participant, the audience is part of the musical performance by creating a live feedback loop in which improvisation of music arrangements can be an important component. Nevertheless, improvisation in music programming is not always practically possible as, during large and spectacular events, a set can be pre-produced due to complex logistics in order to achieve a sense of 'liveness'. Such issues are not new for DJs, whether analogue or digital. However, an increased invisibility of what digital DJs actually do during a performance exacerbates the debate regarding the authenticity of a live DJ set. In addition, the affordances of digital performance technologies have intensified a blurring between music production and music performance, as well as between pre-set composition and improvisation. In short, audience expectations are not only historically shaped, but are also formed by the mediated and technologized contexts of a DJ performance.

## Notes

1 Many thanks to Tobias van Veen (University of Montreal) for final advice on this chapter.
2 Video available here: http://boilerroom.tv/recording/goth-trad/ (accessed 24 February 2015).
3 Final Scratch was developed by DJ-producers Richie Hawtin and John Aquaviva, and after a series of corporate change-overs is now developed by Native Instruments as Traktor Scratch Pro (van Veen, 2001).
4 Video can be watched here: www.youtube.com/watch?v=tfRJhmC-G1Y (accessed 27 February 2015).
5 Video available online here: www.youtube.com/watch?v=hyVq–qZVEI (accessed 6 January 2015).
6 See www.musicradar.com/news/tech/henrik-schwarzs-favourite-music-software-602671 (accessed 27 February 2015) and www.ableton.com/en/packs/schwarz-onator/ (accessed 28 February 2015).
7 For a discussion of authenticity and 'maintaining face' by not replicating performances, see Barbara Bradby's chapter in this volume.
8 For a critique of Auslander's theses, see Bruce Johnson's chapter in this volume.
9 See also Tsioulakis in this volume for a discussion of the importance of live presence for the sociality of performance.
10 For a discussion of the cognitive significance of gesture in musical performance, see Bruce Johnson's chapter in the present volume.
11 Video available here: www.youtube.com/watch?v=Nh9C7nQHmII (accessed 7 January 2015).

# 8 That's me in the spotlight
## Audiences and musicians on screen

*Richard Osborne*

As a popular musician, how do you learn how to perform? One answer is that you watch television, film or video. Most contemporary pop and rock performers will have gained their first impressions of their trade by watching other performers on screen. They will have seen filmed performances before they played live and before they attended a gig. As an audience member, how do you learn how to perform? I believe the answer is the same: the screen is a primary location for discovering what you are expected to do. Most fans first witness other music audiences via mediated sources.

In this chapter I will address ways in which audiences have been represented on screen, exploring uses that have been made of their representations by other fans, by musicians and by media producers. I will examine four periods and four types of filmed audience. First, I will look at Elvis Presley's 1950s television appearances. During the rock 'n' roll era the filming of fans provided an act of *interpretation*. Cameras would zone in on audience reactions to help attach meaning to the music. Second, I will look at the more knowing use of media that was made by artists and audiences during the 'British invasion' years of the mid-1960s. In clips from this era, it can be seen that musicians have a conscious indebtedness to the filmed performances of other musicians, while fans are indebted to the filmed performances of other fans. Nevertheless, the actions of the two parties are not always aligned. As a consequence the audience can be viewed as causing *interference*. Third, I will look at the rock years of the late 1960s and 1970s, a period that witnessed contradictory tendencies towards audiences. On the one hand, the audience was spurned – rock was seen as music of individual artistic genius and claimed opposition to mass media and mass culture. On the other, it was embraced – rock was regarded as music of community. Mediation sat uneasily among these processes; there was *incompatibility* between the rock aesthetic and previous forms of audience representation. Fourth, I will look at the video era of the 1980s and beyond. Video recording brought with it various types of *interaction*. Promotional films drew on live performance, while live performance drew on promotional films. There was also dialogue between genres: pop videos drew upon rock aesthetics, while heavy rock videos drew upon traditions of pop audience presentation. Video technology has also fostered interaction between musicians and audiences: at bigger gigs live performance is filmed while it is happening and is broadcast to the audience on large video screens. Moreover, due to mobile phone technology, many fans now have their own cameras, meaning they too can shoot footage of gigs. These developments have provided new interfaces between artists and their fans.

A main concern of this chapter is representations of male musicians and female audiences. Musical genres have been codified in gender terms. While pop music has been regarded as having feminine qualities, rock music has been depicted as male (Frith and McRobbie, 1990). This binary has been credited to the music itself, through the perceived 'passivity' of pop as opposed to the thrust of 'cock rock' (ibid.: 375–6), as well as to the genre's audiences (pop appeals to a largely female audience while rock is often the preserve of males).[1] In this piece I will explore the role of filmed representations in creating and reinforcing this gendered divide.

## The age of interpretation

Television was the medium that did most to promote Elvis Presley during the early years of his career. Simon Frith has noted that it was 'key to the process in which Elvis Presley became a national American star' (2001: 42), and Peter Mills has written of the 'single mercurial moment' that transformed Presley's career (2010: 55). This moment came on 5 June 1956, when Elvis appeared on the *Milton Berle Show*, singing 'Hound Dog' on television for the first time. The performance featured a spontaneous slowed-down coda to the song, to which Elvis danced in a suggestive manner.

The American press responded with outrage. The *New York Journal-American* regarded the performance as 'a display of primitive physical movement difficult to describe in terms suitable to a family newspaper', while the *Daily News* argued that 'Popular music has reached its lowest depths in the "grunt and groin" antics of one Elvis Presley'. The Catholic newspaper *America* found itself caught in a feedback loop of representation, stating that 'If the agencies (TV and other) would stop handling such nauseating stuff, all the Presleys of our land would soon be swallowed up in the oblivion they deserve' (press reports quoted in Guralnick, 1995: 285–6).

While Elvis's 'Hound Dog' routine was more provocative than his previous TV performances, he had already appeared on seven other variety shows and on each occasion had danced freely. What really differentiated this performance was that it was the first to feature reaction shots of female fans. It was the receptive excitement on the young girls' faces – the fact that they were readily interpreting Elvis's advances – that helped to confirm the sexuality of his routine. David R. Shumway has noted the way this audience was filmed, honing in on 'particular faces whose response tells us of the excitement the performer is generating' (1992: 127). In the 'Hound Dog' clip we can see the conversation that is set up between Elvis and a young fan.

After the singer's first low crouch, the editors switch to a girl with pigtails, who is shown bouncing on her seat and clapping with glee. As he enters the coda, she is returned to, still voicing her approval.

Elsewhere, the show offers a prescriptive course in Elvis reactions. Elvis is featured in a skit with Milton Berle in which he complains about hordes of screaming girls tearing off his clothes. He says he would prefer a sedate woman, such as Hollywood actress Debra Paget. Berle informs Elvis that she is too sophisticated for him (she's the Waldorf, while he's Heartbreak Hotel). Paget is then brought on stage, and responds to the presence of Elvis by screaming, caressing him and kissing him full on the lips. In a second skit young actresses pose as Elvis fans, waiting for a personal appearance by the singer at a record shop. In the melee that surrounds his arrival, the girls mistakenly tear Berle's clothes off.

In the outrage that followed this show, the actions of the female fans – whether spontaneous or staged – were downplayed, as was Berle's own part in the affair. Instead, the blame was placed firmly on Elvis. The response was focused on him too. Elvis appeared in four more variety shows in 1956 and 1957, including the *Steve Allen Show*, 1 July 1956, in which he was humiliated by being made to sing 'Hound Dog' to a basset hound, and the *Ed Sullivan Show*, 6 January 1957, in which he was castrated by being filmed from the waist up only. These neutering strategies have been widely remarked upon. What has been less regularly discussed is that, in these shows, female fans are expunged. After the original 'Hound Dog' performance, Elvis's 1950s TV shows include no further sights of excited young girls. In the *Steve Allen Show* their sounds are excluded too; instead there is an older audience who feign amusement at Allen's lame conceit.

At the start of his programme, Allen states that he wants 'to do a show that the whole family can watch and enjoy'. He twice calls the singer a 'good sport'. Sullivan echoes these sentiments: in his final dialogue with Elvis he refers to him as 'real, decent fine boy', thus reassuring viewers that the performer is safe for consumption. This tendency for television to absorb and nullify musical danger has led to the medium being viewed negatively by commentators, artists and audiences alike. Frith has stated that music viewing that 'provided a bit of a laugh for grown ups' was the 'kind of packaging that rock fans and musicians came to despise' (2003: 283). Nevertheless, as John Hill has pointed out, music television has contradictory tendencies. On the one hand, television has attempted to make popular music 'more acceptable to a family audience', while on the other it has encouraged artists to 'exaggerate, rather than play down, the apparent grotesque of their performances' (1991: 104). Moreover, it is the fact that these performances take place within the context of family viewing that lends them their frisson. Greil Marcus has captured well the shock that persists in Elvis's original 'Hound Dog' performance: ' "My God," I said to myself as I watched him move a quarter-century after the fact. "They let that on television?" ' (1991: 241). However, it is not just artists whose actions are heightened by the presence of cameras and microphones: audiences are also in the habit of exaggerating their behaviour. It has been this out-of-control nature of female studio audiences as much as the pacifying nature of television producers that has led to the rock scorn for music TV.

## The age of interference

As with Elvis, television was the medium that escalated the Beatles' career. The onset of Beatlemania came with the group's performance on *Sunday Night at the London Palladium*, 16 October 1963. An estimated 15 million British viewers witnessed the screams and excitement of their female fans (Davies, 1985: 254). This 'mania' was also witnessed in the United States. Viewers were introduced to the Beatles via news reports from England:

> Jack Paar, who hosted a Friday evening variety program on NBC, marvelled to his TV audience over the unbelievable Beatlemania phenomenon he had observed overseas. Paar then showed a film clip of the Beatles performing 'She Loves You' as the English teens went hysterical.
>
> (Jackson, 1997: 227)

Ehrenreich et al. (1987: 12) have suggested that 'When the Beatles arrived in the United States the fans knew what to do. Television had spread the word from England'. The instruction was 'a license to riot'.

England had also spread the word about how to film these fans (Lynskey, 2013). The Beatles' first American TV performance took place on the *Ed Sullivan Show*, 9 February 1964. In this hour-long special they are given 12 minutes of screen time, during which they perform five songs. Out of this screen time, one and a quarter minutes is devoted to their fans. This is in sharp contrast to the rest of this edition of the variety show, during which the audience cannot be seen. As well as mirroring the film style of British Beatlemania, the American broadcasts had similar effects. Beatles fan Linda Ihle stated, 'Seeing them on the *Ed Sullivan Show*, with the girls screaming in the audience, it was contagious. That, coupled with news reports of girls screaming at the airport, spurred it on' (ibid.).

The filming of the Beatles' audience on the *Ed Sullivan Show* has aspects in common with Elvis's performance on the *Milton Berle Show* eight years earlier. Individual fans or pairs of fans are shown in medium close-up. One girl provides a direct echo of 'Hound Dog': she is shown bouncing up and down and clapping with glee. The performance by the Beatles' audience is more exaggerated, however. Some girls are panting for breath and are close to tears. Others are more brazen: one pokes her tongue out in a lewd manner, while the girl sat beside her puckers her lips.

There are further differences in the responses that the two acts generate. In Elvis's 1950s TV performances, the audiences' reactions are to Elvis's movements. Their screams and sighs are usually at their most intense when he dances to Scotty Moore's guitar solos. Elvis also just about maintains control of this response; he is always ready to tone it down by cracking a corny gag or a giving a sly look. As Shumway has pointed out, the shots of the audience during 'Hound Dog' are the 'equivalent to the shot/reverse shot editing that structures the gaze in narrative cinema' (1992: 127). These sequences establish Elvis as an eroticised object for his female fans. Shumway argues that this editing 'showed other fans how to respond appropriately' (ibid.).

But what was the Beatles' audience responding to? During the *Ed Sullivan Show* the band make little effort to generate or diffuse their fans' behaviour. They remain fairly static. The group had seen Elvis's filmed performances and had chosen not to mimic him. John Lennon stated, 'the Beatles deliberately didn't move like Elvis, that was our policy, because we found it stupid and bullshit' (Wenner, 1973: 34). Consequently, it is only at moments of exciting vocal interplay that the girls' screams appear to be called forth by the group's musical endeavours. As a consequence, the TV crew struggles to find a source for the girls' enthusiasm; they cut between images of fans and band in a somewhat random manner. In fact, the reaction shots during this show are self-generating: they occur because the performance is being filmed. Monitors in the studio provide a live relay of shot selection, hence the fans can see what is being captured. Their largest screams are not for the music, but for moments when band members are featured in close-up, not least because the band subtly respond to these shot selections. The other images that interest the audience are the shots of themselves. When girl fans appear on screen the mania intensifies.

It has been argued that the Beatles' female fans utilised the band's presence for their own needs.[2] Ehrenreich et al. have made a case that Beatlemania 'was the first and most dramatic uprising of *women's* sexual revolution' (1987: 11; emphasis in the original). However, without wishing to denigrate the power of the fans, it should not be forgotten who was controlling their representation. It was the TV producers who elected to devote so much screen time to the Beatles' audience. Nor should it be forgotten that this focus might prove problematic to the artists: why should their act be viewed as a prompt for outlandish behaviour, in contrast to the other performances on Ed Sullivan's programme? The filming does not have the performers' artistry as its main focus, instead its aim is to capture a phenomenon.

The film *A Hard Day's Night* (1964) fictionalises the Beatles' relationship with the broadcast process. The movie climaxes with a TV performance by the group that could almost be described as Brechtian in its execution: cameras are in shot and we witness the activities of the production crew in their control room. The Beatles are shown mocking this crew, but ultimately they concede to their demands. The film's exposure of the filming process is not quite honest, however. While the monitors in the control room show shots from the various cameras that are filming the band, they do not show any footage from the cameras that are trained on their fans' reactions. Moreover, although the film itself includes plenty of footage of the audience in the TV theatre, this crowd is filmed in a different manner to the rest of the TV production, as well as to the way that Beatles' followers would usually be framed. Some of the fan footage is shot documentary-style via hand-held cameras, and the filming takes place among the audience. This filming technique renders the footage of the fans more 'real' than the Beatles' mimed performance. While the Beatles appear to be carrying out pre-meditated roles, the fans' behaviour is for the most part unscripted and wild. By filming the audience differently and denying this footage any presence in the control room, the film suggests that crowd reaction shots were not a usual part of a Beatles' TV production. As with the press reaction to Elvis's Milton Berle performance, there is a denial that the filmed audience helped to establish the meaning of the act. In both instances we witness a fear of female agency. However, whereas in the Berle example the audience's reactions are ignored so that the sexuality of the routine can be regarded as Elvis's responsibility, in *A Hard Day's Night* they are ignored in order to give artistic credit to the Beatles. Here we can see the early stirrings of the rock aesthetic.

*A Hard Day's Night* does nevertheless illustrate the fact that fan behaviour had developed a momentum of its own. It could often be in excess of the musicians' routines. Fans could be more visually spectacular than the artists, and they could be more audibly spectacular as well. In their reminiscences, male 1960s pop performers regularly claim that they could not hear themselves play and that their fans could not hear them either (e.g. Richards with Fox, 2010: 137). The reminiscences of female fans, meanwhile, have indicated that it could be their own actions, and not the presence of the bands or their music, that was of most importance to them. Sheryll Garratt has recalled, 'Our real obsession was with ourselves; in the end, the actual men behind the posters had very little to do with it at all' (1990: 402).[3]

This attitude is captured in The Monkees' self-destructive film *Head*. Their song 'Circle Sky' is about Vietnam, and is accompanied in the film by news footage of the conflict. The clip also shows The Monkees performing the song live, but the way that this footage is intercut with news items suggests that their female fans aren't interested in global politics; instead all they care about is surging towards the band. It is difficult to know whose eyes we are meant to be looking through at the end of the performance, when the band are revealed to be mannequins and are destroyed by their audience. Is this how The Monkees see themselves? Or do they feel that they have glimpsed the way their fans see them? This footage is clear, however, in representing the female audience as interference. A TV viewer who is shown watching at home clicks between images of the fans, news items and adverts as if it was all just static on the screen.

## The age of incompatibility

As it splintered from pop, rock music developed and depicted a different relationship between artists and audiences. The rock aesthetic drew upon a number of earlier artistic movements. From romanticism it gained the idea of individual expressive genius, but also the idea of the rock audience as some form of folk community; from modernism it gained ideas of onward progress and a belief in art for its own sake. What these art movements and rock music had in common was an antipathy towards mass culture and mass media. In doing so, rock shared another quality with modernism: a negative attitude towards the 'feminine' audience.

In his essay 'Mass Culture as Woman', Andreas Huyssen argues that modernism was constructed around a binary. He suggests that modernist discourse 'consistently and obsessively genders mass culture and the masses as feminine, while high culture, whether traditional or modern, clearly remains the privileged realm of male activities' (1986: 47). The solitary artist is male; he is 'objective, ironic, and in control' (ibid.). He stands opposed to large crowds, which in their femininity represent 'nature out of control . . . the unconscious . . . sexuality . . . the loss of identity and stable ego boundaries' (ibid.: 52). Huyssen quotes the nineteenth-century writer Gustave Le Bon, who stated, 'Crowds are somewhat like the sphinx of ancient fable: it is necessary to arrive at a solution of the problems offered by their psychology or to resign ourselves to being devoured by them' (ibid.: 52–3). He also quotes Nietzsche:

> The danger for artists, for geniuses . . . is woman: adoring women confront them with corruption. Hardly any of them have character enough not to be corrupted – or 'redeemed' – when they find themselves treated like gods: soon they condescend to the level of the women.
>
> (ibid.: 51)

Nietzsche was opposed to any form of theatricality in music, because in theatre 'solitude is lacking . . . one becomes people, herd, female, pharisee, voting cattle, patron, idiot' (ibid.). It was this sort of theatricality that TV producers had forced upon the pop artists of the 1950s and 1960s: many filmed performances were characterised by reaction shots of female fans. As some of these musicians turned towards rock, they developed attitudes reminiscent of Nietzsche. Here, for example, is John Lennon, speaking in 1970:

> I resent being an artist . . . I resent performing for fucking idiots who don't know anything. They can't feel; I'm the one that's feeling, because I'm the one expressing . . . I'd sooner be in the audience, really, but I'm not capable of it.
>
> (Wenner, 1973: 105)

Rock performers felt the need to differentiate their screen presence from that of pop performers. One response was to place a distance between artists and audiences. In 1966 the Beatles stopped playing live and devoted more time to the recording studio. They also stopped performing on live TV, creating promotional films for their singles instead. The clips for songs such as 'Penny Lane' or 'Strawberry Fields Forever' have no screaming girls. In fact, they have no audience members at all. This manoeuvre was echoed in British music TV shows. *Ready Steady Go* has been cast as the archetypal British pop show of the early 1960s. As Frith has pointed out, this programme 'simulated a youth group on the screen itself'. He suggests that 'The young people dancing in the studio were the audience among whom we, as viewers, could place ourselves' (Frith, 1988: 209). In contrast, *The Old Grey Whistle Test* typified a 1970's rock approach. Here, the producers elected to film rock acts in a studio that was devoid of audience members. It says much about the complexities of mediation, in particular the disregard for the meaning-making presence of female fans, that the latter TV programme has been viewed as somehow more 'real' than the former. Mills, for example, has argued that it 'set out to show what "*authentic* musicians" looked like, positioned in the reality of a genuine musical performance' (2010: 63; emphasis in the original).

Rock musicians also distanced themselves from TV in general. Just as they eschewed singles in favour of LPs, bands such as Pink Floyd and Led Zeppelin turned away from televised performances, electing to produce feature films instead. The improved sound quality of film was one reason why they chose this medium, but film also gave them greater control over the way they could represent themselves and their audiences. Pink Floyd's *Live at Pompeii* (1972) echoes *The Old Grey Whistle Test*: the band plays live, but to an audience of none. In contrast Led Zeppelin's *The Song Remains the Same* (1976) does feature an audience. This audience is downplayed, however. In this 137-minute film it is given less screen time than the Beatles' fans on the *Ed Sullivan Show*.

Although film helped to support the rock idea of solitary artistic genius, it could also be used to promote the ethos of the rock community. The Beatles are again representative. Two of the group's late 1960's singles, 'All You Need is Love' and 'Hey Jude', feature communal sing-along refrains. As a consequence, they are provided with communal promotional films. In each case the conventional layout of live performance is abandoned. There is no division between audience and band; all share the same stage. Correspondingly, there is little shot/reverse filming. Instead, artists and fans are captured within the same frame. These promos also feature a higher proportion of male fans than earlier films of the Beatles.

Some of the festival films of this period also aim to celebrate the communal nature of the rock audience. *Woodstock* (1970), in particular, is keen to devote much of its time to documenting the hippie audience's worldview. The film faces several problems, however: how to depict rock musicians as artistic deities, while placing their audience on the same level as them; how to depict the huge scale of this audience without dismissing it as a mass; how to celebrate the organic nature of the festival when using mass media.

*Woodstock* addresses these problems by utilising its various 'splits'. Much of the film is edited using split-screen technique. On occasions this technique is used to show musicians in one segment of footage, while alongside them, in a separate screen, audience members are shown listening to their music. This has a different effect to the reaction shots of earlier music TV. Here the performer is not set up as an eroticised object, the focus of a gaze. In addition, the split screen technique disperses visual attention but channels auditory attention: it promotes the music as being the binding agent between musicians and audience. More commonly, *Woodstock* enacts a larger split. Most of the performances are shot without any footage of audience members: the focus is on the artistic expressivity of the musicians. In the film these musical performances are interspersed with non-musical segments. It is in the latter that the audience takes centre stage. They are shown on the fringes of the festival site, forging a rural community.

It was through its mediation – as song, soundtrack album, film and news story – that the Woodstock festival became famous, and yet these artefacts could promote an anti-mediation ethos, suggesting instead the importance of a rooted sense of place. Joni Mitchell, who only experienced the festival second-hand, wrote about Woodstock as an Eden-like paradise. Her song suggests, 'we've got to get ourselves back to the garden', to a pre-fall, pre-mediatised time.[4] As David Brackett has pointed out, Woodstock's triple-LP soundtrack and three-hour film 'required feats of endurance similar to those needed to survive the original event' (2005: 224). In absorbing these artefacts listeners and viewers could believe they were part of the Woodstock nation. This feeling is captured in J. R. Young's review of the album in *Rolling Stone*. It depicts a character called Bill, who failed to make it to the festival, but became so immersed in its mediation that he started to tell people he was there. Moreover, he condemns the 'media trip' that Woodstock has become (Young, 2005: 225). Bill is eventually exposed by someone who had been at the festival, who corrects him that 'the movie was pretty far out. But it wasn't like being there. Nothing was like being there' (ibid.: 226). Woodstock was nevertheless mediated through and through; watching the film it is apparent that the performers are spending some of their time playing directly to camera, as is the audience, even in some of its more unguarded moments.

Steven Connor has noted the disappointing 'authenticity' that became the established norm of 1970s' rock concerts. The 'real corporeal presence' of the performers was facilitated by distance, he has recalled squinting at 'tiny figures performing inconsequentially on a stage half a mile away' (1997: 174). The reverse of this is that, from the performers' perspective, the crowd became tiny figures, reacting inconsequently half a mile away. This represents a turnaround from the 1960s' pop audience, whose presence could visually and audibly compete with the musicians. The audience also had a different composition: while the TV audiences of the 1950s and 1960s had a female bias, the live rock crowd of the 1970s was predominantly male. According to Frith and McRobbie, 'It is boys who become interested in rock as music . . . It is boys who form the core of the rock audience . . . It is boys who experience rock as a collective culture' (1990: 376). They credit this gender bias, in part, to the fact that in the 1970s street life was dominated by boys: 'Teenage girls' lives are usually confined to the locality of their homes; they have less money than boys, less free time, less independence of parental control' (ibid.: 381). A case can be made, however, that this male audience was also the result of successful differentiation on rock's behalf, reflecting a modernist need to escape the feminised mass. Although the male-dominated festival audiences of the 1970s were far larger than the female audiences who populated TV studios and provincial theatres in the 1960s, they were not seen to have the same devouring, Sphinx-like nature.[5] Moreover, although massive, they had shed (some of) the ties with mass media. Huyssen notes that the nineteenth century castigation of the mass as female was connected to a fear of the mass political emancipation of women (1986: 50–51). This should make us think again, both about the suggestion made by Ehrenreich et al. that Beatlemania was an uprising of women's sexual revolution, as well as about the fact that rock musicians generally shunned the filmed presence of female audience members.

## The age of interaction

If television was the main mode of representation for 1960's pop, and film provided the equivalent function for 1970's rock, video has been at the forefront in both genres from the early 1980s onwards. In this closing section I shall examine how this technology has transformed relationships between musicians, audiences and moving images. In particular, I am interested in the extent to which video represents a turn away from the idea that artistry and mass media are incompatible, and has instead provided a mediated domain in which musicians and audiences can interact.[6]

The initial impact of video, particularly in America, was felt via MTV. This national music channel, broadcasting 24 hours a day, seven days a week, transformed notions of the music business, not least in academia. It was viewed as representing a rejection of the rock ethos of unmediated live performance in favour of a concentration on promotional video clips. Several commentators regarded this as a postmodernist turn (Fiske, 1986: 74–9; Kaplan, 1987). Video and MTV were conflating commerce and culture, they were introducing blank parody in place of earnestness, they were disrupting traditional narrative flows. Andrew Goodwin has suggested, on the contrary, that MTV helped to maintain popular music's 'Romantic aesthetic', particularly when it came to the performances of rock musicians in rock videos (1993: 178). While there is much in his argument, video helped to confuse as well as reinforce generic differences. It is notable that both pop and rock benefited from MTV rotation: the first phase of the channel (1981–3) was dominated by British New Pop, while the second phase (1983–5) saw a turn towards heavy rock (ibid.: 132–5).

As well as learning from each other, these two genres reversed earlier taste hierarchies. In Britain, a number of journalists approached, and indeed forged, the New Pop movement with a critical regard that had previously been the preserve of rock (Reynolds, 2005: 361–82). Moreover, it was the visual artistry of these pop performers that 'validated music videos as an expressive form' (Frith, 1988: 210). In contrast, the heavy rock bands that took advantage of the video boom – in particular the 'hair metal' bands from Los Angeles – comprised one of the most critically reviled sub-genres of rock. Although there were a number of aesthetic, cultural and sociological reasons for this dismissal (Thompson, 2001: 227–41), video and MTV were at least partly to blame. Adopting these forms represented an embrace of mass media: MTV was, after all, global in its ambitions. In addition, there is the use these bands made of music video. Here too we can witness a turnaround between pop and rock.

Goodwin notes that many New Pop videos are 'anti-realist' (1993: 133). Artists are situated in dramatic situations, whether created in a film studio (as with the Buggles' 'Video Killed the Radio Star') or via picturesque location shoots (as with Duran Duran's travelogue videos). They are thus distanced from their fans. In contrast, a dominant trope among early rock videos is the 'live' performance, whether this is taking place in a recording studio, rehearsal space or on stage. For Goodwin, these locations serve as a 'guarantor of authenticity', a continuation of the music's romantic and modernist beliefs (ibid.: 77). This is not, however, the authenticity of the earlier rock movement, which vacillated between viewing audiences as interference or as equals. Here, the heavy metal bands take the eroticised gaze of early pop TV and run with it. Female fans are prioritised and are shown responding wildly to the musicians. However, while there is a degree of fan agency in the earlier Elvis and Beatles clips, the images in these videos are more contrived and controlled. Bon Jovi's 'You Give Love a Bad Name', Ratt's 'Round and Round', Def Leppard's 'Pour Some Sugar on Me' and Poison's 'Your Mama Don't Dance' are illustrative of the genre. These 'live' performances feature reaction shots that hone in on young/attractive/ scantily-clad/well-endowed girl fans. Mötley Crüe's 'Girls, Girls, Girls' takes this trope to an extreme: the band performs the song to grateful strippers in a strip club.

With its concentration on the single record and its 24-hour broadcasting policy, MTV increased the repetitiveness of music imagery. Greil Marcus complained about the standardised nature of musicians' video performances: 'the male-rock-performer script . . . everything you see is second-hand, third-hand – received and reified'. For Marcus, the musicians' gestures are empty; they merely signify that bands know 'what male rock stars are supposed to do on stage' (Frith, 1988: 218). In a similar manner, the performances of audience members in both pop and rock videos became increasingly predictable. The video director, record company or artists might select only the most beautiful fans (or even the most beautiful non-fans); these fans might be costumed; their moves choreographed; their actions edited. There can also be a direct echo of the musicians' hackneyed performances, with the audience members singing the words back to them or mimicking their gestures.

It should be noted that 'authentic' 1980s rock performers can be witnessed in anti-realist videos (Peter Gabriel's 'Sledgehammer'; Foreigner's 'I Want to Know What Love Is') while pop artists' videos can show them cutting it live (Wham's 'The Edge of Heaven'; the Eurythmics' 'Sisters are Doin' it For Themselves'). Moreover, regardless of their generic type, these video performances fed into the artists' live routines. Auslander has described the 1980s as being an era of 'simulation': videos imitated live performance and, beyond that, live performance imitated 'music video imitating live performance' (2008: 101). And so, while artists such as Prince and Madonna would enact 'anti-realist' video-type scenarios on stage, the live routines of heavy metal acts would mirror the stagecraft that they had developed for their video performances. In fact, the relationship between live and mediated performance was wound even tighter than Auslander depicts. As I have indicated above, the influence of the moving image on live acts has a longer history, therefore music video wasn't just imitating live performance, it was imitating live performance imitating filmed performance. And what of the audiences? Auslander doesn't mention their role in the live simulation of video or in the video simulation of live performance. They were nevertheless caught within complex webs of representation. In the latter half of the 1980s the 'performance' clip gained ascendancy (Goodwin, 1993: 136). Many of these videos showed idealised images of fans. Consequently, they provided audience members with increased opportunities to see how musicians expected them to look and behave at their gigs.

It was also in this period that concerts first began to regularly incorporate video recording and transmission. Connor compared the 'corporeal' distance of 1970s' music concerts with the simulated closeness of a mediated 1980s' gig:

> [Bruce] Springsteen's appearances on his world tour in 1985, which were rarely to fewer than 50,000 people, made sure that no member of the vast audience could escape the slightest nuance of music or voice. Behind him, an enormous video screen projected claustrophobically every detail of his agonized facial expressions in a close-up which at one and the same time abolished and re-emphasized the actual distance between him and his audience.
>
> (1997: 174)

These video screens have now infiltrated all but the smallest of gigs. In doing so, they have helped to foster the imitative interaction between artists' filmed and live performances. At live concerts, musicians aren't just performing for the fans in front of them; they are also projecting towards the camera. The live audience will also be filmed and broadcast on the screens. This provides another means for closeness and distance. Distance is abolished by means of a common interface. Where artists and audiences previously had the clear division of stage and auditorium, the video screen offers a platform where they can be edited side-by-side. Both parties can be shown in close-up and they can both be brightly lit. Distance is re-established by means of control. Audiences may well receive a greater share of the limelight, but video screens coerce them into further levels of simulation. Cameramen are in search of standardised reaction shots, the preceding promo videos having informed them of the appropriate responses to musicians' actions. And fans know what to do in order to secure a better chance of appearing on screen. It is of benefit to be female/young/attractive/scantily-clad/well-endowed. An example of the standardised nature of fan reactions can be witnessed in concert videos. When gigs are filmed for commercial release it can be convenient to shoot footage of audience members at a separate performance to the one used to compile the shots of the musicians (Plasketes, 2009: 113–14). The fact that this practice usually goes unnoticed is indicative of the extent to which reactions have become reified.

Auslander concludes *Liveness* arguing that live performance will continue to be indebted to televisual performance. This is because, '[a]t present, television is the dominant cultural form' (2008: 187). This statement is included in both the 1999 and 2008 editions of his book, and it possibly remains true for the founding area of his enquiries: theatre of the stage and screen. It is more problematic for popular music. His key measures are 'cultural presence and prestige – and profitability' (ibid.). For many leading musicians, it is arguable that live performance now outperforms television in each of these domains. The fortunes of music video have also fluctuated. In the twenty-first century, MTV is something of a spent cultural force and includes fewer videos in its programming (Hay, 2001: 68–9). Moreover, one of the initial effects of digital downloading – both legal and pirated – was that record companies and artists had less money to spend on promotional videos (Batey, 2010). YouTube, in contrast, has helped to revive the currency of the music video. It has nevertheless meant that these clips are now more commonly seen on computers and phones than on television screens.

Live performance remains indebted to filmed representations.[7] It does, however, draw upon a number of different traditions, rather than being solely in thrall to the artists' promotional videos. It has also developed mediated conventions of its own. The most basic of these is the expectation that fans will gesticulate wildly when realising their presence has been captured on the screen.[8] Here there is something of a return to the Beatles'

TV audiences, whose reactions were heightened by their appearance on studio monitors. Promotional video, meanwhile, provides fewer outlets for excessive fan behaviour.

Another difference between the promotional and live uses of video is that, ironically, live performance now has more layers of mediation than its promotional counterpart. There is a proliferation of mobile phones and digital cameras at gigs. Many fans have the ability to film the concerts that they attend. They can film the live performance and they can film its transmission on video screens. They can also film themselves being filmed. This provides more opportunities for mediated interaction, but questions of agency and influence still remain. Caught within these layers of mediation, do fans behave in accordance with previous modes of representation or are they able to forge new ones?

While digital technology has increased the depictions of fans as consumers, it has also enabled some of them to become producers. Bands such as Nine Inch Nails and Radiohead have endorsed the compilation of their audiences' film footage into concert movies.[9] These two groups have modernist tendencies and it may therefore appear odd that they have embraced fan agency in this way. The footage is telling, however. Although compiled in different manners – the Nine Inch Nails footage is sequenced from '422 individual files from 25+ sources' but edited by representatives of the band, while the Radiohead fans maintained control over the editing stage of their concert film – the outcome is similar.

These amateur filmmakers are not providing usual YouTube-style films. There are no crowd shots of their friends gurning at cameras or transforming themselves into human emoticons, and nor are there any shots of video screens in the venues (if, indeed, any were used). Instead their mobile phones are trained firmly on the live performers. This may be the result of the editing process (the editors' outlook is apparent in the Radiohead footage, which elects to fade to black between each song, rather than show any cheering fans). However, it may also be a representation of the amateur filmmakers' beliefs, or indicative of the way that fans shoot film at gigs, where footage is not usually shot from their own perspective, instead cameras are raised up, so that they can provide a view over the heads of other audience members and over the masses of other mobile phones. Nevertheless, the net effect is that these camera images offer a return to the idea of authentic distance that Connor experienced at 1970s' rock festivals. Out-of-focus footage of tiny figures doesn't have the effect of bringing us closer to the musicians, if anything it renders them more untouchable.

The fan-made Nine Inch Nails and Radiohead films present a solution to some of the dilemmas of the rock era. Live performance and mediation are no longer incompatible. Turning the filmmaking over to the audience supports the idea of rock community and removes the deadening hand of corporate involvement, while the way these films are shot provides the distance needed to preserve the integrity of the artists' lonesome genius. The films also place music at the centre of matters. While the visual output moves skittishly between different viewpoints (similar to the split-screen technique used in *Woodstock*, and again with an absence of shot/reverse shots), the audio output is steady. Moreover, the audio output is superior: while much of the imagery has an expected amateurish quality, the audio is sourced directly from each band. These films are interactive, but only up to a certain point. The fans have agency, but choose to focus their attention on the artists, rather than on themselves. However, they only have agency when it comes to the visual recording of the band. When it comes to the audio, the artists remain firmly in control. We once again have isolated modernist heroes, and we once again have an absence of fans.

## Conclusion

Are we swirling in ever decreasing circles of simulation? At times, it seems as though there is no escape from mediation and there is no escape from popular music's past. Although I have divided this chapter up into four periods and four types of filmed audience, I would not like to give the impression that these tendencies can only be witnessed in their dominant eras. In fact, I argue that the filming of audiences has been of such centrality to popular music practice that three of these forms of representation have persisted. Interpretative camerawork has been in evidence in the filming of punk, rave and other sub-cultures, while the interfering audience has continued to present a dilemma for all boy bands and girl groups who wish to move in an 'artistic' direction. Conversely, the ability to interact with mediated representations has a longer history than some digital theorists would have us believe. What has perhaps disappeared, though, is the idea that performance and mediation are incompatible. The majority of live performances by musicians are indebted to past and present forms of representation, even if those forms of representation try to kid us that they are against the idea of visual display.

The same holds true for many audience members: they behave in a mediated manner. Nevertheless, in this conclusion I do want to urge some caution. This chapter is titled 'That's Me in the Spotlight'. It is the audience members in the first few rows of a gig, video or TV performance who have been my preoccupation, the ones who are most regularly caught in the stage lights and who are liable to be captured on film. Not all members of audiences have received such exposure. As Wendy Fonarow argues, there is 'differential participation and spatial distribution' at gigs (1996: 33). The audience members at the back of the hall operate in a different manner to those hogging the limelight at the front. Here, fan behaviour is learnt as much through regular attendance at gigs as it is by watching audiences on screen. The people at the back have rarely been captured on film, not least because if they were documented they would often display a spectacular degree of inattention to the musicians on stage. As Fonarow has noted, this is a space for 'disparate activities' (ibid.: 35).

Finally, I want to return to the representation of female audiences. Huyssen concludes 'Mass Culture as Woman' on a positive note, arguing that 'the gendering of mass culture as feminine and inferior has its primary historical place in the late nineteenth century', and that 'the old rhetoric has lost its pervasive power because the realities have changed' (1986: 62). The new reality for Huyssen is postmodernism, a cultural condition that has witnessed a merging of high culture and mass culture and a greater proportion of female artists working in each domain. Popular music would perhaps belie his optimism. Although it bears some of the hallmarks of postmodernism, not least in its blurring of the represented and the real, it has not entirely given itself over to this condition. Simon Reynolds has argued that, with its 'isolated modernist hero figures', popular music has in fact held out longer than other art forms 'against the onset of post-modernism' (2011: 173). Its modernist phase didn't happen in the late nineteenth century; it is still happening now. One way of measuring popular music's progress towards the freedoms of postmodernism is via its representations of female audiences. As long as female fans are depicted as sexualised masses or are expunged from view, it can be argued that there still remains some distance to go.

## Notes

1 Statistical evidence shows that this audience split has remained broadly true. In the UK, pop was the dominant genre among women in 2013, making up 37.4% of purchases. Among men, pop accounted for 26% of purchases. The figures were reversed when it came to rock, which was the leading genre among male shoppers, making up 36.3% of their purchases. For women rock accounted for 26.9% of purchases (Green, 2014: 85).
2 See also Barbara Bradby's chapter in this volume.
3 Garratt is recalling her youth as a Bay City Rollers fan. Although a 1970's group, the Rollers were promoted using the conventions of Beatlemania.
4 'Woodstock', written by Joni Mitchell (Sony/ATV Music Publishing).
5 Altamont, the 1969 music festival headlined by the Rolling Stones, has regularly been cast as Woodstock's antithesis. This is partly due to the documentary film of the event (*Gimme Shelter*, 1970). Here the male mass is depicted and it is *devouring*. The film culminates with a male fan brandishing a gun at the Rolling Stones, who are performing on stage. He is murdered by the band's macho security: the Hells Angels. The aggression at the concert represents some sort of culmination of a dilemma that the Rolling Stones' audience faced. From the outset this audience had been more male than that for the Beatles (see, for example, the claims of Mick Jagger in the film *Crossfire Hurricane* (2012)), and yet its examples of fan behaviour had been learnt from watching girl fans on TV. These male fans could go further than the Beatles' female fans – stage invasions were common – and yet they became confused when coming face-to-face with the band. Having been schooled in the erotic gaze/reverse gaze of audience representations, their first impulse was to kiss their heroes. Quickly rejecting this, they would often hit them instead (Coates, 2010: 191).

6   Ioannis Tsioulakis' chapter in this volume also discusses how contemporary online technologies facilitate this interaction in ways which can both intensify and disrupt fandom.

7   See also Laura Leante's examination of filmed performances in this volume.

8   Perhaps the most depressing of all audience interactions is the tradition of the 'boobs shot'. Cameramen will be in search of girls who have been hoisted up onto their partner's shoulders; the crowd will then urge the filmed girl to lift up her top. If she concedes, the crowd will point phone cameras towards the large video screen and film the footage of the girl's display. For an extreme example see Steel Panther, 'Party All Day (Fuck All Night)', www.youtube.com/watch?v=U7ILDT52qrQ (accessed 6 June 2014).

9   For footage of the Nine Inch Nails project, see http://atinylittledot.com/ (accessed 6 June 2014). The Radiohead film can be seen at http://consequenceofsound.net/2012/11/watch-a-fan-made-radiohead-concert-film/ (accessed 6 June 2014).

# 9 'Soon you'll wish they would shut up!'

## The digitised political voices of music stars and their audiences in recession Greece

*Ioannis Tsioulakis*

### Introduction

There is something unsettling about watching my 'native' culture from abroad; an almost unwelcome lucidity, a bitter, disengaged sobriety. I, the 'native ethnographer', feel at once less entitled to commentary and critique, and yet better able and more eager to articulate it. As I observe the radical political developments in Greece since the economic collapse in 2010, I switch between diverse modes of engagement: watching the news (online), reading articles (online), and conversing with friends and family, sometimes through real-time speech (mostly online video-calls) or occasionally through carefully written email texts (still consistently online). These periods of physical absence and virtual presence are juxtaposed with some brief intervals of actual – legitimate, one might say – ethnographic 'being there', steeped in music-making (performances, practices, recordings), political participation (rallies, demonstrations, elections), or occasions that combine both (political concerts and festivals). It is the dialectic between these two configurations of presence/absence that constructs my ethnographic point of departure in this chapter, and it is also this dialectic that most interests me in the present examination of musicians–audience interaction. The interchange of online and physical presence thus serves as both the locus and the method of addressing this question: how do popular musicians and audiences speak to each other about politics in contemporary Greece?

Against the backdrop of turbulent political circumstances in Greece between 2011 and 2014, this chapter aims to analyse the political stance of popular singers, the main personas of the Greek popular music scene, and the way in which it has been received by various audiences and commentators. More specifically, what interests me is how these political speeches (and responses) are articulated through online media, but also how they, in turn, affect physical presences and behaviours in performances and other public domains. This chapter will argue that, while popular singers come out of their political closets and express their views, they reshape their relationship with audiences in ways unprecedented in the past three decades. Simultaneously, through their verbal utterances and physical gestures, audiences forge new avenues of communication, praise or condemnation towards those prominent performers, which effectively construct both positionings anew.

## (Anti)memorandum politics

The chronicle of Greece's radical economic and political change in the past four years has been covered extensively by domestic and international media.[1] Following the global financial crisis that began in the United States in 2008, Greece faced a sovereign-debt crisis in 2009, which resulted in a succession of so-called 'bail-outs' directed by the European Union, the International Monetary Fund (IMF) and the European Central Bank (ECB) (Lapavitsas, 2012). This consortium of power-holders, who have since become known as the *Troika*, implemented a series of economic and socio-political measures that have deeply divided the nation and caused significant upheaval. The most visible political dichotomy concerns the signed bail-out agreement known as the 'Memorandum of Economic Policies'. Two of these memoranda and a number of additional sets of measures have been signed in the past five years, each with more severe terms than the last, deepening the imposed austerity, the recession and the political alienation of Greek citizens. In light of these circumstances, the political spectrum is at first glance divided into two camps: the pro-memorandum politicians (including Conservatives, Neo-liberals and some reluctant but co-operating Social Democrats) and the anti-memorandum campaigners which are dominated by two groups on the opposite side of the spectrum: the Left of the *Syriza* party and the extreme nationalist Right of the party Golden Dawn.

As a consequence of the 'crisis', along with the collapse of the political system and the economy, the narrative of liberal cosmopolitanism, a previous corner-stone of the Social Democrats who were in power for over 20 years since the early 1980s, is also being challenged. Cosmopolitanism, Ulf Hannerz (2004:71) argues, has two faces:

> In its aesthetic and intellectual dimensions, it can become a kind of consumer cosmopolitanism, a cosmopolitanism with a happy face, enjoying new cuisines, new musics, new literatures. Political cosmopolitanism is often a cosmopolitanism with a worried face, trying to come to grips with very large problems.

In the age of Greek prosperity, political and cultural cosmopolitanism had achieved a degree of unproblematic coexistence. This was exemplified, among other traits, by a musical taste for the 'foreign' and the 'exotic' (Tsioulakis, 2011b). Along with this phenomenon, socio-political behaviours of 'Europeanness', linked to tolerance, liberalism, and a rejection of 'petty' nationalism were fostered by both state and media discourses. Granted, the cosmopolitan ideals of the Greek 1990s and 2000s were far from consistent; they were more often contradictory and competing.[2] Along with the state rhetoric of post-nationalism driven by economic neoliberalism, existed other types of cosmopolitanism, some subaltern and counter-hegemonic (Gledhill, 2010) while others purely aesthetic. The generalised feeling of 'growth', however, provided the ideal terrain for 'political projects of creating global networks outside of the stranglehold of nation-states' (Feld, 2012: 48). In contrast, within the current socio-political circumstances feelings of intolerance, discrimination and xenophobia are on the rise (Angouri and Wodak, 2014). These are witnessed in both popular and state discourses and behaviours. Hate crimes against racial, ethnic, religious and sexual minorities is becoming an everyday occurrence, at the same time as the state is resorting to censorship and police brutality (Herzfeld, 2011). These tendencies have been opposed by diverse groups who are largely aligned with the Left and have organised numerous antifascist/antiracist fora and demonstrations, often incorporating music concerts and other performance events.

Popular musicians have not been absent from these discourses. Greek popular music lived the peak of its politicisation between the 1960s and the 1980s. The most celebrated example was that of Marxist composer Mikis Theodorakis, who, following the teachings of Antonio Gramsci, used leftist poetry in combination with folk music idioms in a direct effort to create a musical culture that would shape a revolutionary working class (Papanikolaou, 2007; Tragaki, 2005; Cowan, 1993). Following this aesthetic imperative, a number of singer-songwriters including Manos Loizos and Dionyssis Savvopoulos emerged, who explicitly used music as a means of political struggle, connected to different movements within the broader spectrum of the Greek Left. This artistic and political endeavour was almost completely abandoned in the 1990s and 2000s, a time when musical creativity and political activism were increasingly regarded by the majority of fans and critics as incompatible, and politically-motivated music was often considered banal.

In the wake of economic and social crisis in Greece since 2010, new modalities of political activism and expressions of disobedience are being developed. The internet has been crucial in this course, especially in the way in which it contributed to the disembodiment and re-embodiment of the terrain of political performativity, a phenomenon crucial for the relationship between musicians and their audiences.[3] Although the music scene has yet to produce quintessentially political works apart from some opportunistic and generally low-impact efforts, popular music stars (by which here I mostly mean singers) have not remained silent. On the contrary, by using spoken and written word through online social media and TV they have vocalised their diverse and often radical political views in a way unprecedented in the past 20 years. In turn, audiences have illustrated that they take these utterances seriously, and have found imaginative (virtual and physical) ways of showing both their support and their disdain.

Next I will examine four snapshots of political discourse bringing together all the aforementioned positions from conservative pro-memorandum to leftist and extreme-right anti-memorandum politics coming from popular singers, and examine the digitised and physical reactions that they provoked among audiences. Subsequently, I will propose some ways in which political talk can redefine the nature and quality of contact that artists have with their fans.

## Snapshot one: Dalaras's pro-memorandum controversy

Yiorgos Dalaras has been one of the most prominent singers of the Greek popular music industry in the past 40 years. In a recent article, Dimitris Papanikolaou has summarised Dalaras's case in the phrase 'the singer as nation' (2013: 73), stressing the artist's ability to express in one complex persona all the ambiguities, drifts and self-contradictions of Greek national culture. Dalaras has at various points in his career been involved in, and musically expressed, leftist ideals, but at the time of the first 'bail-out' he was identified with the ruling social-democrat party (PASOK), mainly because his spouse was serving as Deputy-Minister of Labour. During a TV talk show in March 2012, Dalaras was asked about the danger of losing national sovereignty by accepting European political and financial interference. His response was that 'we have to accept it, or else our nation will be destroyed'. The video clip of his interview was instantly uploaded onto YouTube,[4] and was virally disseminated through internet-based social media, accompanied by an almost unequivocal condemnation of his attitude, which was considered to show lack of sensitivity toward a suffering people.

During a live performance a few days after the interview, Dalaras was met by an angry mob who chose to express their indignation in a very traditional Greek way: throwing containers full of Greek strained yoghurt. What is worth noting is that the 'indignant protesters'[5] (as they have come to be known recently, following the movement of the Spanish *indignados*) had gathered at Dalaras's free concert after a call publicised through online social media. In other words, a virtual, digital call for action ensured the very physical presence of angry, threatening bodies, throwing at the famous singer objects that, in their rich symbolism, were also painfully material. Interestingly, the video of Dalaras's ridicule became a new internet sensation in itself,[6] providing a compelling example of how the virtual and the physical can dialogically shape each other. From the initial video interview to the live performance and the dissemination of the recorded incident, we can observe a feedback loop where the virtual becomes physical only to be captured and further circulated again virtually.

After the event, Dalaras published online a long text as a response to the scorn to which he was subjected, dealing specifically with the issue of political voice. In this text he states:

> I am not an orator who tries to impose his views on others, and I never attempted to have an active political role beyond what the trajectory of my whole musical career dictated . . . At the same time, I don't think that a good singer is a mute singer. This is why my work is always connected to my personal and free judgement; it marks and it becomes marked by it.[7]

Dalaras's text illustrates an effort to integrate his recent viewpoints within a consistent narrative, compatible with his lengthy career in the music business. While trying to construct a role for himself where he is allowed to express political opinions without being stigmatised as a quintessentially political figure, he also stresses that his latest views should not be seen as a break from the rest of his history. This, I argue, is a strategic declaration with the intention to undo some of the damage that his political stance caused to the relationship with his very wide audience. By claiming an unbroken continuity between his musical career and his non-musical speech, Dalaras struggles to persuade his fans that – words and yoghurts notwithstanding – essentially nothing has changed between them.

## Snapshot two: Alexiou and the alleged tax evasion

The second example is that of Haris Alexiou, a prominent singer with a long career similar to Dalaras and, according to many, his female alter-ego. In contrast to Dalaras, however, Haris Alexiou had from early on spoken against the memorandum agreements and expressed a rhetoric that affiliated her with the Left. Appearing on a popular TV show in May 2011, she declared her support for the 'indignant movement' (*kinima aganaktismenon*) and in a later interview in *Elle Magazine* she recounted her experience of participating in their demonstrations at Syntagma Square:

> I had people hugging me at Syntagma and saying 'thank you for coming'. But later I read accounts saying 'why did Alexiou go there, what is she "indignant" about?' I do have the right to be indignant, even if it is for different reasons than the worker who makes 600 euro, and that's because I am part of a country that has devastated its people.[8]

What is interesting in Alexiou's account is once more the shift between physicality and virtuality, which is here rhetorically used in her favour. Not insignificantly, she portrays the supportive gestures and utterances as embodied, personal and in 'real' time. On the contrary, the criticisms towards her political participation were presented as anonymous, distant and only appearing after her presence was covered by the media. This rhetoric, I argue, contains an authenticity claim connected to the physicality of the encounter on the streets, especially when juxtaposed with the hostility towards Dalaras' embodied presence.

Following her anti-government declarations, Alexiou was targeted by a mainstream (pro-memorandum) newspaper which published a list of celebrity alleged tax evaders, with her name featuring prominently in the first few lines.[9] After this list was made public, Manolis Kapsis, a very prominent (again pro-memorandum) mainstream journalist wrote on his twitter account: 'The reason why we ended up with the memorandum is because some so-called leftists . . . including bitches like Alexiou, never paid their taxes' (Kapsis, on *Twitter*, September 2012). The utterance was again virally circulated among astonished users who wondered if the famous journalist's Twitter account had been hacked. A shocked Alexiou replied through a Facebook post only a few hours later disputing the tax-evasion accusations and wondering about the purpose of such hostility. In her brief response Alexiou also touched on the issue of the artist's political voice by deliberating: 'Do I not have the right to an opinion about my country, even if I am wrong?' (Alexiou, on *Facebook*)

With this declaration, Alexiou skilfully attempted to switch the discourse from personal issues to the artist's obligation to express herself politically and motivate others. The implication of the existence of virtual audiences is crucial here: by choosing a popular online social network as a medium, Alexiou made clear that she was not responding to the journalist, but rather addressing her online 'friends', in other words the audience that has consciously chosen to 'follow' her – in both the established and web-based sense of the term. In turn, Kapsis answered with a brief online article a few days later, where he apologised for some of his vile language, but retained his opinion that the 'leftists' that are now protesting against austerity were all prominent exponents of the establishment during the times of its artificial prosperity.

## Snapshot three: Ioannidis's blog sensations

Another interesting example comes from Greek-Cypriot singer-songwriter Alkinoos Ioannidis, a prominent musician of the so-called 'art-song' genre.[10] Although quite socially critical with his lyrics, Ioannidis has been known from the beginning of his career in the 1990s for his low-key public appearances and his depoliticised speech. After a concert in England in early 2012, however, Ioannidis decided to publish on his blog an outright political text. This was written as a response to an Englishman who approached him after the end of the concert and told him 'We blame you [Greeks], you know, for the European collapse'. In his long and emotional text, Ioannidis criticised European economic interventions that he connected to a historically established process of colonialism, but also focused on the corrosion of the

Greek socio-political establishment. Within this critique he asserted: 'One of our gravest mistakes was that we allowed the politician and the artist to represent the cheapest, ugliest versions of ourselves' (Ioannidis, 2012).

Interestingly, in Ioannidis's text, the politician and the artist share the blame for mirroring the least enviable qualities of the Greek people. The political voice and the musical voice once again collide into one in Ioannidis's digital social reflexivity. Yet, by using the pronoun 'we', he situates himself within the ranks of 'the people'. As a musical performer, but simultaneously an audience of the 'politicians', Ioannidis appears to admit two kinds of responsibility: one for not shaping a better political system, and another for not incarnating a more ideal artist figure. This could be read as a self-criticism for his previous lack of political engagement, for which evidently this text serves as compensation.

A year after the previous blog entry, Ioannidis published a new text, this time commenting on the infamous (if short-lived) 'NO' of the Cypriot parliament to the European financial elite in March 2013.[11] This loud 'NO', he argued, 'was disastrous and cathartic at the same time, which you Greek memorandum-ists, politicians and journalists will never dare to say. You will prefer to destroy us all the same by saying "YES"' (Ioannidis, 2013). Ioannidis's intervention is significant not least because it was addressing two audiences: the Greeks (in his country of residence) and Cypriots (in his native place). In so doing, Ioannidis managed to assume the role of a dual mediator: between the audiences and power-holders, and between two nations.

Both of Ioannidis's electronic articles appeared within days from their publication on countless political and cultural websites, rendering him a central political voice for the left-leaning anti-memorandum movements. His presence however did not remain virtual. As a result of the political affiliations that he created through his web-speeches, Ioannidis has since sung in numerous anti-memorandum and anti-fascist festivals, renewing with his physical presence the relationship with some of his fans who now see him and the genre that he represents in a different light.

## Snapshot four: Gaitanos and Sfakianakis, the voices of extreme right

Perhaps surprisingly, the neo-fascist trend capitalised in the political terrain by the party Golden Dawn has not been without its music celebrity supporters. Petros Gaitanos is a noteworthy example. First appearing in the early 1990s as a popular music singer, Gaitanos gained substantial visibility later for his performances of Byzantine chants. Although invariably scorned by knowledgeable musicians of the tradition as a mediocre exponent of the genre, Gaitanos's Byzantine chanting became a constant point of reference for mainstream media, especially during the period of Easter festivities.

In a TV interview in late 2012, Gaitanos appeared as an admirer of Golden Dawn's racist and homophobic so-called activism. In an attempt to give a personal touch to his newly-found ideological affiliation with the neo-fascists, Gaitanos states in the video: 'I like the aggressiveness of Golden Dawn ... You know how many times I wanted to take all these [pirate] CDs that the blacks are selling on the streets and smash them on their heads?'[12] Referring to the common practice of selling unauthorised CDs, mostly undertaken by African immigrants in the Greek urban areas, Gaitanos reinforces Golden Dawn's populist rhetoric about 'illegal immigrants' (*lathrometanastes*) harming the Greek economy, and locates himself as a prime victim of their practices.

As expected, the response of internet users was overwhelmingly negative, but not without its own issues of intolerance and discrimination: most responses and comments accompanying Gaitanos's video interview focused on his alleged homosexuality, which was deemed ironic in the context of his support for an outright homophobic political group. But perhaps more interesting is the connection of Gaitanos's racist rant with the Orthodox Church, since many of its supporters have consistently flirted, even if until recently covertly, with extreme nationalism and homophobia. In fact, the Greek Orthodox Church has not remained far from controversial politics verging on extreme nationalism, both before the crisis (Stavrakakis, 2003) and in recent years (Zoumboulakis, 2013; Dragonas, 2013). Significantly, the Orthodox Church even maintained close rapport with the nationalist Dictatorship of the Colonels (1967–1974; see Mavrokordatos, 2003: 126; Zoumboulakis, 2013: 136). In this context, Gaitanos's declaration could be regarded as a conscious effort to address the growing audience of extremely conservative persuasions, an audience compatible with Gaitanos's career in Orthodox religious hymnody. This rhetoric was immediately endorsed by the Golden Dawn party who published an article on their official website referring to Gaitanos as an 'admirable artist, with a commendable contribution to the Byzantine chanting tradition'.[13] This is what a Twitter user, creator of the online mock-poster below (Figure 9.1)[14] intended to comment on, by portraying Gaitanos chanting to a Swastika.

A similar example is that of commercial neo-folk singer Notis Sfakianakis. A commentator who never hid his nationalist feelings or even racist views, Sfakianakis appeared in late 2012 in a series of online and TV interviews as a supporter of Golden Dawn. In one such interview, Sfakianakis stated: 'I have always said that the biggest problem are the illegal immigrants who will one day turn us into a minority in our own country'.[15] Sfakianakis has since then repeatedly reaffirmed his support for the extreme right, both through mediatised interviews and live performances, where he is known for interrupting the flow of the songs in order to intersect his political commentary from the stage to the audience.[16]

These controversies have stigmatised the popular singer in the past few years, to the extent that his name is rarely mentioned without evoking commentary on his relationship with extreme nationalism. In yet another interesting interplay of virtuality and materiality, the wall graffiti from the

*Figure 9.1* Gaitanos is portrayed chanting to a swastika (courtesy of @whiteaxi on *Twitter*)

*Figure 9.2* Sfakianakis portrayed on wall graffiti with a Hitler moustache

centre of Athens pictured above (Figure 9.2) mocks Sfakianakis's political stance. The drawing portrays Sfakianakis with a Hitler-type moustache, and playing with his famous song 'The Eagle Dies in the Air', the caption reads: 'Before he died, the eagle told me that you're a big old fascist scum'. The intertextuality evoked by both mocking pieces of artwork is powerful exactly because it associates the two singers' racist rants with their musical career.

## Musicians and audiences in virtual immediacy

Dilemmas of Europeanism and nationalism, neoliberalism and socialism, and a political spectrum ranging from the fascist right to the radical left have never ceased to be part of the Greek public domain. Artists and specifically popular music celebrities, however, have in recent times moved within this spectrum with their political voices largely muted by their unitary financial interests. Inescapably, this strategy is deemed unacceptable in the wake of economic collapse, with music fans, critics and journalists keeping their ears open (and their screens lit) for political declarations. The ways in which these discourses are taking place and political affiliations between artists and audiences are being negotiated after roughly twenty years of silence are quintessentially new. They are less musical, less poetic, more literal, and yet at the same time more temperamental and momentary. In a recent article about the attitude of 'public intellectuals', writer and journalist Konstantinos Poulis proclaimed that 'once we were calling for artists and intellectuals to speak out, soon we will be wishing that they would shut up' (Poulis, 2013). With the present chapter, I want to argue that the disappointment that many have felt with the singers' political voices is partly due to the raw and unprepared manner that they have been expressed through the TV, social media and online blogging, especially compared to the deeply artistic, and by definition designed and controlled, musical political activism of the 1960s and 1970s.

This disappointment can also be traced in the discrepancy between the singing voice, with all its verbal and sonic mediations by composers, lyricists, producers and so on, and the singer's talking voice, which often appears to fall short of the expectations. Simon Frith argues that

> as listeners we assume that we can hear someone's life in their voice – a life that's there despite and not because of the singer's craft, a voice that says who they really are, an art that only exists because of what they've suffered.
>
> (1996: 185–6)

This performance of suffering becomes harder to maintain while a singer speaks politically to a socially and economically devastated people. Yet, audiences and media are relentless in their search for political declarations by all public figures, who are expected to step up and address the growing anxieties of their followers. As John Street posits,

> Musicians become political as a result of a political process that creates a particular opportunity structure. The musicians' political commitments are, as it were, called into being by the movements that need what the performers have to offer.
>
> (2012: 53)

Political and social formations such as the 'indignant citizens', the anti-memorandum Left, and even the extreme nationalist Right, seem to find in these musicians eager spokespersons with avenues of communication to large audiences. In this process, however, the discursive basis on which relationships between singers and fans were built shifts radically, and new intimacies develop while older ones are being challenged. As a result, audience members recalibrate their affiliation to established popular performers, taking this time into consideration political affinities and the way in which they become expressed and aestheticised, on and off stage.

At the time when the first draft of this chapter was being written, the conservative Greek coalition that governed Greece from 2012 until 2015 had just decided to shut down the National TV and Radio Corporation (ERT) along with its numerous side-projects including orchestras and choirs.[17] In response to what was perceived as an extremely authoritative and undemocratic resolution, journalists and technicians occupied the TV and Radio Headquarters and started broadcasting online, managing to reach audience numbers substantially larger than during their regular programme. As I watched (online) the orchestras giving their last concert outside the National TV Headquarters, attended by a large audience who responded to the journalists' call for solidarity, I pondered again about the interplay of virtual and physical presence. The electronic voices of the occupiers were adamant: 'don't watch us from home; come join us in the courtyard'. Once again, the message reached the audiences directly through the cyberscape, but only their physical presence was deemed loud enough to achieve political ends.

In ethnomusicology and popular music studies, we tend to think of the 'electronic' as a domain of mediation (Wong, 2003; Keil, 1994). So much so, that we often forget its almost opposite primary characteristic: immediacy. Abigail Wood (2008) has successfully illustrated that internet domains need to be investigated by ethnomusicologists as part of a wider web of human and musical interactions, rather than as a separate realm that can be meaningful in isolation.[18] Moreover, in an in-depth study of how online/virtual worlds enhance and channel different manifestations of human musicality, Kiri Miller has argued that 'both digital media and embodied knowledge can bridge space and time, creating connections between dispersed and diverse individual human experiences'. (2012: 4) Anthropologist

Heather Horst (2012) has further elaborated on the interplays between virtuality and physicality that constitute our subjectivity within current socio-political domains. She cautions that:

> While studying patterns and practices in online domains has value, from an ethnographic perspective, the challenge has been to take seriously the relationships between the worlds created in these online spaces and places. Doing so does not necessarily mean privileging one space over the other as more or less authentic but rather understanding how these practices come together and diverge at different points in time.
>
> (2012: 74)

In accordance with the above authors, I see the online domain as an additional facilitator of contemporary socio-political and musical experience, and a factor which, due to its immediacy, becomes catalytic to the dialogues in which musicians and audiences engage.

The examples that I briefly discuss in this chapter, despite their different beginnings and radical contradictions, tell a tale of interconnection between political declaration, commentary and reaction in unprecedented volume and speed. In recounting this, I am not attempting to rejuvenate the old argument of electronic technology as a force of democratisation. If anything, the examples prove that both the utterances and reactions are too scattered, awkward and erratic to form the basis of a democratising process. However, the 'traditional' process of political artists with the well-prepared anthems and the dedicated followers is changed for good. Furthermore, the argument of disembodiment which is overly used in the cultural theory of virtual social spaces[19] can easily overshadow a more complex process. As the examples repeatedly show, the disembodiment of social media easily creates the incentive for physical co-presence. Musicians and their audiences often speak to and about each other through digital media, but their relationships are continuously reaffirmed or broken through embodied physicality such as hugs with Alexiou, yoghurts to Dalaras, and wall-graffiti about Sfakianakis. And it is always this promise and threat of physicality, from presence to violence, which makes relationships between musicians and their audiences appealing and feared.

## Notes

1 This chapter is based on research until 2014 and does not cover the period after SYRIZA took power in 2015. For some critical ethnographic accounts see *Cultural Anthropology*'s 2011 *Hot Spots* online issue entitled 'Beyond the Greek Crisis', especially Dalakoglou (2011), Athanasiou (2011) and Papailias (2011).
2 Turino (2003) and Stokes (2007) have argued that cosmopolitan formations are rarely uniform.
3 Some recent research on political struggle in North Africa and the Middle East has illustrated that new media have a key role to play in revolt strategies

(Allagui, Kuebler et al., 2011; Khondker, 2011). In this article, however, my objective is not to trace the use of social media as a strategic mechanism for political activism, as much as to see how it facilitates conversations between artists and audiences.

4  The video can be accessed here: www.youtube.com/watch?v=nyGaQTWPXQk (accessed 8 June 2015)

5  For an in-depth critical analysis of the Greek anti-austerity protests, see Douzinas (2013a).

6  An extract of that video can be seen here: www.youtube.com/watch?v=xarOc5_WUQs (accessed 8 June 2015)

7  Published on the website aixmi.gr on 26 March, 2012. www.aixmi.gr/index.php/eimaiapo-paidi-sto-dromo-den-anex/ (website accessed on 8 June 2015).

8  *Elle Magazine*, March 2011.

9  Newspaper *Ta Nea*, 10 September 2012.

10  For a discussion of the history and aesthetics of the so-called 'art-song', see Fabbri and Tsioulakis (2016).

11  For a news report of this rejection: www.guardian.co.uk/world/2013/mar/19/cyprus-rejects-eurozone-bailout-savings-tax (accessed 8 June 2015)

12  A version of the video can be accessed here: www.youtube.com/watch?v=8xLYTRggLEY (accessed 8 June 2015)

13  www.xryshaygh.com/index.php/enimerosi/view/petros-gaitanos-mou-aresei-auto-pou-kanei-h-chrush-augh#.UcGDWPlwqT4 (accessed 8 June 2015).

14  Image retrieved from https://twitter.com/whiteaxi/status/258342499091886080/photo/1 (accessed 18 June 2013).

15  A video extract of the interview can be seen here: www.youtube.com/watch?v=HOdprA1XVsA (accessed 8 June 2015).

16  In another article (Tsioulakis, forthcoming), I comment on the intricate relationship between the neo-folk (*laiko*) genre and ideologies of nationalism and intolerance, which is also dependent on structures of power and modalities of spectatorship within Greek night-clubs.

17  See Costas Douzinas' account in the *Guardian*: www.guardian.co.uk/comment isfree/2013/jun/12/ert-greek-state-broadcaster-cultural-calamity (accessed 17 June 2015).

18  Barbara Bradby's chapter in this volume also proposes innovative ways in which we could investigate how video-sharing and anonymous comments on the web can perpetuate the interaction between musicians and audiences off-stage. Also, Richard Osborne's chapter on video-audiences shows successfully that the live performance and its depiction on screen can actually be mutually constitutive. This interaction between liveness and mediatisation becomes more complicated through contemporary internet, which provides significantly more avenues for 'talking back'.

19  See Ajana (2004) for a phenomenological critique of the disembodiment thesis.

# Part 4

# Off-stage discourses and the power of fandom

# 10 'Where are the girls of the old brigade?'

## Vesta Tilley and her female audience in correspondence

*Nancy Bruseker*

## Introduction

In the introduction to this volume, Ioannis Tsioulakis and Elina Hytönen-Ng note the place of the discussion of music not only in providing another vehicle for communicating that which music communicates, but in producing music and the participant musicians and audiences. With recourse to the philosophy of Michel Foucault, they note that 'subjects (by which here we mean both individual persons and concepts) are produced in discourse and cannot be conceived outside it'. Though more common for music after 1950 – see for example Mark Duffett's and Elina Hytönen-Ng's essays in this volume – the discourse of performers and audiences in nineteenth-century popular music has thus far remained in their contemporary historical texts, and been little discussed in popular music studies. Scholars such as Daniel Cavicchi (2012) have written about the popular response to Jenny Lind, and historians working with material relating to music hall and vaudeville (Kift, 1996) or theatre more broadly (Bennett, 1997; Davis, 1991) have attempted to reconstruct the audience of performances. However, bridging the gap between what the historical actors had to say about their subjectivity and the kind of academic analysis which would add to our knowledge of how the relationships between star performers and their audience have developed, has been fragmentary. This is partly due to the difficulties in accessing the views of individual audience members from such a distant time. With the collection of fan letters to one music hall celebrity, Vesta Tilley, it is now possible to recover some of the discursive production of the star and the audience. Encouraged by Vesta, who made a point of constructing a particular *writing* audience in interviews that she gave to the press by repeatedly reporting about her fan correspondence, this audience then responded in kind. The letters, written predominantly by women many of whom came from the working classes, allow a view into the discursively-constructed subjectivities of popular music of the Edwardian period. Using nearly 140 letters written in 1919–20, this chapter shows this construction qualitatively through the subject matters that they included in their letters, and quantitatively through corpus-based linguistics in the volume of positive evaluative adjectives in their correspondence. What emerges is a strong sense that both performer and audience sought a reciprocal relationship and that fans reached for a surprising parity with someone they saw as one of their own.

## Vesta's biography

Vesta Tilley was one of the most famous 'golden age' music hall stars, commanding an international audience and commensurately large salaries for her performances. Born Matilda Powles in Worcester in 1864, she started performing on the music hall stage when she was just three years old. Her father was reputedly the chairman of the music hall in Gloucester and, when she showed a keen interest in performing at that tender age, he arranged for her to have a performance slot. In reality, however, the family came from a working-class background and lived a hand-to-mouth existence until Vesta became a success. By the time when her career was supporting her parents and (eventually, nine surviving) siblings at approximately age ten, her act had settled into a particular type: that of the male impersonator.

This entailed more than just dressing up in men's clothes and singing the male part. Time and again, reviews of her performances describe her as a perfect mimic of mannerism as well. That is, she studied the men whose costume she adopted and, while not altering her voice, did everything else to ensure that her performance served as an effective comedic mirror. Each song had its own particular character and its own costume. The latter evolved from the principal boy costume of the formal theatrical stage plus relevant props, to head-to-toe tailored men's attire. Contemporary commentators, as well as later scholars, describe a performance which trod the fine line between accuracy and mockery. 'There was more than imitation in her mannerisms', wrote Willson Disher in his 1938 *Winkles and champagne: comedies and tragedies of the music hall*. He elaborated:

> There was more than caricature. She was always a very ordinary youth, but she portrayed him in an extraordinary manner. We saw him not how he was in real life, or as he imagined himself, but as he appeared in the eyes of a clever, critically observant woman.
>
> (Disher, 1938: 76)

In her autobiography, she wrote about her experience in playing a raw recruit while the Great War was producing many such lads. The song 'The Army of Today's Alright' had her carrying a regulation-weight rucksack, while marching exaggeratedly back and forth across the stage. After one performance, a couple of soldiers came to speak to her about how they did not approve of her marching. She set them straight and they left, satisfied, having been reminded that the soldier whom Vesta portrayed had only been in the army for a day and thus his/her exaggeration was accurate (De Frece, 1934: 138–139).

In addition to the songs that she sang and characters portrayed in her music hall turns, Vesta was a regular from 1881 to 1901 as the principal boy in the annual pantomime in various cities. Birmingham was a favourite, but she also appeared in Manchester, Glasgow, Liverpool, Newcastle, Brighton, Portsmouth and at Drury Lane in London. While the most economically disadvantaged in Victorian society might not be able to afford regular attendance at the music hall, nearly everyone made a point of at least visiting the halls during the pantomime season. This increased her profile that much more, so that she was known not only nearly in every household in the country, but also in the streets. A week into the run of 'Dick Whittington' in Newcastle, 1893, the papers reported that: 'Miss Tilley's songs . . . are already being whistled all over the town by the street urchins'. In her principal boy costume, Vesta very deliberately was dressed to showcase her femininity in the masculine roles. Further, as everyone came to see the panto, even those whose financial circumstances prohibited regular attendance at the halls, a wider range of people saw her in panto than in her other roles. She toured extensively in the UK, was well known in the northwest and the midlands, and gained a nickname of 'London's Idol'. Subsequently, she crossed the Atlantic for six tours in the United States between 1893 and 1909, where newspaper reports demonstrate that she was immediately equally popular.

In 1911, she was selected to perform in the first Royal Command Performance in part because her off-stage feminine persona was as 'perfect' as her men and boys on the stage. She was also an early experimenter with film, working with Walter Gibbons on one of the first attempts to sync images with sound (Herbert and McKernan, 1996), and in 1916 appeared in a feature film based on her hit 'Jolly Good Luck to the Girl Who Loves a Soldier'. As well as the hundreds of songs sold as sheet music she was also a recording artist, releasing songs even up to the last year of her career (Rust and Debus, 1989: 730–731). She retired in 1920 at the age of 56, then and now a very lengthy career.

She was widely loved and respected, by her peers in the profession – legendary actress Dame Ellen Terry presented her with a bouquet on stage, after her final performance – and by the public at large, at all levels of society. In 1890 she married Walter de Frece, the son of a theatre impresario in Liverpool. They never had any children, but she consistently supported children's charities throughout her career, a fact which served to underline her femininity despite her stage persona and the roles that she undertook. This engagement also took her out of the working class category, by joining middle and upper class women with their charitable work.[1] Nevertheless, she was best known for her working-class female fans, something reflected by both contemporary discussion in the newspapers of the day and in Vesta's own writing. She invited them to see her as accessible, discussing fan behaviour in contemporary interviews, in the process identifying the audience that she most valued. As she wrote in her 1934 autobiography:

> The factory and market girls were my great admirers, and many a humble tribute of their appreciation would they nervously hand to me as I stepped into my waiting cab after the performance. Wet or fine, they would wait in crowds to say good-night, and eventually Mrs Stoll [manager of the Parthenon, a music hall in Liverpool] decided that about ten or twelve of them could wait in the bar at the back of the circle until I had changed and could come up and talk to them.
>
> (1934: 113–114)

They also came to her hotel, waiting around for her to leave for the hall, or came to her lodgings, as they were reported to have done in Liverpool, the night before she sailed for America in 1903.[2] These expressions of devotion, these public gatherings of women in support of a female star are now unfortunately inaccessible to scholars. Luckily, we have been passed through the generations another medium for their appreciation: many dozens of letters written to Vesta and saved (by her) from the rubbish heap. As she received dozens daily at the peak of her career, they are necessarily only a tiny sample. However, they materially reinforce her assertion of her own fan base as being first, predominantly female and second, significantly working class. These letters also show that, despite these social disadvantages, her audience felt empowered to write to her. We know that she wrote back as well, though those letters have unfortunately not survived. Nevertheless, in the letters from her audience we can at least see one exchange: their empowerment to write because of her encouragement and, in that writing, the production of a reciprocal relationship.

## Letters' background

The letters under investigation are taken from a scrapbook documenting Vesta's retirement tour of the UK in 1919 and 1920; the letters speak specifically to this final phase of her career.[3] The majority of the letters carefully pasted in the scrapbooks were written by women;[4] it is upon these that this work focuses. These letters are unique in the annals of music hall history, and are the focus of the following analysis. Not only do they give us a view into star–fan relationships in a previously under-investigated period of music history, but they do so by allowing the fans themselves to speak, as has been possible in more recent times thanks to collections such as Vermorel's *Starlust*, also discussed by Mark Dufett in this volume. These women, who would not otherwise have as individuals a voice in scholarship, will speak on their own terms, just as they did at the point of composition. There is much to be gained in examining these letters as speaking to a community of audience members, a fan base that recognised itself as such, and where hierarchies were produced and/or reinforced. Due to space constraints, however, this chapter focuses solely on the relationship between the letter writers and Vesta Tilley.

The letters are written by women who could socially and economically afford to attend music hall performances.[5] In practice this means that the letters come mainly from women living in the 'provinces'. Of the 138 letters investigated for this chapter, only seven contain no location details about the writer. Forty letters reference or originate from Liverpool and Birkenhead, while 32 come from Birmingham and environs. Manchester and London follow, with 13 and 10 letters respectively. The remaining 32 letters come from other places like Glasgow and Hull, Brighton and Blackpool, Bolton, Southport and Newcastle. There are even a few which reference Vesta's visits to the Isle of Man.

The age range of the authors is vast: even accounting only for those who explicitly state their age, the correspondents span from 12 years at youngest, to the oldest at 75. Women of every age in between are represented in these texts: impassioned letters of teenagers, joint letters from working women in their early twenties, letters from young mothers, mothers with adolescent children, mothers with grown children, and letters from grandmothers. Twelve-year-old Edna Allen had only just been to see Vesta for the first time, on her farewell tour (p. 15, item 18). Annie McKenna wrote a letter from her and an unnamed friend – 'two poor working girls that love you' – to thank Vesta for the photo postcard she sent (p. 11, item 5). Meanwhile, Blanche Brooks wrote, 'I cannot count the numerous times I have seen you' (p. 5, item 5). S. M. Prosser does not give us a number either, except to say 'I have only miss three times seying [sic] you since 1886' (p. 17, item 8).

These women and girls wrote to Vesta because they were encouraged to do so: by Vesta herself, who invoked their letter writing in interviews: 'I receive hosts of letters from girls wherever I go' (Vesta Tilley collection 13801/1/4, p. 288), and from the ubiquitous place of correspondence in everyday life. In drawing attention to the fact that their peers were writing, she encouraged other fans to see this behaviour as normative and indeed necessary in order to be part of the 'in group'. Further, letter writing was a central part of the Victorian world, part and parcel of the concomitant invention of the penny post. One letter-writing style manual from 1864 offered the following guidance to correspondents, to which many of Vesta's audience readily conformed:

> Letter writing is *talking on paper* . . . The greatest charm of a letter is its *individuality*. The best letters – the dearest, the most cherished by the receiver, are the most natural ones – those in which the writer truly pours out his soul upon the paper . . . We rightly expect from him *such a letter as no one else could possibly write*, because no one else has just the same mental organization, or stands in precisely the same relation to us.
>
> (How to write: a pocket manual, 1864: 38–39)

Though it is unlikely that any of the women examined here would have had such a manual, the model outlined here would have been repurposed for, and taught in, schools which they were compelled to attend until at least 12 years of age. What all writers, regardless of age, location or social standing, had in common was their appreciation of Vesta as a public figure and performer, and in writing to her they said something of their own values and identity.

## What can we get from these letters?

As previously noted, the letters are from a particular period in Vesta Tilley's career, and are written in response to two notable, interlinked events. First, she announced her final tour prior to her retirement, in 1919. For this farewell tour, she promised that her salary would be donated to children's charities in the cities and towns where she played. Further, the contemporary fad for picture-postcards would also be put to charitable use; postcards with her picture were sold at the halls, with the proceeds also turned over to local charities. The news of her farewell tour and the details of the charity giving were disseminated in the trade press and local papers. Also in the papers at the time was another important text, namely a multi-instalment auto-biography penned by Vesta for the *Empire News*. All of these texts helped to set the field of discourse in which the letters were written and this is reflected in their structure and content. The evidence also suggests a validation of accommodation theory, which claims that 'we tend to "accommodate" our speech to the speech of the people we are align to, in the hope that they will like us more for doing so' (Hudson, quoted by Bergs, 2007:31). Many of the letters reference one or both of these external events and show the women entering into a perceived – if not also actual – dialogue with Vesta.

In order to evaluate the usefulness of these letters for understanding music hall audiences specifically and popular music audiences in general, I shall examine them through two analytic lenses. In the first instance, I have taken the more conventional approach: a qualitative analysis of the letters themselves, situated in historic context. In the second instance, I have been more experimental, turning to the tools used in the study of corpus-based linguistics. What both these approaches seek to explain is *why* these women were writing to Vesta. Though the use of evidence is different, both show how, by virtue of form and content, the letters served as an opportunity for parity between star and fan.

## Qualitative analysis

One of the key features of Vesta's mini-autobiography is its recapitulation of her lengthy stage career. Unsurprisingly, then, many of the letter writers similarly described their repeated visits to the music halls to see Vesta perform. They wrote themselves into her narrative, re-living on the page their experience of seeing her in the many pantomimes where she performed as principal boy, as well as the numerous turns that she undertook as part of a music hall bill. Mrs Mary Clara Sergeant, from Liverpool, wrote to Vesta in September 1919: 'I have known you for many years, + first saw you at the Pa[r]thenon Gt Charlotte St I was a girl of seventeen then, + I am near 50 now' (p. 11, item 8.). Residents of Birmingham mentioned Vesta's repeated visits, usually in reference to her appearances in the pantomime, Dick Whittington. Mrs Louisa Cooper, the ninth child of Irish immigrants, wrote of her experiences:

> I have looked forward to the times of seeing you since a child I never tired of seeing you as many as five night[s] a week I remember so well when you Played the Part Dick Whittington ... I could not count the times I went to see you and waited outside the theatre to see you enter your carriage and afterwards Prepare to meet a good thrashing when I got home for being late but I did not mind that[.] I was there to see you next night straight from work.
>
> (p. 18, item 2)

Mrs Louisa Bramwell from Liverpool wrote that 'I saw you at the [Parthenon] where you sang Before the lamps are lit – The Shamrocks appeal to the Rose [and] Mary + John ... + remember how excited I used to feel when My Vesta was about to appear' (p. 5, item 1). Mary Clara Sergeant, Louisa Cooper, Louisa Bramwell, by virtue of their letters, have proven to all be in the same place as their idol, Vesta. They expressed this through mutually situating, confessional narratives.

As with Louisa's letter, others also contextualised their knowledge of Vesta's performance career within the larger environment of music hall as an industry. This served to further embed their personal narratives within hers. Widow Catharine Mary Burton wrote from Manchester:

> I have had a gentleman staying with us for twenty years who has been a Musical Director for many years and he has often talked about you to me ... I know he was engaged at some of the Moss Thorntons Hall + I believe he once played for you at the Old Canterbury London.
>
> (p. 12, item 7)

Hettie Halter wrote from Liverpool to express her dismay at Vesta's retirement, explaining:

> I was once a little Pro myself when dear old Mr Harry Defreece[6] often used to book me ... he would say I'll give Hettie next week here [at the old Gaiety] and it seem's [sic] funny does'nt [sic] it but I was known then as 'Little Hettie Halter' Male Impersonator and Dancer[.]
>
> (p. 3, item 5)

Acacia Sullivan is able to go just a little bit further, as she explained: 'I have had the pleasure of been on stage with you several times my first Husband was Paul Wilson the female impersonator + Tenor to [Madame] Marie Rose' (p. 18, item 5). Such claims served to validate their writing to her since they could claim to understand the world in which she lived and worked.

The serialised autobiography did more than recapitulate the highlights of Vesta's stage career, however. It also revealed the figure of Vesta Tilley, woman and wife, someone beyond the male impersonator. Her text answered one of the crucial questions about her final tour: why she was retiring. This was much more a personal than a professional choice; her husband, Walter de Frece, who had been a theatre impresario and her manager since their marriage, was now ready to enter into politics. In 1919, he was standing for election as an MP – a campaign which Vesta helped make successful – but which also spelled the end of her career. Again, the papers carried this story. A brief piece in *The Sketch* magazine read 'we take our hat off to Lady de Frece for seeing that her husband was top of the bill' (25 February, 1920: 295). On the cusp of entering into a largely private life, Vesta was making accommodations that her correspondents recognised and could relate to in their own lives.

In response, the letter writers spoke to her about their husbands, their parents, their children, and the difficulties in balancing their attendance at the halls with their other responsibilities. Emily Coulton wrote:

> It is exactly 10 years ago + you were then as now playing at the Grand [in Nottingham] + I badly wanted to come + see you, my husband promised to . . . take me, but had to work overtime so could not, so I went by myself + if you had seen his face when I came home + heard his sigh of relief you would have smiled, The next day (Saturday) I was taken ill + my little girl was born on Monday morning, but what did it matter, I had seen *Vesta*.
>
> (p. 17, item 19)

Not all of them are cheery stories. Mary Hannah Smith wrote:

> I am only a Poor woman and a broken hearted deserted wife, as my husband a Bradford Corporation Electric Train driver, left me 2 years ago this November to live with his Conductress who was employed on the same car as he was.
>
> (p. 17, item 10)

Another woman, signing herself just 'A Mother', wrote of teaching her son to sing Vesta's song 'The Midnight Son' and her longing to hear Vesta perform it again. 'I felt him so near tonight you will understand perhaps what I am not educated enough to tell you', she wrote, finishing the letter with the heart-breaking last line: 'My boy lies in France' (p. 25, item 11). Mrs Gilchrist, from Manchester, wrote Vesta about her husband and children as well, making it clear that she was responding to Vesta's text: 'I Often Wondered if you were Married, until I Seen Your husband And Yourself in the Sunday Empire and I was Pleased you had Got a Good husband[.]' (p. 3, item 2). In conversation, woman to woman, the authors of the letters produce a confidence in text, as they might do in any friendship. It is possible from this to read a textual production of a measure of equality between them and Vesta.

Here we usefully turn to research done in fan studies to identify further support for how these letters might be read as constructing parity between Vesta and their authors. Research in such disparate fannish moments as Elvis fandom (Duffett, 1998) and KPop has revealed what these letters also suggest: they wanted Vesta to be part of their kinship networks and many had placed her there already. For instance, the oft-repeated northern colloquialism 'our Vesta' made her part of the family. Thus it is no surprise to find this term in the correspondence; Annie McKenna's letter closes with 'God bless you "Our Vesta"', while Flo Bayliss's assessment of Vesta's pantomime success reads 'no one can play Dick Whittington or so idealize the part like "Our Vesta"' (p. 17, item 2). This was a term used not just in the letters investigated here, but in the reported interactions with her inside and outside the music hall, as Vesta herself observed in an American newspaper interview: 'I am the idol for the gallery girls in England. They simply swarm to hear me. . . . To them I am always "'Our Vesta'" or "Our Tilley"' (*The Sun* (New York), 29 November, 1903).

Equally prevalent in the letters is the language of friendship, which the writers use to describe their interactions with Vesta. The word 'friend' appears in textbook usage, letters are addressed to Vesta as 'Dear friend' (p. 13, item 1) and are signed by the writer as 'your True friend' (p. 8, item 3). In between, there are such lines as 'I feel I am personally loosing [sic] a good Friend' (p. 13, item 1) and 'I want you always to think Dear old Friend wherever you are in this big world I will always remember you' (p. 5, item 1). The terms of address they use in their letters echo this. While they might use her formal title – Lady De Frece – it is often qualified by 'my dear', and it equally appears in conjunction with 'Miss Vesta Tilley'. The use of 'my dear' appears in a letter writing manual of the 1860s, specifically when demonstrating the correspondence between family members (Hunter, 1860: 13–20), or as that which would be used 'in more advanced intimacy, especially with gentlemen, as equals' ('The Letter Writer' in *The Youth's Manual*, 1859: 16).[7]

The charitable work done with the proceeds of the farewell tour offered another 'in' for the letter writers, and another chance for connection. Her fans wrote to her to send money alongside their good wishes, and requests for photographs. This also afforded some writers another opportunity of connection, writing with more details of their families and life experiences, as in the case of Miss E. Browning of Birmingham. She wrote to first ask how to purchase photographs, as the theatre had run out on the night when she had been there to see Vesta, and then continued on to write about her brother, who lost a leg to tuberculosis at the age of five. She wrote:

> having seen some of these cripple children undergoing treatment when I was in the Sanatorium I know that taken in time they can be saved the loss of limbs so I hope that you'll get enough funds to erect 2 homes + so safe the lives of suffering children.
>
> (p. 17, item 21)

Agnes Henderson from Liverpool wrote of an experience even closer to her, in her admiration of Vesta: 'It is indeed very kind of you to give your aid to the poor crippled children being a cripple my-self with Hip Joint Disease' (p. 7, item 15). Others wrote to her about caring for children with disability and used it as an opportunity for connection, and as a way of expressing their gratitude.

## Quantitative analysis

As previously discussed, Vesta invited her audience to write to her and also produced a text in the *Empire News* to which they could respond. Thus, there is an element of dialogue in these end-of-career letters sent to Vesta, since there is a text to which they are responding. However, we can expand on this notion of dialogue to show how these letters make Vesta and her audience into peers. In this effort, it is particularly helpful to turn to the results of a corpus-based linguistic analysis. This particular branch of linguistics deals with large volumes of 'natural language', that is, language that has not specifically been produced for linguistic analysis. As a field it has also produced resources for effectively dealing with millions of words requiring analysis. The letters evaluated in this chapter amount to 30,000 words – not quite in the same league as the large corpora, but many words nonetheless.

Douglas Biber, one of the founders of corpus based linguistics, provides a useful working description of the linguistic characteristics of personal letters. He outlines the preponderance of I and you pronouns – unsurprising in letters – the standard WH questions (who, what, where, when, why and how), informal structures such as contractions and what Biber calls 'private verbs' (for example 'feel'or 'love'), indicative of intimacy. Letters also do not have extensive lexical variations and generally use shorter words, featuring few nouns or prepositions. It is what Biber terms 'their affective interactional purpose' (1991: 132–3), however, which is most important for our consideration here.

The focus of this particular analysis is on evaluation, specifically as lexically visible in the use of adjectives. According to Thompson and

Hunston's (2000) foundational text on the subject, evaluation is important in linguistic study as it serves three main functions: (a) to express an opinion, (b) to construct and maintain relations and (c) to organise the discourse. The letters sent to Vesta abound with the writers' opinions and serve to reflect the value system within which they speak. In this process, the mere act of writing upsets the power balance between star and fan. The letter-writer and letter-reader have, Thompson and Hunston point out, two relationships; in this case, star and audience member and simultaneously discourse-producer and discourse-recipient (ibid: 11). As it transpires, this is especially apparent in this collection of letters. It is also important that the letters demonstrate a construction and maintenance of relations with Vesta, as they return her sentiments about them by echoing those same emotions with regards to her stage career. In the process they are also organising the discourse, by producing a text in which they are in control.

The semantic form used to uncover the evaluation in this quantitative analysis is that of affective adjectives. What follows serves as a pilot study for the usefulness of linguistic analysis for fan studies. The evaluative adjectives (as per Dixon's definition) in this collection of letters are: *great*, *good*, *happy*, *wonderful*, *old*, *sweet* and *sincere*. Where relevant, all degrees have been included – the positive, comparative and superlative. Thus, in looking at *great* and *good*, *greater* and *greatest* and *better* and *best* are also considered. Additionally, a term such as 'old' gains its affective meaning when coupled with another adjective, as in 'good old Vesta'. The results (see Table 10.1) are arranged into two categories: (a) those evaluative adjectives which refer to Vesta herself, and (b) those which refer to the letter writers and/or the audience more broadly.

What this table shows with its range of examples is a preference for ascribing evaluative terms to Vesta, though their own feelings have a strong showing as well. Here we can see how they are using evaluative language to express their opinions about Vesta's character and her performances. They are also positively evaluating the investment of time and resource, emotional and otherwise, in their engagement. They have sweet remembrances of happy days, they are sincere about their sentiments and devoted to Vesta. While helpful to note, this is perhaps not the most earth-shattering of conclusions. All of this might have readily been surmised from a qualitative analysis of a selection of the letters. What this methodology provides, in addition to the quantitative confirmation of the qualitative analysis, is something rather more interesting.

In considering Thompson and Hunston's third function of evaluative adjectives – setting the discourse – the results are cast in a rather different light. Looking again at the table, by far the greatest number of affective adjectives come from the 'good' category. The vast majority of these phrases relate to the writers' wishes for Vesta herself: 'good luck', 'good health', 'every good wish', 'best of everything always', and so on. It is for the letter writers to set this discourse, for them to dispense these wishes for Vesta

*Table 10.1* Affective adjectives

| Adjective | Vesta | Audience |
|---|---|---|
| Great/greater/greatest | 16<br>– great little lady<br>– the great kindness and good you have undertaken<br>– wishing you the greatest happiness | 38<br>– great admiration for you<br>– great pleasure of seeing you<br>– greatest thrill of my life |
| Good/better/best | 85<br>– good luck and health<br>– best that can be given to you<br>– best of everything always<br>– best woman | |
| Happy | 9<br>– a long happy life<br>– many happy years<br>– happy and healthy future | 19<br>– happy memories<br>– those happy days<br>– happy days of my girlhood |
| Wonderful | 11<br>– sweet wonderful self<br>– wonderful impersonations<br>– wonderful artist | |
| Old | 4<br>– good old Vesta<br>– dear old time Vesta | 13<br>– dear old city<br>– sincere old admirer<br>– sweet old song |
| Sweet | 10<br>– dear sweet lady<br>– your dear sweet face<br>– how sweet and dainty you were | 2<br>– sweet remembrances |
| Sincere | 6<br>– sincere wish<br>– sincere and loving wish | 10<br>– sincere admirer<br>– sincere regard<br>– sincere regrets |
| Total | 141 | 82 |

and they take that power. Thompson and Hunston (2000) highlight with reference to the work of John Sinclair that evaluation in a monologic text (one with a single narrator) clusters at boundary points. Many of the examples of evaluative language reflected in this table – the good/sincere wishes, the greatest happiness – come at a key boundary point: the closure of the letters. In this way, they answer the implicit 'so what?' of any narrative, the point of evaluation: 'so why are you writing?' (Labov, 1972). The 'so what' here, the purpose of the letters as a group is to bestow, in closing, those good wishes on Vesta. Particularly as she prepared to quit the stage at the end of her career, the end of the letters also functions as the closing of the interaction between this performer and her audience, for which the audience is now in control. If '[i]t is evaluation that enables monologic narrative to be interactive' (Thompson and Hunston, 2000: 13), the adjectives examined here produce just that. Significantly, in their use of these adjectives, the letters operate as texts that structurally insist on an interaction between peers.

## Conclusion

The concerns in this volume centre on the negotiations of relationships and flows of power between musicians and their audiences. Looking back to the nineteenth century these questions are just as alive in British music hall as they are in twenty-first-century jazz clubs, examined elsewhere within this collection of chapters. For instance, many of the letters written to Vesta Tilley apologise to her in their opening lines. Minnie Howard begins with, 'I hope you will pardon me writing to you' and Louisa Bramwell's letter starts 'I hope you will forgive me taking this privilege of writing you'. It could not be clearer that they recognised the imposition that their unsolicited letter might bring. However, the next word in both Minnie and Louisa's letters – 'but' – and the rest of the letter which followed produced a text which insisted on being taken as seriously as Vesta's recounting of her stage career in the *Empire News*. She was 'our Vesta', the girl who had made good in London and in America, who was immensely more successful than the vast majority of her Midlands-born peers, but still 'ours'. Qualitative analysis shows that the women who wrote to Vesta produced a relationship through sharing common experiences, most obviously in discussing the performances that they had witnessed in the halls and theatres around the country, but also in writing about their spouses, as she had done in the autobiography she had addressed to them. She might have been the star but they had made her so, and the making of her was the making of them. Additionally, however, there is the usefulness of considering a qualitative analysis. While letters such as the one by Mrs Cecilia Gilchrist who writes 'Please Excuse the Small v for i am off [sic] my wits End to know how to Make a large One' present women with apparently limited power in language, corpus-based linguistics offers us another lens. The use of linguistics – its corpus linguistics software, and its analysis – provides another way of seeing this power dynamic. Looking closely at the parts of speech in these letters, even where command of the English language is hampered by uneven opportunities for education, demonstrates how these women reached for and achieved an equal relationship through text. They controlled its production and they controlled their self-representation. Close reading of these letters show us how (publicly) important Vesta was to these women and how much power they gave to her. The use of linguistic tools allows us to see how her fans also insisted that they be important to her: their reach for parity legible in the language itself.

## Notes

1   According to Prochaska, '[a]ctive benevolence was most compelling to leisured women who were "compassionate" and "self-sacrificing" and who were traditionally skilled in caring for the young, the sick, the elderly, and the poor ... Many writers argued that it trained women to be better wives and mothers' (Prochaska, 1980: 7).

2   'In Liverpool they discovered where I was staying, and as it had been announced as my last appearance there previous to my going to America, about thirty of them came to the house at midnight to bid me goodbye' (Worcester collection 13801/1/4, p. 288).

3   Primary source material taken from Worcester County Council archives; all letters from their Vesta Tilley collection, 13801/1/13, with page and object number cited in text for letters, and page number for newspaper articles from the same series.

4   Men wrote to her as well and she kept many of those letters. However, since in press interviews she mainly focused on her female correspondents, and as the majority of the letters that she chose to keep were written by women, they are the focus of this study.

5   The financial constraints were only one concern for women being in attendance in the halls; Dagmar Kift draws the distinction between London and the provinces as the major difference (though there is of course much variation in the latter category) as in those centres where women were in public already due to employment outside the home, their presence in leisure spaces was much more readily accepted, and assumptions of dubious morality absent.

6   Vesta's father-in-law.

7   Many of the letter writing manuals of the nineteenth century copy extensively from one another, in the example letters used and sometimes also in the anecdotes conveyed. For example, *Hints on Letter Writing* (1841), *The Youth's Manual or Aids to Study* (1859), and *How to Write* (1864).

# 11  From secret fantasies to social systems

## Re-reading *Starlust* as a portrait of the dedicated popular music audience

*Mark Duffett*

It's not just him and his music, it's the way he involves his audience. And how the audience responds back to him and how people in the audience respond to each other. If someone cries during a particular song, someone, maybe a complete stranger, will put a reassuring hand on their shoulder. Everyone understands what everyone else is feeling. So it doesn't just come from him, it comes from the fans too – it's a combined effort.

(Barry Manilow fan in *Starlust* (Vermorel, 2011 [1985]: 130))

For years after its initial publication, Fred and Judy Vermorel's book *Starlust* (2011 [1985]) provided the main source material for academic discussions about popular music fandom. After considering the book's impact, this chapter uses it as a case study to compare three academic perspectives on dedicated audiences: the mass culture critique, notions of transformative work, and a neo-Durkheimian approach. In many ways, these three perspectives are distinct. Ideas related to mass culture tend to dismiss fans as dreamers, dupes and addicts swindled by commerce. In cultural studies, new ideas emerged in the 1990s to challenge this perception and reposition fans as members of a socially and politically engaged, resourceful community who routinely transform what is given to them by media producers. Neo-Durkheimian approaches provide an alternative explanation for fan behaviour that places emphasis on mutual understanding between fans and their heroes: a 'combined effort'. From this viewpoint, fandom and celebrity are different aspects of a larger psycho-social system that redistributes inter-personal attention in pleasurable ways. Durkheim's work can be used to hypothesize an affective motive for fan behaviour that contradict tenets of the mass culture critique and fill gaps in the transformative works paradigm. While the Vermorels' book prompted reviews guided by mass cultural thinking, this chapter explores the extent to which statements offered by *Starlust*'s contributors might be used to support a neo-Durkheimian perspective.

It is hard to over-estimate *Starlust*'s importance in the first two decades after it was written and its impact still resonates.[1] In 1997, Timothy Scheuer included it in his academic bibliography of 'The Best Books on Popular Music Since 1971'. Five years later, Tony Grajeda (2002: 250) claimed in the edited volume *Rock Over the Edge* that *Starlust* remained 'the key text on fandom'. In 2006, it was listed eighth in *Observer Music Monthly*'s '50 Greatest Music Books Ever' (Garfield, 2006). Faber and Faber published a Faber Finds reprint edition in 2011, and noted on their blog that the high profile music journalist Simon Reynolds had called it 'a lost classic of pop culture critique'.

The book's epistolary and fragmented contents offered a particular frame suggesting that readers were looking at the (almost) unmediated truth about fandom. Yet there is evidence that Vermorel's eight-year long process of data collection and selection heavily slanted the material.[2] Music critics, however, took the vignettes in *Starlust* as straight description and understood the book as a gripping combination of imaginative, resentful and disturbing empirical evidence. Robert Christgau (1995) for instance, said, 'In these mash notes gone bonkers, craven entreaties are often indistinguishable from empowered fantasies'. Jude Rogers (2012: 38) explained:

> [The] first [book] to tell me how obsessive the fan's inner life could get became my favourite – Fred and Judy Vermorel's jawdropping *Starlust*. Long out of print, and chock-full of interviews, answer-phone messages, questionnaires, diaries and dream journals, *Starlust* shows how murky, and mucky, fan fantasies can get. Many are saucy, some shocking, others unbearably sad.

In her review of the book excerpt that appeared in *The Adoring Audience*, Holly Kruse (1993: 206) elaborated: 'Fred and Judy Vermorel's compilation of fan letters written to stars like David Bowie and Barry Manilow is both fascinating and disturbing; the letters which appear to be written by the most deranged fans are also the most beautiful and poetic.' Because popular discourses conflated all fandom with a temptation to social pathology, *Starlust* was widely used to argue that popular music culture was characterized by atypical forms of behavior.

## *Starlust* and the mass culture critique

Between the 1930s and 1990s, various exponents of the mass culture critique promoted a negative image of media fandom in the public sphere (see Duffett, 2014a). It is important to understand that mass culture criticism often began from the Marxist premise that industrial practices – including media production – not only exploited communal resources but were also tools for governance. This premise was then aligned to elitist conceptions of culture that questioned the intellectual capacities of audiences for popular culture. As the most ardent fraction of these audiences, fans were dismissed as subservient consumers whose passions were, in effect, the end products of an industrial process. Commentators from a variety of perspectives drew repeatedly on common ideas to suggest that media consumers were dreamers, dupes and addicts – distracted, immature or insane individuals who were incapable of separating fantasy from reality and had an obsession with celebrity idols (see Jenkins, 1992: 11; Duffett, 2014a). They had relinquished their individual autonomy and begun to embrace irrational fads and fancies. Popular music phenomena were apprehended as manias: contagious public disorders in which overly excited females displayed a form of mass hysteria.[3] In *On the Fetish Character of Music*, for instance, Theodor Adorno distinguished between two broad types of music fan:

> Whenever they attempt to break away from the passive status of compulsory consumers and 'activate' themselves, they succumb to pseudoactivity. Types rise up from the mass of the retarded who differentiate themselves by pseudoactivity and nevertheless make the regression more strikingly visible. They are, first, the enthusiasts who write fan letters to radio stations and orchestras and, at well-managed jazz festivals, produce their own enthusiasm as an advertisement for the wares they consume. They call themselves jitterbugs, as if they simultaneously wanted to affirm and mock their loss of individuality, their transformation into beetles whirring around in fascination . . . The opposite type appears to be the eager person who leaves the factory and 'occupies' himself with music in the quiet of his bedroom. He is *shy and inhibited, perhaps has had no luck with girls, and wants in any case to preserve his own special sphere.* He seeks this as a radio ham. At twenty, he is still at the stage of a boy scout working on complicated knots to please his parents.
>
> (Adorno, 2001 [1938]: 52–3; emphasis mine)

In passages like this one, the mass culture critics used their polemics to suggest that fans were a group of infantilised, alienated individuals who were separated from cultural production and assembled in unstable crowds ('the mass of the retarded') to pursue attachments to simplistic cultural forms, interests that represented either a clinical obsession, an outpouring of repressed sexual energy, or a misguided way of seeking spiritual transcendence. Because of the emotional nature of their interests and the way that they entered the public sphere, pop and rock fans were an easy focus for mass cultural interpretations.

The Vermorels implicitly made two problematic arguments about the fans who contributed to *Starlust*. The first was that they were locked in a form of unrequited fantasy relationship. A focus on fan fantasies evokes the idea of fans as fantasists: people who preferred imagination to reality, and are, perhaps, lost in the throes of imagined relationships with idealized celebrity figures not physically there for them. In this formulation, solipsistic spectators fall for the social cues offered by their heroes and start believing in an imagined personal relationship. This idea was formulated by the psychiatrists Donald Horton and Richard Wohl, who argued that broadcast media provided the 'illusion' of a face-to-face relationship with the performer: 'We propose to call this seeming face-to-face relationship between spectator and performer a *para-social relationship*' (1956: 215; emphasis in original). In *Starlust*, Fred Vermorel invited music fans to discuss their sexual fantasies. Reviewing the book, Vermorel (2008) explained that '*Starlust* was about what happens when fans take stars' sexual advances literally'.

Second, mass cultural thinking did not just influence the book's compilation. It also permeated the responses of contributors. One area in which fans seemed to be adopting mass cultural assumptions was in assuming that their relationships with celebrities were unrequited. Such assumptions implied that fans' lives were based on daydreams, delusions and fantasies, and that they focused on imagined relationships to compensate for a personal inadequacy. Vermorel reported in the book's afterword:

> To begin with we were astonished by the degree of *hostility and aggression*, spoken and unspoken, shown by fans towards stars. Later we realized this was one necessary consequence of such *unconsummated*, unconsumable passion . . . Pop is a frustration machine. And one of its most interesting mechanisms is the tension between the star's incitement of desire and passion (not to mention hysteria) and the bureaucratic and ideological apparatus erected to protect stars from the consequences of this incitement.
>
> (Vermorel, 2011 [1985]: 249; emphasis mine)

However, hostile responses from fans towards their heroes were neither quite as common nor as intense in *Starlust* as one might have expected from such claims. Sometimes there were resentful statements, such as this one from a Bowie fan:

> And you do, because you're absolutely gullible. It's almost pathetic that kind of idol thing. But then he was extraordinary and he deserved all that idolatry, even though he's probably laughing now. So I don't regret any of the money I spent or any of the things I used to do, the obsessions I had. I think it was part and parcel of what I am now. I'd like to talk to him about it some time, I really would . . . I just wonder if he doesn't think that everyone's a sucker. He's riding the crest of a wave and he's a legend . . . I actually believed that I could have a relationship with him. This was his influence and it was rather damaging. And I think he's so detached now from what he's done to people that he doesn't realize in all his wealth how he's influenced them. Because he's actually walked away from them

and has lived a life of cream because we've allowed him to. It's a terrible thing he did really. He's got a lot to answer for.

(Vermorel, 2011 [1985]: 107–8)

One way to read such responses is that the fans themselves would sometimes use the mass culture paradigm as a discursive resource to speak to outsiders or interrogate their passions. The issue here is that the parasocial relationship is a theoretical artefact of mass culture thinking rather than actual behaviour. It is evident that ordinarily fans were not *stuck* in a parasocial bind, mistaking fantasy for reality. As one fan explained of Michael Jackson, 'Having his posters, having his records is not really as good as the real thing'. (Vermorel, 2011 [1985]: 46)

## Transformative works perspectives

*Starlust* can alternatively be framed from the perspective of an active or 'producerly' fandom. This approach has emerged from the work of Henry Jenkins, who, inspired by his mentor John Fiske, wrote a book in 1992 called *Textual Poachers*. Jenkins contested *Starlust* for the way that it duplicitously claimed to represent the authentic voices of music fans and at the same time voyeuristically offered up their emotions to its readers as a form of spectacle. In the paradigm pursued by Jenkins, fans were portrayed as creative, productive and networked individuals. *Textual Poachers* for example showed how fans of the TV show *Miami Vice* (1984–1989) edited together their own videos of the series. According to Jenkins, these video reworkings both commented on the original series and helped to bond the fan community. They were simultaneously a testament to the dedication of the people who made them and an expression of the fan community's mutual interests, shared understandings and collective fantasies (Jenkins, 1992: 248–9).

Before the internet era, such fan videos were, in effect, *new* narrative art forms. While official music videos for *Miami Vice* emphasized the consumer dream of driving through the city, fan-edited footage focused more on the bond between the two male leads (see Jenkins, 1992: 234). In effect the show was re-imagined as a soap opera that explored camaraderie. Jenkins showed that fans could appropriate the products of commercial culture for their own ends. To do that they created new meanings, discourses and cultures across a range of phenomena from 'filking' (making up folk songs whose lyrics referred to their favourite texts) to slash fiction (erotic stories about intimacy between male characters). In an age of social media, Jenkins has taken his approach to the active audience further by exploring the ways that fans participate in community networks to enhance their pleasures, promote their interests, and pursue forms of political activism. The strand of research into ardent audiences inspired by his concepts and interests could broadly be called a *Transformative Works* approach.[4]

Jenkins' emphasis on communal and 'producerly' activity – from fiction writing to fan art – finds its own reflection in a few of the accounts in *Starlust*. Some of the fans talk in the book about their fandom as a pretext for socializing. One of them says, 'So my life is very Barry orientated, from corresponding with other fans, meeting friends locally, to arranging functions, planning for concerts, conventions, etc, etc' (Vermorel, 2011 [1985]: 189). Equally, rather than dismissing fans' imaginative statements as compensatory fantasies, they can be seen as creative real person fiction. For example, one Adam Ant fan wrote about her ideal show:

> I am at an Ants gig with a couple of my mates and I somehow wander away from them . . . I see a lot of other punkettes [who] have noticed and are really randy for the sexy bastard, just like me! But he isn't eyeing them up. He's looking at me.
>
> (Vermorel, 2011 [1985]: 77)

Despite such examples, fanfic and fan networks are not the focus of many of the entries in *Starlust*. We are invited to read the correspondence as personal fantasies from individuals, not texts aiming to create connections between different members of a community. In other words, the epistles in *Starlust* seem to be expressions of personal identities rather than letters from people interested in receiving recognition from fan communities. It is not necessarily the case that the fans contributing to *Starlust* were individualistic or apolitical, but – with the exception of some imaginative written contributions – the book did not generally demonstrate ways in which fans were remaking the cultural forms that they consumed.

## Neo-Durkheimian approaches

*Starlust* can be interpreted in a way that does not succumb to the objectionable elistism of the mass culture paradigm or focus on fan productivity at the expense of fan motivation. Émile Durkheim's combined notions of effervescence and totemism may help us understand why fans get excited by real or imagined interactions with prominent performers.

Durkheim examined the social ecology of Australian clans who practiced idol worship in his classic 1912 book *Elementary Forms of Religious Life*. His account was premised on the idea that the spiritual realm was set apart from ordinary life and deemed sacred. Durkheim's research then described how the emotional charge of the collective is expressed in these sacred spaces through individual excitation, something he called 'effervescence'. He argued that 'The very fact of assembling is an exceptionally powerful stimulant. Once individuals are assembled, their proximity generates a certain kind of electricity that quickly transports them to an extraordinary degree of exaltation' (2008 [1912]: 162). This electricity was only part of Durkheim's understanding of religion, however:

By gathering together almost always at fixed times, collective life could indeed achieve its maximum intensity and efficacy [i.e. effervescence], and give a man a more vivid sense of his dual existence and his dual nature [i.e. transport him into and out of a sacred realm]. *But this explanation is still incomplete.* We have shown how the clan awakens in its members the idea of external forces that dominate and exalt them. But we have yet to understand how these forces were conceived in the form of the totemic species, that is, as an animal or plant.

(ibid: 165)

Durkheim realized that each tribe had a totem – an animal, plant, person or object – which mediated the emotional charge of the collective. In a section on the 'genesis of the totemic principle' he explained that 'Within a crowd moved by common passion, we become susceptible to feelings and actions of which we were incapable on our own' (ibid: 157). As he further elaborated:

By definition, it [the totem] is shared by everyone. During the ceremony, all eyes are upon it ... Because religious force is nothing but the collective and anonymous force of the clan, and because this *can be imagined only in the form of the totem*, the totemic emblem is like the visible body of god. Therefore it seems to be the source of actions, benevolent or dreaded, which the cult's purpose is to invoke or prevent.

(ibid: 166; emphasis mine)

Totemic religion is therefore a thrilling belief system accepted by those who assume energy moves from the collective *through* its leader, back towards each follower. Since the totem has a mediating role, he or she is also energized by participating in the social process. In Durkheim's words:

This unusual surplus of forces is quite real: it comes to him from the very group he is addressing. The feelings provoked by his speech return to him inflated and amplified, reinforcing his own. The passionate energies he arouses echo back to him and increase his vitality. He is no longer a simple individual speaking, *he is a group incarnate and personified.*

(ibid: 158; emphasis mine)

If the totem's role in transforming collective attention determines its social significance, its role as 'the body of god' is made meaningful by suggesting that the totem occupies the boundary between the sacred realm and daily life. The totem occupies a leading role precisely because he or she both symbolizes the powerful force of the collective (in an 'energetic' sense) and governs the boundary between the sacred and the secular (in a semiotic one). Whoever comes into contact with him or her gets magically and contagiously connected to the source: the energy of the collective expressed as something sacred. Individual followers experience this as a jolt of effervescence through their contact with the totem. Partaking of this social energy not only offers a mood-raising personal boost. Shared beliefs, values and behaviour emerge from the communal experience of effervescence and in turn act to maintain the social system. Durkheim's work on religion therefore sees through divine mystery and finds human sociology.

Attention to Durkheim's theory raises the issue of its relevance beyond tribal religion. The sociologist himself argued that religious assembly was not the only means of creating heightened emotion. Citing the events of the French Revolution as an example, he described secular instances of 'general effervescence' (ibid: 158). Celebrities occupy the centre of media spectacles and generate heightened emotions in the public sphere, but their performances are often produced through alienating technology (caught on audio or video recording). If we want to understand the strength of fan connections as part of a Durkheimian symbolic economy, then we must first recognize that contemporary social 'tribes' find their collectivity reflected through such apparatuses.[5] We do not, of course, need to be in the middle of a live crowd to recognize our participation in collective life. Notions such as 'the mass audience' and 'the fan base' enable that recognition, while – from music chart positions to Twitter following figures – statistical measures diagnose its magnitude.

A variety of post-war scholars have commented on Durkheim's work (see Pickering, 2009 [1984]). Two rather sparse scholarly traditions have applied Durkheim's ideas to popular music. On one hand, there are researchers schooled in theology or religious studies who have been applying Durkheimian concepts to social phenomena that appear secular and to them in some ways also resemble religious practice (see Partridge, 2014 and Jennings, 2014). Their scholarship attempts to faithfully apply Durkheim's original notion of sacredness to music fandom as a ritualistic, neo-religious practice of sanctification. On the other hand, Durkheim's original work has been drawn upon more loosely or modified by a small number of scholars such as Martin (1979) and Riley (2005) to fit the music fans whom they are studying. Neo-Durkheimian approaches begin from the assumption that the symbolic economy of fandom is a generative phenomenon: for fans who feel a connection, commercial music has a 'magical' ability to create realms of affective experience because it facilitates the redistribution of human attention. My own work has been of that latter type because, I suggest, Durkheim's thought was not originally designed to understand commercial popular music culture.[6] It therefore has limitations. For example, mainstream rock and pop music is generally created for secular not 'sacred' sociological uses, and fans are not a clan of 'worshippers'.[7] We should be aware that, if a religious vocabulary is used indiscriminately, it might cast fans in a particular light (Duffett, 2015). This does not mean, however, that researchers should ignore how celebrity performers play key roles in economies that redistribute attention in very particular ways. Stripping Durkheim's schema down to the singular mechanism of effervescence allows us to create as a hypothesis that has little to do with religiosity or sacredness, but everything to do with the affective resonances experienced in pop fandom as a specific cultural field. Durkheimian ideas can therefore be used as a working hypothesis or template from which to examine fan phenomena. Fan comments in Vermorel's compilation not only indicate that there is evidence to support a neo-Durkheimian reading, but pursuing such a reading also allows us to illuminate *Starlust's* fan contributions in new ways. I will demonstrate these two claims in the next part of this section.

Effervescence depends on recognizing oneself as part of a larger collective. The first challenge was therefore to find instances of fans who understood that they were participating in a larger social experience.[8] In *Starlust*, Barry Manilow fans in particular emphasized that they had collective unity as a fan base. For example:

> Because I've been to lots and lots of concerts, but I've never felt that kind of atmosphere and that kind of closeness. Complete strangers catch hold of your hands. And you are united, united as one. And to think that one man can do that to so many people. I mean, he must be special to be able to do that, to create this atmosphere and this special feeling. He can't be ordinary, can he? So many people can't be wrong.
>
> (Vermorel, 2011 [1985]: 18–19)

It is important to point out here that comments such as this one are relatively typical of celebrity orientated music fan bases in general. The fact that in *Starlust* they most often come from Barry Manilow fans is quite possibly, I think, an artefact of the Vermorels' diverse methods of data collection.

Second, the entries in *Starlust* reflect fans' desires to give attention to, and receive attention from, their favourite performers. These expressions of desire indicate the role played by 1980s pop heroes and supply further evidence of a fit with neo-Durkheimian thinking. For example, according to one Nick Heyward fan:

> There you were right in front of us. I just couldn't stop screaming and calling your name. I went all hot and cold and I felt completely drained. The moment I had been waiting for two years had finally arrived. I screamed your name. You looked at me and smiled. (I know you smiled at me because you looked straight at me.) Well, at that point I went crazy. It was like a dream.
>
> (Vermorel, 2011 [1985]: 132)

The concern for attention was not unusual. Another fan, this time of Boy George, explained: 'On my way in on the train I listen on the little stereo headphones. Listening like that makes me feel better. Makes me feel he's singing it to me, that he's thinking of me' (Vermorel, 2011 [1985]: 60). A David Bowie fan recalled a live show, saying, 'At one point during the song "Breaking Glass" he points to a member of the audience who then has a pointing match with him. And that was me at one of the gigs – we were pointing at each other' (Vermorel, 2011 [1985]: 63).

When fans get near their heroes, their exchange of attention creates thrilling jolts of social electricity and feelings of heightened emotion that are, in effect, manifestations of effervescence. Affirming neo-Durkheimian expectations, they occur at precisely the point when the fan feels a personal connection to the performance. One fan of the female performer Nena recalled:

> When Nena first touched me it felt like a current passed through my arm. My body had come into contact with the star. The star and you, you've both had a point in your lives where you've been together. That's how it felt for me. You've had that one moment.
>
> (Vermorel, 2011 [1985]: 135)

Similar responses happened to fans of other artists. A follower of the group Classix Nouveaux described a close encounter with her hero: 'I thanked him and as I set next to him, my leg touching his, it was like electricity. I felt excited by his nearness' (Vermorel, 1985 [2011]: 114). Interactions did not have to be absolutely proximate for fans to feel different; they only have to be *closer*. After all, being in the same (big) room as one's favourite musician at a live event is a moment of increased intimacy and mutual participation. One satisfied Police fan recalled, 'I was on cloud nine after the concert for about three weeks. I couldn't come down . . . That night after the concert I lay in bed shivering and shuddering. I kept thinking: "God, it was brilliant!"' (Vermorel 1985 [2011]: 162).

So far, we have seen examples of the way in which fan statements in *Starlust* have affirmed motives for interaction with pop stars that can easily be accounted for within a neo-Durkheimian framework. Taking things further, we can use that framework to offer a fresh perspective on particular aspects of fan behaviour. I will support this claim in two ways: by thinking about fan anxiety and fan mail. The practice of pop fandom at live events is not simply a matter of getting excited. For some it can contain an undercurrent of anxiety too. This undercurrent cannot be fully accounted for the perspective of the mass cultural critique, which dismisses fans as hysterical, but can also assume to the contrary that they are passive or lost in fantasy. In contrast, the neo-Durkheimian model offers a stronger explanation: because the totemic person is so socially valued by his or her fans, the possibility of a meeting can be both exciting *and* provoke anxiety. Almost all fans are absolutely thrilled with the prospect, but – rather like having stage fright – they can also be anxious that they might be rejected. Sally, a Kajagoogoo fan observed:

You get this knot in your stomach and with the beat of the music your chest starts to pound. It's just amazing. A great feeling. You're on such a high, you really are, just the atmosphere around you. Then you come out into the cold night air and then it's finished. You just feel empty, like you've used all your energy up. You just feel weak. Then you come home. You get into bed and your ears are ringing. They hurt sometimes, your ears, from the noise.

(Vermorel, 2011 [1985]: 131)

In effect, then, the book offers ample evidence that forms of music fandom centring on celebrity-following involve a shared socio-cultural process that redistributes attention from the fan base, through the performer, back to individual fans. Attention to totemism helps us to understand a whole raft of fan comments that indicate insecurities and anxieties in relation to favourite performers. On one hand, we can now see why pop stars are immensely significant to their fans. On the other, dedicated followers recognize that the chance of meeting their hero and establishing a meaningful relationship is slim. Framing *Starlust* in this way, we can also examine the fan mail that forms much of the book and understand it as a process of *audition* in which fans individually attempt to attract their star's attention. Since many fans make declarations of desperation that have a kind of beseeching function in fan mail, the medium should not be taken as objectively reflecting tormented states of mind. Instead it is a special kind of writing, adroitly crafted for maximum psychological impact in service of its aim to make a personal connection with the star. As one Nick Heyward fan lamented: 'I hope that soon you will reply to one of my letters. It's a terrible feeling when you're ignored, you know!' (Vermorel, 1985 [2011]: 32).

The notion of it being 'a terrible feeling when you're ignored' raises another issue. Fans contributing to *Starlust* had limited discursive resources available to explain their own behaviour. In this final part of the section, I will discuss the relationship between popular interpretational frameworks offered by the mass culture critique and the motives for fan behaviour suggested by neo-Durkheimian theory. I wish to suggest that a particular approach was sometimes manifested in *Starlust* whereby fans frame their patterns of behaviour by referring to mass cultural ideas when they are in fact consistent with neo-Durkheimian motivations. We should not be surprised at this finding, as mass culture ideas dominated the public sphere for many decades, and to some extent still do (see Hills, 2012).[9] Since neo-Durkheimian approaches are only just now emerging within academia, they were simply not available in the public sphere. While the pop fans in *Starlust* saw their stars as important people and wanted to get closer to them, some had also accepted a key assumption from parasocial interaction theory that they were alone in the world and their heroes were forever separated from them. One David Bowie fan said, 'I wouldn't like to go through life and think he was never aware of who I was' (Vermorel, 2011 [1985]: 86). A Michael Jackson fan said, similarly:

> It seems unreal, but it's not. It's reality. Because he's living at the moment. He's alive that very second. And I think: What's he doing? And then it really gets to me. It makes me cry because it's so impossible. And I know what it is never to be able to talk to him.
>
> (Vermorel, 2011 [1985]: 45)

This fan believes that she and Michael Jackson are two individuals who live in discrete and painfully distant private worlds. Implicitly, the media industry has lured her into a trap in which the intimacy she desires with Michael can never actually be. It is important to understand this kind of existential, melancholic thinking as reflecting mass cultural assumptions because the fan laments the lost possibility of a 'real' relationship with her hero, rather than understanding her fandom in other ways: as a vital part of a shared conversation, as an opportunity to enter a vast community, as an ethical inspiration, as a training ground for acquiring new skills, as a therapeutic tool, or even as a means of simply amassing knowledge and understanding about another individual in the same way that we do about everybody – including those who are intimate with us rather than remote. Instead of her fandom being understood as any of those things, the fan uses mass cultural thinking as a kind of communicative platform from which to share her predicament. In sum, neo-Durkheimian theoretical approaches can quite accurately predict patterns of fan behaviour but cannot necessarily tell us how people will view their fannish practices, identities or motivations.

There is a final issue here that warrants some discussion. The fact that fans can simultaneously pursue totemic interests and adopt socially accepted mass culture assumptions suggests that the mass culture critique can also, knowingly or unknowingly, be levered by fans themselves. Those who wish to express their own pathologies can draw on popular views of media fandom as an alibi. Many of the discussions about the book mentioned a Barry Manilow fan called Rosie as their key example. In *Starlust*, Rosie claimed that she did not sleep with her own husband as she felt 'unclean' with any man except Barry (Vermorel, 2011 [1985]: 80). From the perspective of the mass culture critique, thoughts of encounters with powerful, socially valued pop stars are framed as lustful temptations to reject one's normal (civilized) ethics. In contrast, Neo-Durkheimian readings pinpoint that the force drawing fans toward stars is not something mysterious or destructive, perhaps not even a cathartic escape from sexual repression. Instead such readings suggest that celebrities matter because they their performances have drawn enough attention to them to make them socially valuable. Such thinking questions the idea that fans are blinded by love into believing that they fully know (or, worse, think that they are already with) the apparently inaccessible objects of their attention. It does not assume

Manilow is the sole reality in the lives of his dedicated fans, but it does suggest that he is a popular, important and appealing person. Crucially, it also says that when fans are fascinated by their stars, they are not tempted to reject the various forms of sociability around them. Instead they ordinarily acquire values that support the star and maintain a positive picture of his fan base. Many of Barry Manilow's fans pay him attention and offer their love and support, but from this perspective Rosie's confession of deep romantic 'love' for Barry is atypical insofar as it actually functions as way to excuse her own fear of intimacy. Parasocial interaction theory assumed that interest in celebrities substituted for 'real' social interactions. Drawing on such thinking, mass culture critique arguments cast Rosie as a case example of fan culture's potential dangers. On the contrary, however, although Barry Manilow fans may go to great lengths to meet him or watch him perform, their urges have nothing to do with whether or not they sleep with their spouses.

In conclusion, although reviews of *Starlust* in the 1980s and 1990s portrayed pop fans as having lives characterized by twisted fantasies and unhealthy obsessions, with the benefit of hindsight it is possible to re-interpret contributions to the book from other angles. Examining *Starlust* as a source text from the world of 1980s pop culture, my own theoretically informed rereading has enabled the comparison, contrasting and mutual situation of three different academic approaches: the mass culture critique, transformative works paradigm and neo-Durkheimian perspective. To deal with each of these in turn, within the shared context of the mass culture critique, a limited stock of explanations was available to music enthusiasts. As a way to access wider audiences, many of the Vermorels' respondents therefore interrogated their actions by using mass cultural assumptions. It is evident that a tiny minority of contributors used accepted notions of pop fandom as a means to play out their own insecurities and pathologies. In contrast to this, other fans pursued creative and imaginative writing experiments inspired by their fan passions.[10] Such projects that can be framed as examples of fannish transformative labour. While there were elements of 'producerly' fandom at play in the fan responses in *Starlust*, the transformative works paradigm has relatively little to say about fan motivations. There were, in contrast, signs that celebrity-following music fans were motivated by the emotional rewards described by a neo-Durkheimian analysis. Fans were thrilled by the thought of close attention from their heroes. Attention to this particular thesis – which hypothesizes that fandom is about participation in a shared symbolic economy based on totemic interest – offers us a way to begin exploring fan rationality and therefore separating *ordinary* desires to follow celebrities from the ways that eccentric individuals can lever established expectations about fandom to express their own personal quirks and insecurities. It offers a different perspective on the passions of Vermorel's 1980s pop enthusiasts.

## Notes

1   Excerpts were reprinted in influential edited volumes such as Simon Frith and Andrew Goodwin's *On Record* (1991), Lisa Lewis's *The Adoring Audience* (1992), and Hanif Kureishi and John Savage's *Faber Book of Pop* (1996). The book was widely referenced in academic work on celebrity and fandom by writers such as Chris Rojek (2007: 171), Nick Couldry (2003: 86), Henry Jenkins (1992: 15), Matt Hills (2002) and Cornel Sandvoss (2005). In popular music studies, *Starlust* was referenced by Mavis Bayton (1997: 40), appeared in Roy Shuker's textbook *Understanding Popular Music* (1994: 214) and was discussed several times in detail by Simon Frith (see Frith and Horne, 1987: 170; Frith, 1988: 165–7 and 1998: 329).

2   One of the formative theoretical influences on *Starlust* was Jacob Goldstein and Hans Toch's 1956 article about 'eccentric' fan mail sent to the United Nations. Vermorel (2014: 87) said that the article was 'not shy about the ambivalence and "dirty" aspects of such communication'.

3   See Chapter 8 by Richard Osborne in the present volume.

4   Since 2008, contributors to the online journal *Transformative Works and Cultures* have been pursuing the study of media fan practices in ways broadly proposed by Henry Jenkins.

5   Maffesoli (1996) discusses the concept of contemporary social 'tribes'. I use the term more loosely here to mean fan bases.

6   See, for instance, Duffett (2015).

7   What I am suggesting here is really that even if the term 'sacred' registers the affective charge of fan objects, it has been too loosely adopted by some theorists (see Duffett, 2003). There are, of course, exceptions to the idea that popular music is not sacred, such as the gospel tradition and Christian music. These need more investigation in relation to totemism.

8   On the development of social cohesion and collectivity among audiences, see Bradby's, Johnson's and Pace's chapters in this volume.

9   Elsewhere I have contrasted parasocial interaction and neo-Durkheimian approaches (see Duffett, 2014b).

10  For a discussion of fans' letters historically, see Nancy Bruseker's chapter in this volume.

# Afterword

## 'Moved to the point where she could no longer contain herself': Ellington and audience interaction at the Newport Jazz Festival

*Walter van de Leur*

A famous incident in jazz history may serve to show the value of the work done in *Musicians and their Audiences*. It is the story of Duke Ellington and his Orchestra at the Newport Jazz Festival, July 7, 1956, a wealthy summer retreat at Rhode Island. At the time, jazz festivals were a fairly new phenomenon, and in 1956 Newport saw the third annual rendition of its outdoor event. As with most music festivals, people were partly drawn to Newport for the overall experience, for the event as such, and not necessarily for Ellington. In fact, the popularity of big bands was on the decline: their heyday had been from the mid-1930s to the end of the Second World War. Big bands played dance music for swing dancing teenagers and that had been the key to their success. But swing dancing, and consequently the accompanying music, got replaced by other genres; such is the fate of teenage culture. In the 1950s, youngsters danced to rock 'n' roll, while many of Ellington's one-time fans were raising kids and watching TV in the rapidly expanding suburbs. Reportedly, his orchestra had been operating at a loss for the better part of the early-1950s; many of his contemporaries had been forced out of the music business.

That night at Newport, Ellington would reconnect with his audience in a now legendary concert. The music was (partly) issued on what would be his best-selling LP-record (*Ellington at Newport*), and re-issued in full on a CD that claimed to deliver the real thing, without the 'non-musical shenanigans that include tons of overdubbed, phony applause.' The event furthermore led to a monograph dedicated to the concert, John Fass Morton's *Backstory in Blue: Ellington at Newport '56*. Such was its importance that Ellington would maintain for the remainder of his life: 'I was born in Newport in 1956' (Morton, 2008: 6).

The relevance of 'Newport '56' to the present volume is that, for the first time in the historiography of the orchestra, the active role of the audience was recognized and made part of the narrative. In fact, the larger share of the original liner notes serves to underline that the success of the concert relied on the 'support of the crowd', in general, and one audience member in particular.

That night, Ellington started to perform around 11:45 pm, after an earlier failed attempt because four key band members had gone missing. The band opened with its signature theme, Strayhorn's *Take the 'A' Train*, after which the Ellingtonians segued into a newly composed, longer work, titled *Newport Jazz Festival Suite* (co-written by Ellington and Strayhorn, see Van de Leur, 2002). Two more numbers later it was well past midnight and part of the audience, apparently not too taken by what had been offered so far, was heading for the parking lot. Then, Ellington called for *Diminuendo and Crescendo in Blue*, a two-part work from the 1930s which had recently developed into a feature for his star-tenorist Paul Gonsalves. On the road, Gonsalves had started to bridge the two movements with a lengthy solo over the blues, with just rhythm section accompaniment. At Newport, the band went into the same routine, and that's where the concert became an 'epic moment in American cultural history', as the blurb on Morton's book informs the reader.

While Ellington's rhythm section – Jimmy Woode, bass and Sam Woodyard, drums – provided a driving background of swinging blues, Gonsalves embarked on a string of deeply inspired solo-choruses that built in intensity. According to the liner notes of the original LP, 'at about the seventh chorus, the tension, which had been building both on-stage and in the audience ... broke. A platinum blonde girl in a black dress began dancing in one of the boxes (the last place you'd expect that in Newport).' In the words of Clark Terry,

> as this begins to build, some gorgeous voluptuous lady in the audience, decided that she was being moved to the point where she could no longer contain herself, so she jumped up on the stage and started to allowing herself to be flounced around a bit. And Ellington kind of liked that, and it inspired him, and he in turn inspired the band ... and Sam Woodyard started pounding a little heavier, so things began to build up to a real frenzy.
>
> (Burns, 2001)

The remaining spectators began to cheer her on, while others followed her example and started to dance as well, drawing further shouts from the crowd. As the noise started to rise from the festival grounds, some of those on the way out returned to their seats. The woman, immortalized with a picture on the back of the record sleeve, captioned 'the girl who launched 7,000 cheers' (Avakian, 1956), was Elaine Anderson. With her dancing, Anderson became a *trait-d'union* between the band and the audience, as her movements visually translated what was sonically coming from the stage. As such, she made herself part of the overall performance and became instrumental in what transpired next. 'Everybody crowded around to see the dancing of this woman,' festival producer George Wein reminisced (Burns, 2001). Photographs show that the audience indeed was cheering her on while looking at Anderson rather than at the band.

Fully in the flow, Gonsalves continued to play. When he was done he had completed an astonishing 27 choruses. As the story goes, by then the crowd was so heated up, that festival producer George Wein feared that things might spin out of control and wanted Ellington to stop (in fact, the audience only protested when Wein tried to get the band off stage later). Understandably, Ellington would have nothing of it and continued playing to an elated audience. The story got out quickly that the performance had been a sensation: 'within an hour, reporters and critics were buzzing about it' (Avakian, 1956).

Since the band had been under-rehearsed at the concert, the *Newport Jazz Festival Suite* was recorded again two days later in the studio (Heaney, 2002), at the behest of Ellington. Columbia Records producer George Avakian understood that the record's success would rely on the buzz surrounding the performance and saw to it that the studio recordings were doctored to bring the audience back in ('the phony applause'). Clearly, the ambiance created by the crowd and the enticing story of the young beautiful woman whose dancing inspired both band and public were part of the experience for the (mostly male) record buying public too. To great effect, since the record sold better than any other Ellington LP, even though it did not contain his most accessible music. Furthermore, the extended Gonsalves section drew on the improvised blues which, in the context of the usually highly pre-charted music of Ellington, was only partly representative of his style.

Phil Schaap, the producer of the 1999 *Ellington at Newport 1956 (Complete)*, takes issue with the original recording, which he sees as a hybrid of 'studio recordings with bits of Newport reality' that does not present the concert 'as performed'. In pretty loaded language ('post-production goosing of the audio', 'transmogrified with scripted announcements', 'marred initial releases') Schaap subscribes to romantic fantasies of the unmediated, spontaneous and authentic performance that can be captured on tape as is. It becomes somewhat hilarious when later in his liner notes Schaap explains how two separate mono recordings of that night, one made by the Voice of America, and the other by Columbia engineers, were painstakingly synchronized to create post-production stereo for the reissue. In keeping with the by now historical status of the concert, the reissue feeds into the mythology of the near-riot that broke out, with track titles such as 'Announcements, Pandemonium' (disc 1, track 20), 'Duke Calms Crowd' (disc 2, track 4; Ellington merely announces Ray Nance) and 'Riot Prevention' (disc 2, track 6). In the end, the two record projects, even though more than 40 years apart, differ less than Schaap wants us to believe. Like the original Columbia LP, the reissue fits the recording into the overarching narrative of how Ellington, with the help of a young woman, won back his audience overnight.

The significance of *Musicians and their Audiences* is that it provides us with tools to unpack the complex and layered cultural encounters between performers and their audiences, as exemplified by Ellington at Newport. Most jazz histories duly note that the music's legacy is partly to be found in Africa – where music is a group effort and the boundaries between music and dance, and performers and audiences, are permeable, if not non-existent – to happily embark on linear 'great men' historiography. This volume invites us to rethink how the different roles of the various actors in music are forged, what ideologies are at play, and how such roles may shift. In the stories surrounding Ellington at Newport, some tried-and-true tropes and binaries pop up, which revolve around gender, class, age and race. A young, beautiful, upper-class, white woman (or 'girl') becomes possessed by the music of black, middle-aged jazzmen. Both the original record and the reissue show pictures of an enchanted Anderson, hair flinging, mouth open, eyes shut, hands in the air. It is not the complex, composed music (the suite) that Ellington has brought to the festival that transfixes her, but the swinging blues (deemed more authentic) played by an equally possessed Gonsalves. With her dancing, Anderson channels the music to the audience. It had lost its interest in the concert, but is offered a way to understand the performance in a new manner. Consequently, in true romantic fashion, the orchestra which was close to folding, emerges in triumph.

The ensuing debate is about authenticity, about who can claim ownership of the performance and who has wrongfully appropriated it. Schaap, for one, subscribes to the old hierarchical models and power structures in music production, where Ellington is the mastermind: 'Duke put it all together in a single stroke' (Schaap, 1999). His view reduces this rich interaction to the work of a single author where actually many participated. All present played different yet significant roles in shaping the event and its aftermath, from Ellington and his orchestra to Gonsalves, from the festival and its producer Wein to the recording engineers and Columbia producer Avakian, from the dancers in the audience to the record-buying public.

When Elaine Anderson passed away in 2004, the Boston Globe obituary mentioned that 'she made her mark in jazz by dancing near the stage as Duke Ellington's band performed at the Newport Jazz Festival in 1956' (Levene, 2004). The piece refers to her as an 'ex-dancer', even though Anderson danced publicly only once: by July 9, 1956 her dancing career was over. To Ellington, there was no doubt that *Newport* was a collaborative effort. As Anderson remembered, 'in later years, I attended a concert [of sacred music] in Grace Cathedral [in 1965] at the invitation of Duke Ellington and he admitted that I was the force that put his band back on the Jazz Map at that time' (Heany, 2002).

# Bibliography

Abbott, J. 2012 Has David Guetta been caught faking it? *Mixmag*. 13 August 2012. http://staging.mixmag.net/words/news/has-david-guetta-been-caught-faking-it. Accessed 20 August 2012.

Adorno, T. 2001 [1938] On the fetish-character of music and the regression of listening. In *The Culture Industry: Selected Essays on Mass Culture*. New York: Routledge.

Advisory Editors. 2005 Can we get rid of the 'popular' in popular music? A virtual symposium with contributions from the International Advisory Editors of *Popular Music. Popular Music*, Vol. 24, No. 1, pp. 133–145.

Ajana, B. 2004 Disembodiment and cyberspace: a phenomenological approach. *Electronic Journal of Sociology*, Vol. 7.

Alamango, A. 2000 Etnika, *Sunday Times of Malta*. 27 August, p. 63.

Alamango, A. 2013 Etnika – Żifna. https://filflarecordsmusic.bandcamp.com/album/etnika-ifna. Accessed 11 November 2014.

Allagui, I., J. Kuebler, et al. 2011 Feature: the Arab Spring and the role of ITCs. *International Journal of Communication*, Vol. 5, pp. 1435–1442.

*Amsterdam Editor*. 2013 Red Bull Music Academy FT. Henrik Schwarz. *Red Bull Studios Network*. 27 June 2013. www.redbullstudios.com/articles/red-bull-music-academy-session-ft-henrik-schwarz-0. Accessed 27 February 2015.

Angouri, J. and R. Wodak. 2014 'They became big in the shadow of the crisis': The Greek success story and the rise of the far right. *Discourse & Society*, Vol. 25 No. 4, pp. 540–565.

Anonymous. 2012a Music review: Van Morrison. *Belfast Music*, 7 February. www.belfastmusic.org/article/4748/music-review-van-morrison. Accessed 6 February 2014.

Anonymous. 2012b Posa dilonoun oi star tis pistas (The declared income of the music stars). *Ta Nea Newspaper*, 10 September.

Anonymous. 2013 The Barrakka lift. http://vassallohistory.wordpress.com/the-barrakka-lift. Accessed 3 November 2014.

Appadurai, A. 1990 Disjuncture and difference in the global cultural economy. *Public Culture*, Vol. 2, No. 2, pp. 1–24.

Asanuma, Y. 2014 Goth-Trad: a new epoch. *Ableton Artists*. 30 April www.ableton.com/en/blog/goth-trad-after-dubstep-a-new-epoch/. Accessed 28 February 2015.

Athanasiou, A. 2011 Becoming precarious through regimes of gender, capital, and nation. *Fieldsights – Hot Spots, Cultural Anthropology Online*. www.culanth.org/fieldsights/250-becoming-precarious-through-regimes-of-gender-capital-and-nation. Accessed 8 June 2015.

Atkinson, M. 1984 Public speaking and audience responses: some techniques for inviting applause. In J. M. Atkinson and J. Heritage (eds), *Structures of Social Action*. Cambridge: Cambridge University Press.

Attias, B. A. 2013 Subjectivity in the groove: phonography, digitality and fidelity. Attias, B. A., Gavanas, A., and Rietveld, H. C. (eds), *DJ Culture in the Mix: Power, Technology, and Social Change in Electronic Dance Music*. London and New York: Bloomsbury Academic.

Attias, B. A. and van Veen, t. c. 2012 Off the record: turntablism and controllerism in the 21st century (Part 2). *Dancecult*, Vol. 4, No. 1. https://dj.dancecult.net/index.php/dancecult/article/view/332/328. Accessed 1 July 2015.

Auslander, P. 1999 *Liveness: Performance in a Mediatized Culture*. London: Routledge.

Auslander, P. 2008 *Liveness: Performance in a Mediatized culture*. (2nd edn.) London and New York: Routledge.

Auslander, P. 2011 Afterword: is there life after liveness? In S. Broadhurst and J. Machon (eds) *Performance and Technology: Practices of Virtual Embodiment and Interactivity*. Basingstoke and New York: Palgrave Macmillan.

Avakian, G. 1956 Liner Notes. *Ellington at Newport*. Columbia CL 934.

Bakhtin, M. 1984 [1968] *Rabelais and His World*. Translated by Hélène Iswolsky. Bloomington, IN: Indiana University Press.

Ball, D. M. and M. B. Kuhlman (eds) 2010 *The Comics of Chris Ware: Drawing is a Way of Thinking*. Jackson, MO: University Press of Mississippi.

Barker, M. 2003 Crash, theatre audiences, and the idea of liveness. *Studies in Theatre Performance*, Vol. 23, No. 1, pp. 21–39.

Bateson, G. 1973 *Steps to an Ecology of Mind*. London: Fontana.

Batey, A. 2010 So Solid Crew: what we're doing now is bigger than music. www.theguardian.com/music/2010/jan/14/so-solid-crew-interview. Accessed 1 July 2015.

Baudrillard, J. 1988 *The Ecstasy of Communication*. New York: Semiotext(e).

Baym, N. 2012 Fans or friends?: Seeing social media audiences as musicians do. *Participations: Journal of Audience and Reception Studies*, Vol. 9, No. 2, pp. 286–316.

Bayton, M. 1997 Women and the electric guitar. In S. Whiteley (ed.), *Sexing the Groove: Popular Music and Gender*. London: Routledge.

Becker, H. S. 1951 The professional dance musician and his audience. *American Journal of Sociology*, Vol. 57, No. 2, pp. 136–144.

Becker, H. S. 1982 *Art Worlds*. Berkley, LA: University of California Press.

Becker, J. 2002 Anthropological perspectives on music and emotion. In J. A. Sloboda and P. N. Juslin (eds), *Music and Emotion: Theory and Research*. Oxford: Oxford University Press.

Beebe, S. A. and S. J. Beebe. 2012 *Public Speaking: An Audience-Centred Approach*. (8th edn) Upper Saddle River, NJ: Allyn & Bacon.

Beebe, S. A. and J. T. Masterson. 2006 *Communicating in Small Groups: Principles and Practices*. (8th edn) Boston, MA: Pearson/Allyn and Bacon.

Benjamin, W. 1968 The work of art in the age of mechanical reproduction. In W. Benjamin, and H. Arendt (eds), *Illuminations*. (Trans. by H. Zohn.) New York: Harcourt Brace and World.

Bennett, J. 2010 *Vibrant Matter: A Political Ecology of Things*. Durham and London: Duke University Press.

Bennett, S. 1997 *Theatre Audiences: A Theory Of Production and Reception.* (2nd edn) London: Routledge.

Bergs, A. 2007 Letters: a new approach to text typology in Nevalainen, Terttu and Sanna-Kaisa Tanskanen (eds). *Letter Writing.* Amsterdam: John Benjamins.

Berliner, P. 1997 *Thinking in Jazz: The Infinite Art of Improvisation.* Chicago, IL: Chicago University Press.

Biber, D. 1991 *Variation across Speech and Writing.* Cambridge: Cambridge University Press.

Billig, M. 2005 *Laughter and Ridicule: Towards a Social Critique of Humour.* London: Sage.

Bohlman, P. V. 2001 Vernacular music. In S. Sadie (ed.), *New Grove Dictionary of Music and Musicians – Volume 26.* (2nd edn) London: Macmillan.

Boissevain, J. 2000 Changing Maltese landscapes: from utilitarian space to heritage? In C. Vella (ed.), *The Maltese islands on the move.* Valletta, Malta: Central Office of Statistics Malta.

Borg, S. 2000 The sound of Maltese folklore. *Sunday Times of Malta: Weekender.* 26 August.

Borg Cardona, A. 2002 *A musical legacy: Malta-related music found in foreign libraries.* Malta: The author.

Borg Cardona, A. 2007 *Daqq, għana u żfin Malti.* Malta: Publishers Enterprises Group.

Borg Cardona, A. 2014 *Musical instruments of the Maltese islands: history, folkways and traditions.* Malta: Fondazzjoni Patrimonju Malti.

Born, G. 2005 On musical mediation: ontology, technology and creativity. *Twentieth Century Music*, Vol. 2, No. 1, pp. 7–36.

Boym, S. 2001 *The Future of Nostalgia.* New York: Basic Books.

Brackett, D. (ed.) 2005. *The pop, rock, and soul reader: histories and debates.* New York and Oxford: Oxford University Press.

Bradby, B. 2008 Hello Dublin! The live event as local interaction order. Paper delivered to IASPM (International Association for the Study of Popular Music) UK and Ireland biennial conference, University of Glasgow.

Bradby, B. 2011 The business of informality: interaction, ritual, and emotional effervescence in the rock concert. Paper delivered to conference on 'The Business of Live Music', Edinburgh University.

Brand, G., J. Sloboda, B. Saul and M. Hathaway. 2012 The reciprocal relationship between jazz musicians and audiences in live performances: a pilot qualitative study. *Psychology of Music*, Vol. 40, No. 5, pp. 634–651.

Brewster, B. and F. Broughton. 2006 *Last Night a DJ Saved My Life: The History of the Disc Jockey.* 3rd Edition. London: Headline.

Brown, M. 2012 Making our own – two ethnographies of the vernacular in New Zealand music: tramping club singsongs and the Māori guitar strumming style. Unpublished doctoral dissertation: Victoria University of Wellington/Massey University New Zealand.

Burland, K. and S. E. Pitts. 2010 Understanding jazz audiences: listening and learning at the Edinburgh Jazz and Blues Festival. *Journal of New Music Research*, Vol. 39, No. 2, pp. 125–134.

Burns, K. 2001 *Jazz.* Documentary. PBS.

Butler, J. 1993 *Bodies That Matter: On The Discursive Limits of 'Sex'.* Abingdon, Oxon and New York: Routledge.

Butler, J. L. and Baumeister, R. F. 1998 The trouble with friendly faces: skilled performance with a supportive audience. *Journal of Personality and Social Psychology*, Vol. 75, No. 5, pp. 1213–1230.

Butler, M. J. 2014 *Playing with Something that Runs: Technology, Improvisation and Composition in DJ and Laptop Performance*. Oxford and New York: Oxford University Press.

Butsch, R. and S. Livingstone (eds) 2014 *Meanings of Audiences: Comparative Discourses*. London and New York: Routledge.

Cascone, K. 2002 Laptop music–counterfeiting aura in the age of infinite reproduction. *Parachute Contemporary Art*. Issue 107, pp. 52–60. www.zotero.org/pedroliveira/items/itemKey/8QM5JPHV. Accessed 4 April 2015.

Casey, E. 2000 *Remembering: A Phenomenological Study*. (2nd edn) Bloomington, IN: Indiana University Press.

Cassar, E. 2003 Bum Bum Show. *Times of Malta* (online) 7 August. www.timesofmalta.com/articles/view/20030807/letters/bum-bum-show.143947. Accessed 1 August 2013.

Cavicchi, D. 1998 *Tramps Like Us: Music and Meaning Among Springsteen's Fans*. New York: Oxford University Press.

Cavicchi, D. 2012 *Listening and Longing: Music Lovers in the Age of Barnum*. Middletown, CT: Wesleyan University Press.

Chandler, M. A. 2013 Finger talking good for early baby babbling. *Sydney Morning Herald* 5 August. www.smh.com.au/national/education/finger-talking-good-for-early-baby-babbling-20130804–2r7do.html#ixzz2b4W8Pj3J. Accessed 1 August 2014.

Christgau, R. 1995 Idle worship: how pop empowers the weak, rewards the faithfull and succours the needy. www.robertchristgau.com/xg/bkrev/idle-95.php. Accessed 1 August 2014.

Clark, A. 2011 *Supersizing the Mind: Embodiment, Action, and Cognitive Extension*. Oxford and New York: Oxford University Press.

Clark, A. and D. J. Chalmers. 2010 The extended mind. In Richard Menary (ed.), *The Extended Mind*. Cambridge MA, London: Bradford/MIT Press.

Clarke, E. 2011 Lecture: Sound-Space-Psyche: Musical proxemics. 8 November 2011, University of Oxford.

Clayman, S. 1993 Booing: the anatomy of a disaffiliative response. *American Sociological Review*, Vol. 58, No. 1, pp. 110–130.

Clayton, M. 2007 Time, gesture and attention in a *khyal* performance. *Asian Music*, Vol. 38, No. 2, pp. 71–96.

Clayton, M. and L. Leante. 2015 Role, status and hierarchy in the performance of North Indian classical music. *Ethnomusicology Forum*, Vol. 24, No. 3, pp: 414–442.

Coates, N. 2001. Whose tears go by? Marianne Faithfull at the dawn and twilight of rock culture. In L. Stras (ed.), *She's So Fine: Reflections On Whiteness, Femininity, Adolescence and Class in 1960s Music*. Farnham: Ashgate.

Cohen, A. P. 1985 *The Symbolic Construction of Community*. London: Routledge.

Cohen, S. 1991 *Rock Culture in Liverpool: Popular Music in The Making*. Oxford: The Clarendon Press.

Collins, R. 2004 *Interaction Ritual Chains*. Princeton, NJ: Princeton University Press.

Connor, S. 1997. *Postmodernist Culture: An Introduction to Theories of The Contemporary*. (2nd edn) Oxford: Blackwell.

Cortazzi, M. and L. Jin. 2000 Evaluating evaluation in narrative. In S. Hunston and G. Thompson (eds), *Evaluation in Text: Authorial Stance and the Construction of Discourse*. Oxford: Oxford University Press.

Cottrell, S. 2004 *Professional Music-Making in London: Ethnography and Experience*. Aldershot: Ashgate.

Couldry, N. 2003 *Media Rituals: A Critical Approach*. London: Routledge.

Cowan, J. 1993. Politics, identity and popular music in contemporary Greece. *Kampos: Cambridge Papers in Modern Greek*, Vol. 1, No. 1, pp. 1–22.

Cox, A. 2006 Hearing, feeling, grasping gestures. In A. Gritten and E. King (eds), *Music and Gesture*. Aldershot: Ashgate.

Crawford, G. 2005 *Consuming Sports: Fans, Sport, and Culture*. London and New York: Routledge.

Dalakoglou, D. 2011 The irregularities of violence in Athens. *Fieldsights – Hot Spots, Cultural Anthropology Online*. www.culanth.org/fieldsights/251-the-irregularities-of-violence-in-athens. Accessed 8 June 2015.

Davies, H. 1985. *The Beatles: The Only Authorised Biography*. London: Jonathan Cape.

Davis, T. C. 1991 *Actresses as Working Women: Their Social Identity in Victorian Culture*. New York: Routledge.

Dawoud, A. 2014 Egyptian audiences of *Musalsalat* in the eye of the beholder. In R. Butsch and S. Livingstone (eds), *Meanings of Audiences: Comparative Discourses*. London and New York: Routledge.

De Frece, M. 1934 *Recollections of Vesta Tilley*. London: Hutchinson and Co.

Disher, W. 1938 *Winkles and Champagne: Comedies and Tragedies of The Music Hall*. London: BT Batsford.

Dixon, R. M. W. 1982 *Where Have All Adjectives Gone? And Other Essays in Semantics and Syntax*. The Hague: Mouton.

Dixon, S. 2007 *Digital Performance: A History of New Media in Theater, Dance, Performance Art, and Installation*. Cambridge, MA and London: MIT Press.

Douzinas, C. 2013a *Philosophy and Resistance in the Crisis: Greece and the Future of Europe*. Cambridge: Polity Press.

Douzinas, C. 2013b The loss of ERT, the 'Greek BBC', is a cultural calamity. *Guardian*, 12 June. www.theguardian.com/commentisfree/2013/jun/12/ert-greek-state-broadcaster-cultural-calamity. Accessed 7 July 2015.

Dragonas, T. 2013 Religion in contemporary Greece – a modern experience? In A. Triandafyllidou, R. Gropas and H. Kouki (eds), *The Greek Crisis and European Modernity*. New York: Palgrave Macmillan.

Duffett, M. 1998 'Understanding Elvis', Unpublished PhD Thesis. University of Wales, Aberystwyth.

Duffett, M. 2003 False faith or false comparison: a critique of the religious interpretation of Elvis fan culture. *Popular Music and Society*, Vol. 26, No. 4, pp. 513–522.

Duffett, M. 2009 'We are interrupted by your noise': heckling and the symbolic economy of popular music stardom. *Popular Music and Society*, Vol. 32, No. 1, pp. 37–57.

Duffett, M. 2013 *Understanding Fandom: An Introduction to The Study of Media Fan Culture*. London: Continuum.

Duffett, M. 2014a Introduction. In M. Duffett (ed.), *Popular Music Fandom: Identities, Roles and Practices*. New York: Routledge.

Duffett, M. 2014b Celebrity: the return of the repressed in fan studies? In L. Duits, K. Zwaan and S. Reijnders (eds), *The Ashgate Companion to Fan Cultures*. Farnham: Ashgate.

Duffett, M. 2015 Elvis's gospel music: Between the secular and the spiritual? *Religions*, Vol. 6, No. 1, pp. 182–203.

Durkheim, E. 1965 [1915] *The Elementary Forms of the Religious Life*. New York: Free Press.

Durkheim, E. 2008 [1912] *The Elementary Form of Religious Life*. Oxford: Oxford University Press.

Edwards, D. and J. Potter. 1992 *Discursive Psychology*. London: Sage.

Ehrenreich, B., E. Hess, and G. Jacobs. 1987 *Re-making Love: The Feminization of Sex*. Glasgow: Fontana.

Ehrenreich, B., E. Hess and G. Jacobs. 1992 Beatlemania: girls just want to have fun. In L. Lewis (ed.), *The Adoring Audience: Fan Culture and Popular Media*. London: Routledge.

Ekman, P. 2003 *Emotions Revealed: Understanding Faces and Feelings*. London: Weidenfeld & Nicolson.

Ekman, P. and W. V. Friesen. 1975 *Unmasking the Face: A Guide To Recognizing Emotions From Facial Clues*. Englewood Cliffs, NJ: Prentice-Hall.

Evans, M. 2006 *Open Up the Doors: Music in the Modern Church*. London: Equinox.

Fabbri, F. and I. Tsioulakis (2016). Italian *canzone d'autore* and Greek *entechno tragoudi*: a comparative overview. In K. Williams and J. A. Williams (eds), *The Cambridge Companion to Singer-Songwriters*. Cambridge: Cambridge University Press.

Faulkner, R. R. and H. S. Becker. 2009 *'Do You Know . . . ?': The Jazz Repertoire in Action*. Chicago, IL: University of Chicago Press.

Feld, S. 1988 Aesthetics as iconicity of style, or "lift-up-over-sounding": getting into the Kaluli groove. *Yearbook for Traditional Music*, Vol. 20, pp. 74–113.

Feld, S. 1994 Communication, music and speech about music. In C. Keil and S. Feld (eds), *Music Grooves: Essays and Dialogues*. Chicago, IL: University of Chicago Press.

Feld, S. 2012 *Jazz Cosmopolitanism in Accra: Five Musical Years in Ghana*. Durham, NC: Duke University Press.

Ferreira, P. P. 2008 When sound meets movement: performance in Electronic Dance Music. *Leonardo Music Journal*. Special Issue: *Why Live? Performance in the Age of Digital Reproduction*, Vol. 18, pp. 17–20.

Fikentscher, K. 1997 The DJ as performer. In H. Järviluoma and T. Hautamäki (eds), *Music on Show: Issues of Performance*. Tampere: Department of Folk Tradition, University of Tampere Press.

Fikentscher, K. 2000 *'You Better Work!' Underground Dance Music in New York City*. Hanover, NH and London: Wesleyan University Press.

Fikentscher, K. 2001 The DJ as composer, or how I became a composing DJ. *Current Musicology*, Vol. 65, pp. 93–98.

Fikentscher, K. 2003 'There's not a problem I can't fix, 'cause I can do it in the mix': on the perfomative technology of 12-inch vinyl. In R. T. Lysloff and L. C. Gay (eds), *Music and Techno Culture*. Middletown, CO: Wesleyan Univeristy Press.

Fikentscher, K. 2013 'It's not the mix, it's the selection': music programming in contemporary DJ culture. Attias, B. A., Gavanas, A. and Rietveld, H. C. (eds),

*DJ Culture in the Mix: Power, Technology, and Social Change in Electronic Dance Music.* London and New York: Bloomsbury Academic.

Finnegan, R. 1988 *The Hidden Musicians: Music-making in an English Town.* Cambridge: Cambridge University Press.

Fiske, J. 1986 MTV: post structural post modern. *Journal of Communication Inquiry*, Vol. 10, No. 1, pp. 74–79.

Fonarow, W. 1996 Spatial distribution and participation in British contemporary musical performances. *Issues in Applied Linguistics*, Vol. 7, No. 1, pp. 33–43.

Fonarow, W. 2006 *Empire of Dirt: The Aesthetics and Rituals of British Indie Music.* Middletown, CT: Wesleyan University Press.

Foucault, M. 1982 The subject and power. In H. L. Dreyfus and P. Rabinow (eds), *Michel Foucault: Beyond Structuralism and Hermeneutics.* Brighton: Harvester Press.

Frith, S. 1986 Art versus technology: the strange case of popular music. *Media, Culture & Society*, Vol. 8, pp. 263–279.

Frith, S. 1988 *Music for Pleasure: Essays in the Sociology of Pop.* Cambridge: Polity Press.

Frith, S. 1998 *Performing Rites: Evaluating Popular Music.* Oxford: Oxford University Press.

Frith, S. 2001 The popular music industry. In S. Frith, W. Straw and J. Street (eds), *Cambridge Companion to Pop and Rock.* Cambridge: Cambridge University Press.

Frith, S. 2003 Look! Hear! The uneasy relationship of music and television. *Popular Music*, Vol. 21, No. 3, pp. 277–290.

Frith, S. and A. Goodwin. 1991 *On Record: Rock, Pop and the Written Word.* London: Routledge.

Frith, S. and H. Horne. 1987 *Art into Pop.* London: Methuen.

Frith, S. and A. McRobbie. 1990 Rock and sexuality. In S. Frith and A. Goodwin (eds), *On Record: Rock, Pop and the Written Word.* London: Routledge.

Galea Debono, F. 2001 Traditional Maltese music being fused with flamenco and jazz. *Times of Malta*, 17 September, pp. 24–25.

Galea Debono, F. 2002 Vilhena Palace forecourt transformed into 'dignified space'. *Times of Malta* (online) 15 July. www.timesofmalta.com/articles/view/20020715/local/vilhena-palace-forecourt-transformed-into-dignified-space.170982. Accessed 8 June 2015.

Gallagher, S. 2012 How to DJ on a laptop: a beginner's guide to DJing on a laptop. *How To DJ Fast.com.* www.howtodjfast.com/how-to-dj-on-a-laptop/. Accessed 4 November 2014.

García Quiñones, M., A. Kassabian and E. Boschi. 2013 *Ubiquitous Musics: The Everyday Sounds That We Don't Always Notice.* Farnham: Ashgate.

Garfield, S. 2006 The 50 greatest music books ever. *Observer Music Monthly*, 18 June. http://observer.guardian.co.uk/omm/story/0,,1797455,00.html. Accessed 8 June 2015.

Garratt, S. 1990 Teenage dreams. In S. Frith and A. Goodwin (eds), *On Record: Rock, Pop and the Written Word.* London: Routledge.

Giorgi, A. and Giorgi, B. 2003 Phenomenology. In J. A. Smith (ed.), *Qualitative Psychology: A Practical Guide to Research Methods.* London: Sage.

Gledhill, J. 2010 Hegemonic, subaltern and anthropological cosmopolitics. In D. Theodossopoulos and E. Kirtsoglou (eds), *United in Discontent: Local Responses to Cosmopolitanism And Globalization.* New York: Berghahn Books.

Goffman, E. 1959 *The Presentation of Self in Everyday Life*. New York: Doubleday Anchor.

Goffman E. 1963 *Behavior in Public Places: Notes on the Social Organization of Gatherings*. New York: The Free Press.

Goffman, E. 1967 [1955] On face-work: an analysis of ritual elements in social interaction. In *Interaction Ritual: Essays on Face-To-Face Behavior*. New York: Anchor Books.

Goffman, E. 1967 [1956] The nature of deference and demeanor. In *Interaction Ritual: Essays On Face-To-Face Behavior*. New York: Anchor Books.

Goffman, E. 1981a [1978] Response cries. In *Forms of Talk*. Oxford: Oxford University Press.

Goffman, E. 1981b The lecture. In *Forms of Talk*. Oxford: Oxford University Press.

Goffman, E. 1981c Replies and responses. In *Forms of Talk*. Oxford: Oxford University Press.

Goffman, E. 1990 [1959] *The Presentation of the Self in Everyday Life*. London: Penguin.

Goldin-Meadow, S. 2003 *Hearing Gesture: How Our Hands Help Us Think*. Cambridge MA and London: The Belknap Press of Harvard University Press.

Goldstein, J. and H. Toch. 1956 An analysis of a sample of eccentric mail to the United Nations. *American Imago*, Vol. 13, pp. 149–187.

Goodwin, A. 1993 *Dancing in the Distraction Factory: Music Television and Popular Culture*. London: Routledge.

Gordon, K. 2009 *Media Audiences: Television, Meaning and Emotion*. Edinburgh: Edinburgh University Press.

Gordon, S. 2006 *Mastering the Art of Performance: A Primer for Musicians*. Oxford: Oxford University Press.

Gourlay, K. 1980 Alienation and ethnomusicology. In N. McLeod and M. Herndon (eds), *Ethnography of Musical Performance*. Norwood: Norwood Editions.

Grajeda, T. 2002 The feminization of rock. In R. Beebe, D. Holbrook and B. Saunders (eds), *Rock Over the Edge: Transformations in Popular Music Culture*. Durham, NC: Duke University Press.

Green, C. (ed.) 2014 *BPI yearbook 2014*. London: BPI.

Gregory, R. L. 1987 *The Oxford Companion to the Mind*. Oxford: Oxford University Press.

Guralnick, P. 1995 *Last Train to Memphis: The Rise of Elvis Presley*. London: Abacus.

Gwertzman, M. 2004 With a nod to vinyl, CDs take over the turntable. *The New York Times*. 23 September. www.nytimes.com/2004/09/23/technology/circuits/23basi.html?_r=0. Accessed 5 January 2015.

Hairston, M. 2008 Gender, jazz, and the popular front. In N. T. Rustin and S. Tucker (eds), *Big Ears: Listening for Gender in Jazz Studies*. Durham, NC and London: Duke University Press.

Hall, S. 1997 *Representation: Cultural Representations and Signifying Practices*. London and Thousand Oaks, CA: Sage in association with the Open University.

Hamilton, J. 2000 Theatrical enactment. *The Journal of Aesthetics and Art Criticism*, Vol. 58, No. 1, pp. 23–35.

Hannerz, U. 1996 *Transnational Connections: Culture, People, Places*. London and New York: Routledge.

Hannerz, U. 2004 Cosmopolitanism. In D. Nugent and J. Vincent (eds), *Companion to the Anthropology of Politics*. Oxford: Blackwell.

Harré, R. and P. Stearns. 1995 Introduction: psychology as discourse analysis. In R. Harré and P. Stearns (eds), *Discursive Psychology in Practice*. London: Sage.

Hay, C. 2001 Proper role of music TV debated in the US. *Billboard*, 17 February: 1, pp. 68–69.

Heany, J. 2002 Dance to Duke. *DEMS Bulletin* (August/November). http://depanorama.net/dems/02dems2b.htm. Accessed 18 November 2015.

Hebdige, D. 1979 *Subculture: The Meaning of Style*. London: Routledge.

Heller, W. 2014 *Music in the Baroque*. New York: W. W. Norton and Company.

Henriques, J. 2011 *Sonic Bodies: Reggae Sound Systems, Performance Techniques, and Ways of Knowing*. London and New York: Continuum.

Herbert, S. and L. McKernan. 1996 *Who's Who of Victorian Cinema: A Worldwide Survey*. London: BFI publishing.

Herring, S. 1996 Posting in a different voice: gender and ethics in computer-mediated communication. In C. Ess (ed.), *Philosophical Perspectives on Computer-Mediated Communication*. Albany, NY: State University of New York Press.

Herzfeld, M. 2011 Crisis attack: impromptu ethnography in the Greek maelstom. *Anthropology Today*, Vol. 27, No. 5, pp. 22–26.

Hesmondalgh, D. and K. Negus. (eds) 2002 *Popular Music Studies*. London: Arnold.

Hill, J. 1991 Television and pop: the case of the 1950s. In J. Corner (ed.), *Popular Television in Britain: Studies in Cultural History*. London: British Film Institute.

Hills, M. 2002 *Fan Cultures*. London: Routledge.

Hills, M. 2012 'Twilight' fans represented in commercial paratexts and inter-fandoms: resisting and repurposing negative fan stereotypes. In A. Morley (ed.), *Genre, Reception, and Adaptation in the 'Twilight' Series*. Farnham: Ashgate.

Hitchcock. H. W. 1969 *Music in the United States: A Historical Introduction*. Englewood Cliffs, NJ: Prentice Hall.

Hoggart, S. 2013 Simon Hoggart's week: let's end this obsession over Ed Miliband, *Guardian*, Saturday 30 November 2013. www.theguardian.com/theguardian/2013/nov/30/simon-hoggarts-week-ed-miliband. Accessed 8 June 2015.

Holt, F. 2010 The economy of live music in the digital age. *European Journal of Cultural Studies*, Vol. 13, No. 2, pp. 243–261.

Horst, H. 2012 New media technologies in everyday life. In H. Horst and D. Miller (eds), *Digital Anthropology*. Oxford: Berg.

Horton, D. and Wohl, R. 1956 Mass communication and parasocial interaction: observations on intimacy at a distance. *Psychiatry*, Vol. 19, pp. 215–229.

Hunter, J. 1860 *A School Manual of Letter-Writing*. London: Longman, Green, Longman and Roberts.

Huyssen, A. 1986 *After the Great Divide: Modernism, Mass Culture and Post-modernism*. Basingstoke: Macmillan.

Hytönen-Ng, E. 2013 *Experiencing 'Flow' in Jazz Performance*. Farnham: Ashgate Publishing.

Hytönen-Ng, E. 2014 Gender at play in jazz venues in Britain. In A. Arvidsson (ed.), *Jazz, Gender, Authenticity*. Proceedings of the 10th Nordic Jazz Research Conference Stockholm August 20–31 2012. Stockholm: Svenskt visarkiv/Statens musikverk. http://carkiv.musikverk.se/www/epublikationer/Online_publ_Jazz_Gender_Authenticity.pdf. Accessed 8 June 2015.

Ihde, D. 2007 *Listening and Voice: Phenomenologies of Sound*. (2nd edn) Albany, NY: State University of New York Press.

Illich, I. 1981 *Shadow Work*. Boston: Marion Boyars.

Inda, J. X. and R. Rosaldo. 2008 Tracking global flows. In J. X. Inda and R. Rosaldo (eds), *The Anthropology of Globalization: A Reader*. (2nd edn) Malden, MA: Blackwell.

Ioannidis, A. 2012 We blame you! *Alkinoos.gr* online blog: http://alkinoos.gr/el/news/196-news-mar-2012.html. Accessed 8 June 2015.

Ioannidis, A. 2013 Eleutheroi kataktimenoi (Liberated and conquered) *Alkinoos.gr* online blog: www.alkinoos.gr/el/news/200-news-mar-2013.html. Accessed 8 June 2015.

Jackson, J. A. 1997 *American Bandstand: Dick Clark and the Making of a Rock 'n' Roll Empire*. New York and Oxford: Oxford University Press.

Jackson, M. (ed.) 1996 *Things as They Are: New Directions in Phenomenological Anthropology*. Bloomington and Indianapolis, IN: Indiana University Press.

Jenkins, H. 1992 *Textual Poachers*. London Routledge.

Jennings, M. 2014 *Exaltation: Ecstatic Experience in Pentecostal Religion and Popular Music*. Bern: Peter Lang.

Jenson, J. 1992 Fandom as pathology: the consequences of characterization. In L. Lewis (ed.), *The Adoring Audience: Fan Culture and Popular Media*. London: Routledge.

Johnson, B. 1996 Arts policy and vernacular music. Unpub. Report for the Third Annual Assembly of the Music Council of Australia, Canberra.

Johnson, B. 2002 Jazz as cultural practice. In M. Cooke and D. Horn (eds), *The Cambridge Companion to Jazz*. Cambridge: Cambridge University Press.

Johnson, B. 2008 'Quick and dirty': sonic mediations and affect. In C. Birdsall and A. Enns (eds), *Sonic Mediations: Body, Sound, Technology*. Newcastle-Upon-Tyne: Cambridge Scholars Publishing.

Johnson, B. 2013 I *hear* music: popular music and its mediations. In *IASPM@Journal Online*. Vol. 3, No. 2, Special Issue: Popular Music Studies in the Twenty-First Century, pp. 96–110. www.iaspmjournal.net/index.php/IASPM_Journal/issue/view/55/showToc. Accessed 8 June 2015.

Johnston, C. 2013 Big day over? *Sydney Morning Herald*, 20 October 2013. www.smh.com.au/entertainment/big-day-over-20131019–2vtq0.html. Accessed 8 June 2015.

Kaplan, E. A. 1987 *Rocking Around the Clock: Music Television, Postmodernism and Consumer Culture*. London: Methuen.

Kassabian, A. 2013 *Ubiquitous Listening: Affect, Attention, and Distributed Subjectivity*. Berkeley, CA: University of California Press.

Katz, M. 2012 *Groove Music: The Art and Culture of the Hip-Hop DJ*. Oxford and New York: Oxford University Press.

Keil, C. 1987 Participatory discrepancies and the power of music. *Cultural Anthropology*, Vol. 2, No. 3, pp. 275–283.

Keil, C. 1994 Music mediated and live in Japan. In C. Keil and S. Feld (eds), *Music Grooves*. Chicago: University of Chicago Press.

Khondker, H. 2012 Role of the new media in the Arab Spring. *Globalisations*, Vol. 8, No. 5, pp. 675–679.

Kift, D. 1996 *The Victorian Music Hall: Culture, Class and Conflict*. Cambridge: Cambridge University Press.

Krueger, A. B. 2005 The economics of real superstars: the market for rock concerts in the material world. *Journal of Labor Economics*, Vol. 23, No. 1, pp. 1–30.

Kruse, H. 1993 The Adoring Audience: Fan Culture and Popular Media by Lisa Lewis [review]. *Popular Music*, Vol. 19, No. 2, pp. 205–206.

Kureishi, H. and J. Savage 1996 *Faber Book of Pop*. London: Faber & Faber.

Kytö, M. 2011 'We are the rebellious voice of the terraces, we are Çarşı': Constructing a football supporter group through sound. *Soccer & Society*, Vol. 12, No. 1, pp. 77–93.

Labov, W. 1972 *Language in the Inner City: Studies in the Black English Vernacular*. Philadelphia, PA: University of Pennsylvania Press.

Laing, D. 1991 A voice without a face: popular music and the phonograph in the 1890s. *Popular Music*, Vol. 10, No. 1, pp. 1–9.

Lapavitsas, C. 2012 *Crisis in the Eurozone*. London: Verso.

Lawrence, T. 2003 *Love Saves the Day: A History of American Music Culture, 1970–1979*. Durham, NC and London: Duke University Press.

LeBlanc, A., J. Y. Chang, M. Obert and C. Siivola. 1997 Effect of audience on music performance anxiety. *Journal of Research in Music Education*, Vol. 45, No. 3, pp. 480–496.

LeDoux, J. 1999 *The Emotional Brain*. London: Phoenix.

Lester, P. 2011 The worst gig we ever played: musicians on their on-stage lows. *Guardian* 4 August. www.theguardian.com/music/2011/aug/04/musicians-worst-gigs. Accessed 8 June 2015.

Levene, A. 2004 Elaine Anderson, 80; activist, ex-dancer. *Boston Globe*. 21 April. www.boston.com/news/globe/obituaries/articles/2004/04/21/elaine_anderson_80_activist_ex_dancer/. Accessed 18 November 2015.

Lewin, K. 1951 *Field Theory in Social Science: Selected Theoretical Papers*. Oxford: Harpers.

Lewis, L. 1992 *The Adoring Audience*. London: Routledge.

Lipsitz, G. 2007 Footsteps in the Dark: The Hidden Histories of Popular Music. Minneapolis, MN: University of Minnesota Press.

Löbert, A. and Duffett, M. 2015 "Trading offstage photos: celebrity following as participatory fan culture." In S. Baker (ed.), *Preserving Popular Music Heritage: Do-it-Yourself, Do-it-Together*. New York: Routledge.

Lynskey, D. 2013 Beatlemania: 'the screamers' and other tales of fandom. www.theguardian.com/music/2013/sep/29/beatlemania-screamers-fandom-teenagers-hysteria. Accessed 8 June 2015.

Macdonald, D. 1957 A theory of mass culture. In B. Rosenberg and D. Manning White (eds), *Mass Culture: The Popular Arts in America*. New York: Macmillan.

Mackintosh, I. 1993 *Architecture, Actor and Audience*. Florence, KY: Routledge.

Maffesoli, M. 1996 *Time of the Tribes: The Decline of Individualism in Mass Society*. London: Sage.

Maitland, H. 2009 Understanding audiences for jazz. *EmJazz Report*. www.jazzsteps.co.uk/emjazz_report/1%20Overview%20of%20audiences%20for%20jazz%20in%20the%20East%20Midlands.pdf. Accessed 2 March 2013.

Manderson, L. 2011 *Surface Tensions: Surgery, Bodily Boundaries, and the Social Self*. Walnut Creek, CA: Left Coast Press.

Manzoor, S. 2013 Bob Dylan, Clyde Auditorium, Review. *Daily Telegraph*, 18 November. www.telegraph.co.uk/culture/music/bob-dylan/10458128/Bob-Dylan-Clyde-Auditorium-review.html. Accessed 8 June 2015.

## 210 Bibliography

Marcus, G. 1991. *Mystery Train: Images of America in Rock 'n' Roll Music*. (4th edn.) Harmondsworth: Penguin.

Martin, B. 1979 The sacralization of disorder: symbolism in rock music. *Sociological Analysis*, Vol. 40, No. 2, pp. 87–124.

Mavrokordatos, G. 2003 Orthodoxy and nationalism in the Greek case. *West European Politics*, Vol. 26, No. 1, pp. 117–136.

Maxwell, I. 2002 The curse of fandom: insiders, outsiders and ethnography. In D. Hesmondalgh and K. Negus (eds), *Popular Music Studies*. London: Arnold.

McCall, M.1938 Handy concert for Milk Fund. *Daily Worker*, November 24, 1938.

McGillion, C. 2013 Unpub. Draft Report on Seeds of Life (SoL) program, Timor Leste Ministry of Agriculture and Fisheries.

McNeill, D. 2005 *Gesture and Thought*. Chicago and London: University of Chicago Press.

Meintjes, L. 2004 Reaching 'overseas': South African sound engineers, technology, and tradition. In Thomas P. (ed.), *Wired for sound: engineering and technologies in sonic cultures*. Middletown, CT: Wesleyan University Press.

Menary, R. (ed.) 2010 *The Extended Mind*. Cambridge MA, London: Bradford/MIT Press.

Merriam, A. P. and R. W. Mack. 1960 The jazz community. *Social Forces*, Vol. 38, No. 3, pp. 211–222.

Michael, L. 2004 Audience experience during Italian opera performances in Italy in the 18th and 19th century vs. audience experience during Italian opera performances in North America today, or Why we should ditch the concert hall and hit the bar. www.music.mcgill.ca/~benson/liederwolfe/Files/Liederwolfe_essay.pdf. Accessed 8 June 2015.

Middleton, R. 1990 *Studying Popular Music*. Milton Keynes: Open University Press.

Middleton, R. 2006 'Last Night a DJ Saved My Life': avians, cyborgs and siren bodies in the era of phonographic technology', *Radical Musicology*, Vol. 1, pp. 1–31.

Mifsud Chircop, G. 2004 *Il-folklor Malti*, Vol. 1. Malta: Pubblikazzjonijiet lndipendenza.

Miller, K. 2012 *Playing Along: Digital Games, YouTube, and Virtual Performance*. New York: Oxford University Press.

Mills, P. 2010 Stone fox chase: the *Old Grey Whistle Test* and the rise of high pop television. In I. Inglis (ed.), *Popular Music and Television in Britain*. Farnham: Ashgate.

Minga, M. 2013 Këngë Korçare: song making and musical culture in the city of Korçë during the twentieth century. Unpublished PhD thesis, University of Milan.

Mitchell, J. P. 2002 *Ambivalent Europeans: Ritual, Memory and the Public Sphere in Malta*. London: Routledge.

Moran, N. 2013 Social co-regulation and communication in north Indian duo performances. In M. Clayton, B. Dueck and L. Leante (eds), *Experience and Meaning in Music Performance*. New York: Oxford University Press.

Morris, C. 2010 Digital diva: opera on video. *The Opera Quarterly*, Vol. 26, No. 1, pp. 96–119.

Morton, J. F. 2008 *Backstory in Blue: Ellington at Newport '56*. Newark, NJ: Rutgers University Press.

Napier, J. 2004 Re-organization and rhetoric: changes in the social organization of North Indian classical music. *Musicology Australia*, Vol. 27, No. 1, pp. 35–53.

Napier, J. 2007 The distribution of authority in the performance of North Indian vocal music. *Ethnomusicology Forum*, Vol. 16, No. 2, pp. 271–301.

Napoli, P. M. 2003 *Audience Economics: Media Institutions and the Audience Marketplace*. New York: Columbia University Press.

Napoli, P. M. 2011 *Audience Evolution: New Technologies and the Transformation of Media Audiences*. New York: Columbia University Press.

Nettl, B. 2005 *The Study of Ethnomusicology: Thirty-One Issues and Concepts*. Urbana, IL: University of Illinois Press.

Neuman, D. 1990 [1980] *The Life of Music in North India*. Chicago and London: Chicago University Press.

Neuman, D. 2004 *A House of Music: The Hindustani Musician and the Crafting of Traditions*. PhD dissertation, Columbia University.

Nevalainen, T. 2007 Introduction. In Nevalainen, T. and S. K. Tanskanen (eds), *Letter Writing*. Amsterdam: John Benjamins.

Niesel, J. 2013 Concert Review: Bob Dylan at EJ Thomas Hall in Akron. *Cleveland Scene* online magazine, April 20. www.clevescene.com/scene-and-heard/archives/2013/04/20/concert-review-bob-dylan-at-ej-thomas-hall-in-akron. Accessed 6 February 2014.

Nora, P. 1989 Between memory and history: les lieux de mémoire. *Representations*, Vol. 26, pp. 7–24.

Nora, P. 2002 Reasons for the current upsurge in memory. *Eurozine*, www.eurozine.com/pdf/2002–04–19-nora-en.pdf. Accessed 8 June 2015.

Owen, W. 2000 Etnika, Nafra. *Rambles: A Cultural Arts Magazine*. www.rambles.net/etnika_nafra.html. Accessed 8 June 2015.

Pace, A. 2011 Representing traditional Maltese music as world music: Maltese identity in a Mediterranean soundscape. Unpublished MA thesis, City University London.

Page, W. and C. Carey 2010 Adding up the UK music industry. *Economic Insight*, Vol. 23. http://prsformusic.com/creators/news/research/Documents/AddingUpThe UKMusicIndustry2010.pdf. Accessed 8 June 2015.

Pandian, J. 2001 Symbolic inversions. An interpretation of contrary behavior in ritual. *Anthropos*, Vol. 96, No. 2, pp. 557–562.

Papailias, P. 2011 Witnessing the crisis. *Fieldsights – Hot Spots, Cultural Anthropology Online*. www.culanth.org/fieldsights/246-witnessing-the-crisis. Accessed 8 June 2015.

Papanikolaou, D. 2007 *Singing Poets: Literature and Popular Music in France and Greece*. London: Legenda.

Papanikolaou, D. 2013 Pali symmetehei o Yiorgos Dalaras (Once again featuring Yiorgos Dalaras). *Unfollow Magazine*, Vol. 14.

Partridge, C. 2014 *The Lyre of Orpheus: Popular Music, the Sacred and the Profane*. New York: Oxford University Press.

Pattie, D. 2007 *Rock Music in Performance*. New York: Palgrave Macmillan.

Perls, F. 1976 *Gestalt Therapy Verbatim*. New York: Bantam Books.

Phelan, P. and J. Lane (eds) 1998 *The Ends of Performance*. New York: New York University Press.

Pickering, M. and T. Green (eds) 1987 *Everyday Culture: Popular Song and the Vernacular Milieu*. Milton Keynes: Open University Press.

Pickering, W. 2009 [1984] *Durkheim's Sociology of Religion: Themes and Theories*. Cambridge: James Clark and Co Ltd.

Pini, M. 2001 *Club Cultures and Female Subjectivity: The Move from Home to House*. London: Palgrave.

Pitts, S. E. 2005 What makes an audience? Investigating the roles and experiences of listeners at a chamber music festival. *Music and Letters*, Vol. 86, No. 2, pp. 257–269.

Pitts, S. E., M. C. Dobson, K. Gee and C. P. Spencer. 2013 Vire of an audience: Understanding the orchestral concert experience from player and listener perspectives. *Participations – Journal of Audience & Reception Studies*, Vol. 10, No. 2. pp. 65–95.

Plasketes, G. 2009 *B-sides, Undercurrents and Overtones: Peripheries to Popular in Music, 1960 to the Present*. Farnham: Ashgate.

Plastino, G. 2003a Introduction. In G. Plastino (ed.), *Mediterranean Mosaic: Popular Music and Global Sounds*. London: Routledge.

Plastino, G. 2003b Inventing ethnic music: Fabrizio De André's Creuza de Mä and the creation of musica mediterranea in Italy. In G. Plastino (ed.), *Mediterranean Mosaic: Popular Music and Global Sounds*. London: Routledge.

Pomerantz, A. 1984 Agreeing and disagreeing with assessments: some features of preferred/ dispreferred turn shapes. In J. M. Atkinson and J. Heritage (eds), *Structures of Social Action*. Cambridge: Cambridge University Press.

Porcello, T. 1991 The ethics of digital audio-sampling: engineers' discourse. *Popular Music*, Vol. 10, No. 1, pp. 69–84.

Porcello, T. 2005 Music mediated as live in Austin: sound, technology, and recording practice. In T. Porcello (ed.), *Wired for Sound: Engineering and Technologies in Sonic Cultures*. Middletown, CN: Wesleyan University Press.

Poulis, K. 2013 Oi agrioi, oi dianooumenoi kai oi agrioi dianooumenoi (The savages, the intellectuals, and the savage intellectuals). *Kyriakatiki Eleutherotypia Newspaper*, 3 March.

Pressing, J. 1987 The micro- and macrostructural design of improvised music. *Music Perception*, Vol. 5 No. 2, pp. 132–172.

Prochaska, F. K. 1980 *Women and Philanthropy in Nineteenth-century England*. Oxford: Oxford University Press.

Pullicino, G. C. and C. Camilleri. 1998 *Maltese Oral Poetry and Folk Music*. Malta: Malta University Publishers Ltd.

Quilliam, S. 2008 *Body Language: Actions Speak Louder Than Words: Crack The Unspoken Code Of Body Language*. London: Carlton.

Quinn, K. G. 2009 *Sports and Their Fans: The History, Economics and Culture of the Relationship Between Spectator and Sport*. Jefferson, NC: McFarland.

Qureshi, R. 1987 Musical sound and contextual input: a performance model for musical analysis. *Ethnomusicology*, Vol. 31, No. 1, pp. 56–86.

Qureshi, R. 1995 [1976] *Sufi Music of India and Pakistan. Sound, Context and Meaning in Qawwali*. Chicago and London: Chicago University Press.

Ragonesi, A. and G. Mifsud Chircop. 1999 *Maltese Folksong 'Ghana': A Bibliography and Resource Material*. Msida, Malta: Malta University Press.

Reynolds, S. 2005 *Rip It Up and Start Again: Postpunk 1978–1984*. London: Faber and Faber.

Reynolds, S. 2011 *Retromania: Pop Culture's Addiction to Its Own Past*. London: Faber and Faber.

Richards K. with J. Fox. 2010 *Life*. London: Weidenfeld & Nicolson.

Rietveld, H. C. 1998 *This Is Our House: House Music, Cultural Spaces and Technologies*, Aldershot: Ashgate.

Rietveld, H. C. 2004 Ephemeral spirit: sacrificial cyborg and soulful community. St John, G. (ed.), *Rave and Religion*, London and New York: Routledge.

Rietveld, H. C. 2007 The residual soul sonic force of the vinyl 12″ dance single. In C. Ackland (ed.), *Residual Media*. Minneapolis, MN and London: University of Minnesota Press.

Rietveld, H. C. 2011 Disco's revenge: house music's nomadic memory. *Dancecult: Journal of Electronic Dance Music Culture*, Vol. 2, No. 1, pp. 4–23.

Rietveld, H. C. 2013a Introduction. In A. B. Attias, A. Gavanas, and H. C. Rietveld (eds), *DJ Culture in the Mix: Power, Technology, and Social Change in Electronic Dance Music*. London and New York: Bloomsbury Academic.

Rietveld, H. C. 2013b Journey to the light? immersion, spectacle and mediation. In A. B. Attias, A. Gavanas and H. C. Rietveld (eds), *DJ Culture in the Mix: Power, Technology, and Social Change in Electronic Dance Music*. London and New York: Bloomsbury Academic.

Riley, A. 2005 The rebirth of tragedy out of the spirit of hip-hop: a cultural sociology of gangsta rap. *Journal of Youth Studies*, Vol. 8, No. 3, pp. 279–311.

Ritzer, G and N. Jurgenson. 2010 Production, consumption, prosumption: the nature of capitalism in the age of the digital 'prosumer'. *Journal of Consumer Culture*, Vol. 10, No. 1, pp. 13–36.

Robertson, B. J. 2011 Music, terrorism, response: the conditioning logic of code and networks. In J. P. Fisher and B. Flota (eds), *The Politics of Post-9/11 Music: Sound, Trauma, and the Music Industry in the Time of Terror*. Farnham, Surrey, UK: Ashgate Press.

Rogers, J. 2012 Starlust [review]. *Caught by the River: A Music Book Reader*. http://issuu.com/neilscott/docs/cbtr-mbr-18052012/search. Accessed 8 June 2015.

Rojek, C. 2007 Celebrity and religion. In S. Holmes and S. Redmond (eds), *Stardom and Celebrity: A Reader*. London: Sage.

Ross, A. 2005 Applause: a *Rest is Noise* special report. On *Alex Ross: The Rest is Noise* website. www.therestisnoise.com/2005/02/applause_a_rest.html. Accessed 8 June 2015.

Rust, B. and A. G. Debus. 1989 *The Complete Entertainment Discography: From 1897 to 1942*. New York: Da Capo Press.

Sacks, H. 1995 *Lectures on Conversation*. Oxford: Blackwell.

Sacks, H., E. A. Schegloff and G. Jefferson. 1974 A simplest systematics for the organization of turn taking for conversation. *Language*, Vol. 50, pp. 696–735.

Sandvoss, C. 2005 *Fandom: The Mirror of Consumption*. Cambridge: Polity Press.

Sant Cassia, P. 1999 Tradition, tourism and memory in Malta. *Journal of the Royal Anthropological Institute*, Vol. 5, No. 2, pp. 247–263.

Sant Cassia, P. 2000 Exoticizing discoveries and extraordinary experiences: 'traditional' music, modernity, and nostalgia in Malta and other Mediterranean societies. *Ethnomusicology*, Vol. 44, No. 2, pp. 281–301.

Saul, J. R. 2005 *The Collapse of Globalism and the Reinvention of the World*. Melbourne: Viking.

Schaap, P. 1999 Liner Notes. *Ellington at Newport 1956 (Complete)*. Columbia C2K 64932.

Schegloff, E. 1968 Sequencing in conversational openings. *American Anthropologist,* Vol. 70, No. 6, pp. 1075–1095.

Schegloff, E. 1988 Goffman and the analysis of conversation. In P. Drew and T. Wootton (eds), *Erving Goffman: Exploring the Interaction Order.* Cambridge: Polity Press.

Schechner, R. 1985 *Between Theater and Anthropology.* Philadelphia, PA: University of Pennsylvania Press.

Schechner, R. 1988 *Performance Theory.* New York: Routledge.

Schechner, R. 1998 What is performance studies anyway? In P. Phelan and J. Lane (eds) *The Ends of Performance.* New York: New York University Press.

Schechner, R. 2002 *Performance Studies: An Introduction.* London: Routledge.

Scheuer, T. 1997 The best books on popular music since 1971: a bibliography. *Popular Music and Society,* Vol. 21, No. 1, pp. 117–121.

Schutz, A. 1976 *Collected Papers II: Studies in Social Theory.* Edited and introduced by Arvid Brodersen. Hague: Martinus Nijhoff.

Shank, B. 1994 *Dissonant Identities: The Rock 'n' Roll Scene in Austin, Texas.* Hanover, NH: University Press of New England.

Shuker, R. 1994 *Understanding Popular Music Culture.* London: Routledge.

Shumway, D. R. 1992. Rock & roll as a cultural practice. In A. DeCurtis (ed.), *Present Tense: Rock & Roll and Culture.* Durham and London: Duke University Press.

Silver, B. 1984 The adab of musicians. In B. D. Metcalf (ed.), *Moral Conduct and Authority. The Place of Adab in South Asian Islam.* Berkeley, CA: University of California Press.

Sim, A. 2011 *Life in Tudor Palaces and Houses: From 1485 to 1603.* Andover: Pitkin.

Sloboda, J. and B. Ford. 2012 What classical musicians can learn from other arts about building audiences. *Understanding Audiences* Working Paper 2. Guildhall School of Music and Drama.

Small, C. 1998 *Musicking: The Meanings of Performing and Listening.* Hanover, NH: University Press of New England.

Soames, C. (ed.) 2003 *Oxford Compact English Dictionary.* (2nd edn). Oxford: Oxford University Press.

Spiteri, S. 2003 Etnikafe – Bumbum at Fort St Elmo. *Times of Malta* (online) 21 July. www.timesofmalta.com/articles/view/20030721/local/etnikafe-bumbum-at-fort-st-elmo. Accessed 8 June 2015.

Spurrett, D. and S. Cowley 2010 The extended infant: utterance activity and distributed cognition. In Richard Menary (ed.), *The Extended Mind.* Cambridge MA, London: Bradford/MIT Press.

St John, G. 2009 *Technomad: Global Raving Countercultures.* London and Oakville: Equinox.

Stagno-Navarra, K. 2009 Piano unveils 25-year-old dream for Valletta. *Malta Today* (online) 28 June. http://archive.maltatoday.com.mt/2009/06/28/t6.html. Accessed 8 June 2015.

Stasik, M. 2012 *DISCOnnections: Popular Music Audiences in Freetown, Sierra Leone.* Bamenda, CMR: Langaa.

Stavrakakis, Y. 2003 Politics and religion: on the 'politicization' of Greek church discourse. *Journal of Modern Greek Studies,* Vol. 21, No. 2, pp. 153–181.

Stebbins, R. A. 1969 Role distance, role distance behaviour and jazz musicians. *The British Journal of Sociology,* Vol. 20 No. 4, pp. 406–415.

Stokes, M. (ed.) 1994 *Ethnicity, Identity and Music: The Musical Construction of Place*. Oxford: Berg.

Stokes, M. 2007 On musical cosmopolitanism. *The Macalester International Roundtable 2007*.

Street, J. 2012 *Music and Politics*. Cambridge: Polity Press.

Sutton, J. 2010 Exograms and interdisciplinarity: history, the extended mind, and the civilising process. In R. Menary (ed.), *The Extended Mind*. Cambridge MA, London: Bradford/MIT Press.

Temple, P. 2013 On 'Colonized', Live 9, and Push. *Ableton Artists*. 3 June. www.ableton.com/en/blog/paula-temple-colonized-live-9-and-push/. Accessed 28 February 2015.

Thompson, B. 2001. *Ways of Hearing: A User's Guide to the Pop Psyche, From Elvis to Eminem*. London: Orion.

Thompson, G. and S. Hunston. 2000 Evaluation: an introduction. In S. Hunston and G. Thompson (eds), *Evaluation in Text: Authorial Stance and the Construction of Discourse*. Oxford: Oxford University Press.

Thornton, S. 1995 *Club Cultures: Music, Media and Subcultural Capital*. Cambridge: Polity Press.

Thurley, S. 1993 *The Royal Palaces of Tudor England: Architecture and Court Life, 1460–1547*. New Haven, CT: Yale University Press.

Tilley, V. 1919 My life story: related by Vesta Tilley. *Empire News*. 6 July, p. 7.

Tragaki, D. 2005 Humanizing the masses': enlightened intellectuals and the music of the people. In D. Cooper and K. Dawe (eds), *The Mediterranean in Music: Critical Perspectives, Common Concerns, Cultural Differences*. Lanham, MD: Scarecrow Press.

Tribble, E. B. and N. Keene (eds) 2011 *Cognitive Ecologies and the History of Remembering: Religion, Education and Memory in Early Modern England*. Basingstoke: Palgrave Macmillan.

Tsioulakis, I. 2011a At first I saw it as a toy: life stories, social consciousness and music ethnography. *Irish Journal of Anthropology*, Vol. 14, No. 1, pp. 19–28.

Tsioulakis, I. 2011b Jazz in Athens: frustrated cosmopolitans in a music subculture. *Ethnomusicology Forum*, Vol. 20, No. 2, pp. 175–199.

Tsioulakis, I. 2013 The quality of mutuality: jazz musicians in the Athenian popular music industry. In C. Wergin and F. Holt (eds), *Musical Performance and the Changing City*. New York: Routledge.

Tsioulakis, I. (forthcoming) Music *pistes*: socio-musical dystopia and the cultivation of neo-fascism. In D. Dalakoglou and G. Angelopoulos (eds), *Crisis in Greece: Critical Anthropological Explorations and Ethnographic Approaches*.

Tuan, Y. 1990 *Topophilia: A Study of Environmental Perception, Attitudes, and Values*. New York: Columbia University Press.

Tulloch, J. and H. Jenkins. 1995 *Science Fiction Audiences: Doctor Who, Star Trek, and Their Fans*. Florence, KY: Routledge.

Turino, T. 2003 Are we global yet? Globalist discourse, cultural formations and the study of Zimbabwean popular music. *British Journal of Ethnomusicology*, Vol. 12, No. 2, pp. 51–80.

Turino T. 2008 *Music as Social Life: The Politics of Participation*. Chicago and London: University of Chicago Press.

Turner, E. 2012 *Communitas. The Anthropology of Collective Joy*. New York: Lamgrave Macmillan.

Turner, J. 2001 The microsound scene: an interview with Kim Cascone. *CTheory*. https://journals.uvic.ca/index.php/ctheory/article/view/14586/5431. Accessed 8 June 2015.

Turner, V. 1977 Variations on a theme of liminality. In S. F. Moore and B. G. Myerhoff (eds), *Secular Ritual*. Assen/Amsterdam: van Gorcum.

Turner, V. 1982 *From Ritual to Theatre: The Human Seriousness of Play*. New York City: Performing Arts Journal Publications.

Van de Leur, W. 2002 *Something to Live For: The Music of Billy Strayhorn*. New York: Oxford University Press.

van Veen, T. C. 2002 Digital DJing: Richie Hawtin and (the) Final Scratch, from *Discorder, Jancember. Quadrant Crossing*. www.quadrantcrossing.org/papers/DigitalDJing%28Hawtin%2902-Disc-tV.pdf. Accessed 4 December 2014.

Van Zijl, A. 2014 *Performers' Emotions in Expressive Performance: Sound, Movement, and Perception*. Jyväskylä: University of Jyväskylä.

Veblen, K. 2014 Dancing at the crossroads remixed: Irish traditional musical identity in changing community contexts. In M. Fitzgerald and J. O'Flynn (eds), *Music and Identity in Ireland and Beyond*. Farnham: Ashgate.

Vermorel, F. 2008 Starlust: love, hate and celebrity fantasies. Obscenity law stops fans from thinking aloud. *The Register*. 12 November. www.theregister.co.uk/2008/11/12/fred_vermorel_girls_aloud/. Accessed 8 June 2015.

Vermorel, F. 2014 Fantastic voyeur: lurking on the dark side of biography. In M. Duffett (ed.), *Popular Music Fandom: Identities, Roles and Practices*. New York: Routledge.

Vermorel, F. and J. Vermorel. 2011 [1985] *Starlust: The Secret Life of Fans*. London: Allen.

Vinton, K. L. 1989 Humor in the workplace: it is more than telling jokes. *Small Group Research*, Vol. 20, No. 2, pp. 151–166.

Wardhaugh, B. 2008 *Music, Experiment and Mathematics in England, 1653–1705*. Farnham: Ashgate.

Webster, E. 2012 One more tune! The encore ritual in live music events. *Popular Music and Society*, Vol. 35, No. 1, pp. 93–112.

Weiner, R. G. 1999 *Perspectives on the Grateful Dead: Critical writings*. Westport, CT: Greenwood Press.

Weingarten, G. 2007 Pearls before breakfast: can one of the nation's great musicians cut through the fog of a D.C. rush hour? Let's find out. *Washington Post*, 8 April. www.washingtonpost.com/wpdyn/content/article/2007/04/04/AR2007040401721.html. Accessed 8 June 2015.

Wenner, J. 1973. *Lennon Remembers: The Rolling Stone Interviews*. Harmondsworth: Penguin.

Whelan, A. 2008 *Breakcore: Identity and Interaction on Peer-to-Peer*. Cambridge: Cambridge University Press.

Wicke, P. 1990 *Rock Music: Culture, Aesthetics, and Sociology*. Cambridge: Cambridge University Press.

Wong, D. 2003 Plugged in at home: Vietnamese American technoculture in Orange County. In R. T. Lysloff and L. C. Gay (eds), *Music and Technoculture*. Middletown, CN: Wesleyan University Press.

Wood, A. 2008 E-fieldwork: A paradign for the twenty-first century? In H. Stobart (ed.), *The New (Ethno)Musicologies*. Lanham, MD: Scarecrow Press.

Wu, J. C. 2014 From Qunzhong to Guanzhong: the evolving conceptualization of audience in mainland China. In R. Butsch and S. Livingstone (eds), *Meanings of Audiences: Comparative Discourses*. London and New York: Routledge.

Xu, G. 2014 The articulation of audience in Chinese communication research. In R. Butsch and S. Livingstone (eds), *Meanings of Audiences: Comparative Discourses*. London and New York: Routledge.

Young, J. R. 2005. Review of various artists, *Woodstock*. In D. Brackett (ed.), *The Pop, Rock, and Soul Reader: Histories and Debates*. New York and Oxford: Oxford University Press.

Yu, J. 2013 Electronic Dance Music and technological change: lessons from actor-network theory. In A. B. Attias, A. Gavanas and H. C. Rietveld (eds), *DJ Culture in the Mix: Power, Technology, and Social Change in Electronic Dance Music*. London and New York: Bloomsbury Academic.

Zahra, R. 2006 *A Guide to Maltese Folk Music*. Malta: PBS Malta and Soundscapes.

Zajonc, R. B. 2004 *The Selected Works of R. B. Zajonc*. New York: Wiley.

Zammit, R. 2004 Quest for revival of musical heritage. *Times of Malta*, 26 August, p. 12.

Zoumboulakis, S. 2013 The Orthodox church in Greece today. In A. Triandafyllidou, R. Gropas and H. Kouki (eds), *The Greek Crisis and European Modernity*. New York: Palgrave Macmillan.

## Discography

Alamango, A. 2010 *Malta's lost voices 1931–1932*. [CD] Valletta, Malta: Filfla Records.

Etnika, 2000 *Nafra*. [CD] Valletta, Malta: self-produced.

Etnika, 2003 *Żifna*. [CD] Valletta, Malta: Marsovin / UNESCO.

Etnika, 2004 *Etnika: in search of our lost voice*. [DVD] Valletta, Malta: Drunken Angel Entertainment.

Etnika, 2005 *EtnikaFé: port cabaret*. [DVD] Valletta, Malta: self-produced.

Schwarz, H. and Kuniyuki. 2010 *Once Again* [Vinyl LP]. Tokyo, Japan: Mule Music.

# Index

Locators in italics refer to figures